D0272508

BROOKLANDS COLLEGE LIBRARY
305965

animation

A GUIDE TO ANIMATED FILM TECHNIQUES

animation

A GUIDE TO ANIMATED FILM TECHNIQUES

Roger Noake

MACDONALD ORBIS

A Macdonald Orbis BOOK

First published in Great Britain in 1988
by Macdonald & Co (Publishers) Ltd
London & Sydney

A member of Maxwell Pergamon Publishing Corporation plc

British Library Cataloguing in Publication Data
Noake, Roger
Animation
1. Cinematography. Animation, Techniques
I. Title
778.5'347

ISBN 0–356–15872–1

Filmset by Wyvern Typesetting Ltd, Bristol
Printed and bound in Italy by OFSA SpA

Senior Editor: Catherine Rubinstein
Text Editor: Reg Grant
Art Director: Linda Cole
Designer: Bob Burroughs
Picture Researcher: Sarah Connearn
Photographer: Susanna Price
Illustrator: Coral Mula

Illustrations on pp 1, 3, 5 from Big Hands, Sarah Strickett, West Surrey College of Art & Design
Illustration on p 6 from The Horse, Witold Giersz

Macdonald & Co (Publishers) Ltd
Greater London House
Hampstead Road
London NW1 7QX

CONTENTS

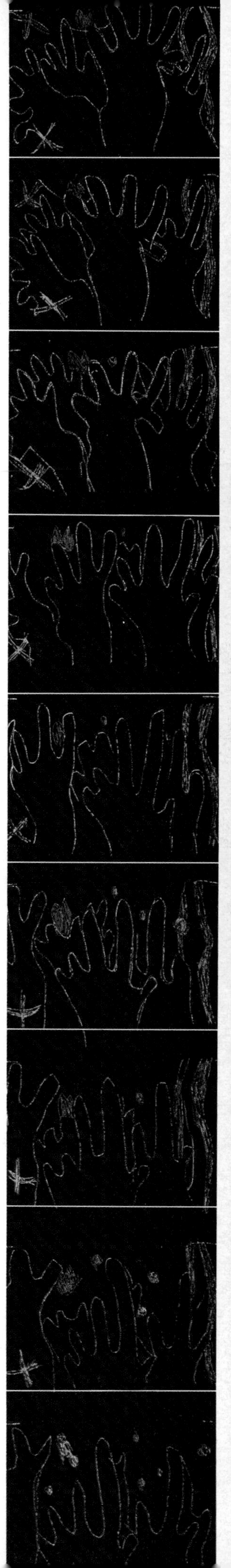

INTRODUCTION

Whichever of the many and varied techniques is used, making an animated film always involves constructing it frame by frame. When projected, these frames create an illusion of movement. This quite simple quirk of human perception which causes us to paper over the joins and to strive to see a continuum where none exists has made possible the art form, the industry and the craft of animation.

The two elements of construction and of illusion are central to the many concerns and arguments which surround the production of animated film, as well as to the process of making itself. In some kinds of animation, clearly inanimate objects are made to move—this has been likened to alchemy and magic. Other kinds of illusion have more correspondence to what is thought of as real life. Stories are constructed that have such authenticity they are perceived as real, even though we know they are only cartoons.

Animators are storytellers and magicians who can transport an audience into new and undreamed of worlds, transform the base objects of drawing and model into a living thing, or hold our attention with the way they tell an excessively old tale. But animation is also a craft. If the storytellers and magicians are to communicate, patient work must take place. Without the skills of drawing, model-making and, increasingly, programming, the animated film would not exist. Even so, the skills are secondary to the process of communication. There is always a technique that creative individuals can discover which will enable them to make the animation they want.

Drawing remains the main studio skill and as such it has great importance in animation production. It is the ability to communicate the sense of movement through a single line that is the essence of good classical studio animation technique. Other traditional skills which have their place in the studio perspective are rendering and model-making, used by the animator of three-dimensional films.

Animation is built piece by piece, sometimes over a long period of time. At each stage new elements are introduced, some directly related to animation, others belonging to film and video production in general. This process of building, while at the same time keeping the final purpose in mind, is the element of the work which fascinates the animator and appears as incomprehensible drudgery to the uninitiated. Why sit at a light box producing hundreds of drawings for a product that lasts only a short time and certainly does not make the animator a fortune?

The animator is in complete control of this small world which has been created. The control spreads over every detail and all aspects of production. Yet this degree of control over the materials and processes has its own problems. The repetitive nature of production, whether in the industrial process or individual creation, can result in a lifelessness and a lack of energy far from the original notions of animation breathing life into the inanimate. Animation struggles against this inertia. It takes on the Sisyphian task and, by skill and sometimes by humour, moves it.

For both the beginner and the experienced animator, there are inevitably times when the machine will not move, no matter how much energy is applied to it. These blockages can be dispiriting when a great deal of hard work seems to have had no effect. For the beginner, such blockages are often the result of not knowing how to do it, or of not being able to think through the problems or even to identify why 'it won't work'. Each of the chapters in this book takes one stage in the production of animation and thinks it through. If some of the elephant traps awaiting the intrepid animator can be negotiated or at least climbed out of, the adventurer may even wish to start a second journey.

The great animator Norman McLaren defined animation as 'the space between the frames'. This holds even as, with the development of the electronic technology of animation, the frame becomes conceptual rather than real. It is a space in which anything that can be imagined can happen.

1
THE STORY SO FAR

Contemporary animators in search of ideas and inspiration have a rich tradition they can turn to, stretching back to the origins of cinema itself. The history of animation has been shaped by technology, by the demands of the entertainment industry and, above all, by the skill and imagination of individual artists.

Rainbow Dance, Len Lye
Lye used solarized images of figures combined with abstract shapes in a film which prefigures much of the recent work that uses new technology. Lye also wrote prophetically at this period on the potential of the television medium for visual experimentation.

Animation images are all around us. In the West animated films sell banks and beer; in Japan cartoon stories of superheroes and cute animals flood prime-time television. In Eastern Europe animated films spin subtle allegories; in India they promote literacy and health. Animation can hook children on cheap dolls or it can tell great stories. It provides us with both sophisticated computer graphics and dumb stereotypes.

Animation can give us magic and illusion, but also moments of intense and moving realism. In no other medium is there so much potential for industrial methods of production and yet at the same time so much flexibility for the individual artist to create personal statements. The form can be used by a large number of people working as a team or by the

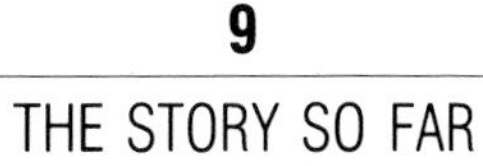

single determined animator, ready to invest the long hours of hard work required to produce a film that will probably never be seen by more than a handful of enthusiasts.

But whatever the kind of animation in question, there is always the same search for a suitable technique and production practice, and for the right voice to address an audience. Because at the end of the long production road, it is the audience's reaction that counts – whether they are amused, challenged, transformed or just plain indifferent.

Beginnings

Although the pre-history of the cinema is full of wonderful illusionary devices based on the phenomenon of the persistence of vision – Zoetropes, Phenakistiscopes, and so on – it was the Frenchman Emile Reynaud's Praxinoscope, invented in the 1880s, which presented the world with the first sequence of movements shown to an audience in a form approaching a cinema performance. The Praxinoscope consisted of a series of painted slides mounted on a huge perforated leather belt, held on two large drums. As the belt was wound through the machine, a lamp projected the moving images through a lens onto a screen. The Praxinoscope pre-dated photographic film, so it was impossible to reproduce the images. The slides had to be made by hand, and although backgrounds could be superimposed during the projection, this cumbersome production process made a large output or widespread exhibition impossible. The 'films' were limited to performances at Reynaud's own theatre, the Théâtre Optique, opened in Paris in 1892.

Reynaud's images have a unique power, occurring as they do at the moment when cinema, perhaps the most influential form of communication of the twentieth century, was about to be created. The sequences from Reynaud's *Autour d'une Cabine* (1895), showing a beach scene complete with bathing hut and naughty male voyeur, have not yet developed a way of dealing with changing space and time except through exaggerated perspective. But there is no reason to be patronizing. The speed of technological change may mean that we will soon look back on present-day computer animation with the same sympathy we now reserve for the films of the pioneers. After all, for them the answers were just around the corner.

Within a decade of the first showing of moving photographed images in Paris, film had progressed from scientific research and novelty performance to the point where a whole series of films could be shown as a programme in a theatre. A language of the cinema was developing quite different from that used by the earlier experimenters, and both a system of production and an audience were being rapidly defined.

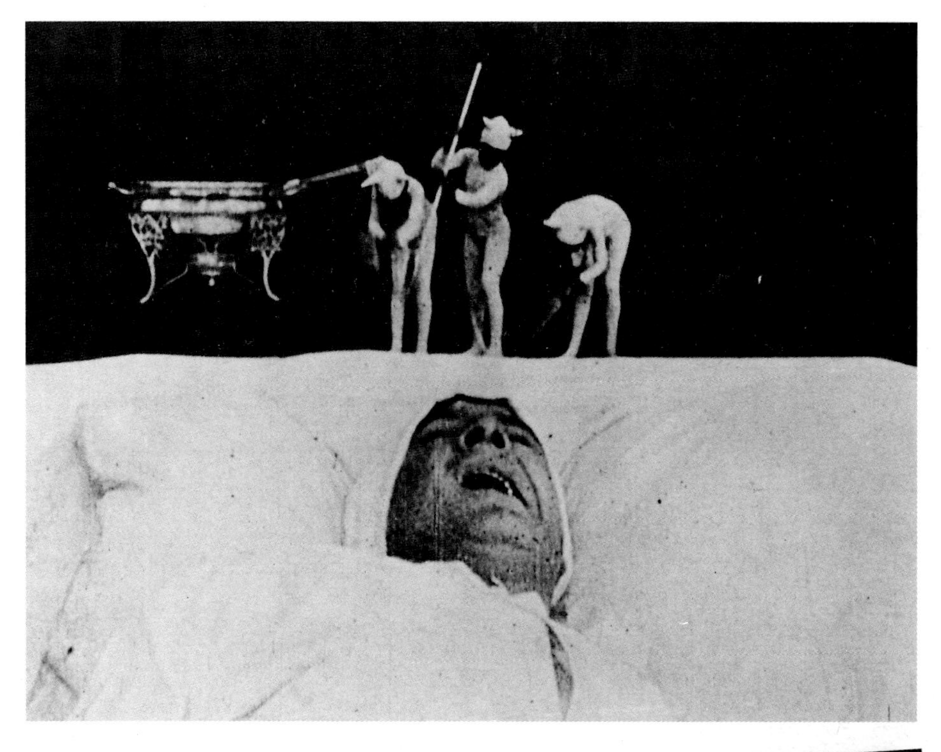

Above: *Dreams of a Rarebit Fiend,* Winsor McCay
The strong graphic technique used by McCay in his newspaper work provided a style which adapted well to his dramatic and fantastic animation themes.

Right: Fantasmagorie, Emile Cohl
Cohl achieved remarkable fluidity of movement with his simple stick figures.

Animation had at first a minor place in this new, still shifting system. A British-born American, James Stuart Blackton, extended his own stage performances with animation routines on film, such as *Humorous Phases*, and Arthur Melbourne Cooper and Walter Booth used trickfilm to animate objects for early publicity films like *Matches Appeal* (1899). There has been a recent re-evaluation of the place of trickfilm in the growth of the language of cinema. We have learned to see how films that appeared aberrant and marginal, that failed to become central to the development of the language, can be as important as what survived to become the dominant form. This has ensured the place of these pioneers in film history. At the time, however, they remained eccentrics specializing in novelty films. Interesting as they are, these works had little effect on the main developments in the production of animated film.

Animation emerged in its own right through the persistence of two great figures, the Frenchman Emile Cohl and the American Winsor McCay. They laid the foundations of animation as an art and an industry. For a short time, both had a clear view of the potential of this new medium, of the technical needs of production and, significantly, of the audience. Both ultimately failed as technique and audience moved rapidly to a more sophisticated and demanding stage and as the process itself became industrialized.

Emile Cohl, who already had a firmly established reputation as an illustrator, was able to bring a well-worked-out visual style to his first animated film, *Fantasmagorie* (1908). For the first time an animated film went beyond the mere insertion of tricks into live-action material or extension of music-hall routines

Above: Gertie the Dinosaur, Winsor McCay
The first famous dinosaur of animation has just been scolded by the animator. Even with the very simplified drawing, McCay is able to describe not only the movement of the character but also its weight and mass.

into the cinema. Only two minutes long, *Fantasmagorie* consists of a stream of images appearing in a dreamlike way, without a narrative structure but determined by an inner logic. Cohl continued to produce films well into the 1920s, including the *Fantoches* series, but died in poverty in 1938. He still holds a fascination for animators, who recognize the grasp he had of the mysterious power of the medium to transform and distort the world of figures and objects.

Winsor McCay also still has an influence on present-day film-makers. Like Cohl, he was well established as a major graphic artist with a considerable reputation, working for the *New York Herald* on a popular comic strip series, *Little Nemo.* The comic strip was a successful form among the booming newly arrived European immigrant population of the American cities, who spoke little if any English and who were trying to come to terms with their new lives and location quickly. The visual narratives of these early strips gave the recently displaced audience a non-verbal form of their own which was familiar to them, coming as it did from the mid-European tradition, but had in addition the boldness of the New World. The early comic strip owed much to its European roots. McCay, however, transformed the expressionistic style into a graphic form which, even had he not ventured into animation, would have earned him a place among the very great graphic artists of the century.

Cohl had adapted his graphic technique to suit the production conditions of the new medium. He believed the sheer amount of artwork that was needed demanded a much simpler line. McCay made no such compromise with his style. All of his great power as a draughtsman is displayed in his films from the very start. The first, *Little Nemo* (1909), has the fine line drawing shown in his comic-strip works. In the most well known of his films, *Gertie the Dinosaur* (1909), all of the features of McCay's greatest work come together – the showmanship, the revelation within the film of the production process behind it, and above all the sharply defined drawing. In *Gertie*, McCay achieved a control over animation that was not equalled again for some time. He was also beginning to develop some of the production techniques, such as cycling and repeats, that remain important elements in the animator's repertoire today.

One element, however, was missing, an element which has become synonymous with classic animation: 'cel'. It was the introduction of cel – acetate sheets – that permitted animation to develop into an effective method of production. Cel allowed the animator to combine a number of different pieces of artwork carrying out different routines and made duplication of the static elements of the animation figure unnecessary. It also made it possible to combine foreground action with a drawn background.

Both Cohl and McCay worked on their early films by drawing one frame after another painstakingly onto paper without the aid of such devices. Working without cel and drawing onto rice paper, as McCay did, gives a

Below: Carmen, Anson Dyer
A rare still from one of the pioneers of British animation.

tension to the line which flickers and 'boils' when projected. The later work of McCay and of the animators following him set out to eliminate this error, which was seen as another aberration holding back progress towards greater realism.

The industrialization of animation

While Cohl and McCay pursued their endeavours alone as craftsmen, producing one-off works, the trend of other industries was in a quite opposite direction. In all industries production methods were being rationalized, time-and-motion study and product control were becoming accepted as the most efficient methods of production, and it was not long before these methods were applied to animation. Indeed, the production line seemed to be eminently suitable for animation, with its many discrete components which required quality control and careful timing and scheduling. At the same time, the growing demands of the distributors for more quality production could only be met by the application of modern industrial techniques.

While these new systems were being pioneered in the United States, in Europe the tradition established by Cohl was overtaken by the events of World War I. Animation production on both sides in the conflict now went over to meeting the needs of the war effort through the making of propaganda and instructional films. Meanwhile, entertainment films were imported from America and developed a strong following among European audiences. Some excellent propaganda and instructional films were produced – Lancelot Speed made *Bully Boy* (1914) and Anson Dyer, who was to play an important part in the development of British animation, collaborated with Dudley Buxton to produce films for the war effort. Although Dyer, with a prodigious effort, set about making a number of entertainment films, starting with *The Three Little Pigs* in 1918, the damage caused by the diversion from entertainment films during the war could not easily be repaired.

Although there were determined attempts to develop series production in Great Britain after the war, such as the *Bonzo* series made by G. E. Studdy, the British could not match American production for quality or its availability through the increased output made possible by industrial techniques. In Germany, advertising began to make extensive use of animation, and two great experimental animators, Walter Ruttmann and Oskar Fischinger, produced a series of abstract films, most notably Ruttmann's *Opus* series. These films were both abstract experiments with sound and image and, at the same time, popular with mass audiences. They began to explore the formal possibilities of animation and sound long before it became technically feasible to bring the two together on a single strip of film.

In the newly founded Soviet Union, film-maker Dziga Vertov commissioned animation for his revolutionary newsreels. Entitled *Kino-Pravda*, these had begun as a film newspaper for the Bolshevik agit-trains. The animators who received commissions included Bushkin, Ivanov and Beliakov, whose *Soviet Toys* (1924) drew on the strong tradition of Russian satirical political illustration. It was a tradition that was to continue and expand in later animated films.

A Russian emigré who was now living in Paris, Ladislas Starevitch, developed the area of puppet films with remarkable works, notably *La Voix du Rossignol* (*The Voice of the Nightingale*, 1923). He continued in his own unique style until the 1960s, as did Lotte Reiniger. *The Adventures of Prince Achmed* (1926) established Reiniger at the forefront of two-dimensional, cut-out animation.

But while Europe continued to produce great individual works, both popular and experimental, extending the boundaries of the art and the craft, in America these decisive years saw the basis laid of an animation industry which was to dominate the international market even more certainly in the future. An American called John Randolph Bray established patents on all the known

Above: Soviet Toys, Dziga Vertov
The film uses cut-out and transformations to portray the evil of the New Economic Policy and the re-introduction of private enterprise into the Soviet Union. The struggle between the heroic peasants and the NEP is resolved by the final destruction of the adherents of the NEP.

Left: The Adventures of Prince Achmed, Lotte Reiniger
Reiniger's mixture of oriental and expressionist traditions created a powerful style. The cut-out technique permitted a detail which could not be achieved using the line animation techniques of the time.

animation techniques existing at that time, including a method for getting rid of the 'defects' of paper animation by using cel overlays. He signed lucrative production and marketing deals with Paramount and Goldwyn, and established new industrial management practices in the studio. Thus the 'studio system' was born. This system of production, becoming increasingly sophisticated, was to dominate the future of animation. Max Fleischer, Paul Terry and Walter Lantz all learnt their studio skills from Bray and went on to form their own studios run on similar lines. To an extent, the procedures which were established then are still at the root of any animation work involving a group today, even when, because of its small scale, the operation might at first sight seem to lie outside the area of large-scale studio production.

The studio system was required to produce a consistent and recognizable product to meet the needs of the distributors and the growing cinema audiences. A guaranteed product required series of films, and a series required a cast of identifiable characters. In the early 1920s, Fleischer produced the *Out of the Inkwell* series with Koko the Clown, Paul Terry made *Aesop's Fables*, and Pat Sullivan and Otto Messmer began to turn out the most successful of the silent animation series, *Felix the Cat*.

Above: Felix Knight Errant, Pat Sullivan, courtesy of Felix The Cat Creations Inc
Felix duels with the mouse. In this pre-cel animation, the background and the action are separated and do not overlap.

Below: Bad Luck Blackie, Tex Avery, © 1949 Loew's Inc, Ren 1976 Metro-Goldwyn-Mayer Inc
Another piece of good fortune strikes the bulldog villain in the form of a flowerpot.

The impact of Disney

In Hollywood a young animator called Walt Disney set out to create a series of films based on the character of Oswald the Rabbit, which quickly established his reputation for very high-quality work and tightly structured scripts, though not at this point for business acumen. He lost the rights to his character to the distributor, together with most of his hard-earned money. From then on Disney set out to control not only production but all of the aspects of the marketing, distribution and exploitation of the product.

Disney was not an innovator. He did not invent the studio system, nor was he the first to make colour or sound animation. He was, however, the first to harness these elements to a high quality of animation and a close attention to narrative and characterization. As a result, he trumpeted, or to be precise tooted, animation into the spotlight with his first sound film in 1928. Disney applied the same precision to the synchronization of sound to image in *Steamboat Willie* that he had applied to the narrative structure of his earlier films. The sound was far removed from the 'terrible noise' that accompanied his competitors' animations. In addition the characters moved freely, unlike early live-action sound films in which the technical requirements of the 'sound stage' constrained the movement of actors and camera.

Disney and the group he gathered in the studio consistently pursued the imperative of quality production. The result was a series of classic short films: *Skeleton Dance* (May 1929), *Flowers and Trees* (July 1931), *The Three Little Pigs* and *The Band Concert* (February 1935). From 1931 for eleven years Disney won every Academy Award for animation. He used his distributors to maintain control over the use of the product with increasing effect until he finally assumed control of his own distribution.

There were, of course, other successful studios but none was able to dominate the animation of the 1930s as Disney did. The Fleischer studio was producing the Popeye and Betty Boop series, but these characters never gained the enormous following that the Mouse-star had. The Fleischer cartoons maintained the links with European style, at times gothic in its preoccupation with expressionist nightmares and threatening gloomy settings. The films' structures seemed loose, even improvised, compared to Disney's tight control of the script. Many classics did emerge from the Fleischer studios, however, such as *Snow White* (1931), a Betty Boop film.

Both Disney and Fleischer now believed that the production techniques of animation and the skills of the animators were sufficiently developed to make the first feature-length animated film. Disney, of course, won the race, releasing *Snow White and the Seven Dwarfs* in 1938. Fleischer's impressive first feature, *Gulliver's Travels*, was not released until the following year.

In the meantime Disney was ready to release two other masterpieces, arguably the best work to come out of his studio: *Pinocchio* (1939) and *Dumbo* (1941). Also in 1941 he produced *Fantasia*, drawing unusually, if not wholly successfully, on European high-art traditions, though in the process extending the development of the relationship of music to animation. Then in 1941 came the Disney strike. The production team was divided and an uncertainty entered the work. There are many reasons given for the strike, but it does seem that, whatever the claims and counterclaims, the system had become so rigid that a significant number of the workforce had come to resent Disney's paternal hand. An attempt was made to revitalize production afterwards, but the progressive element of the work had vanished. Some animators like John Hubley left to set up new studios; others joined the existing well-established teams at Warner Brothers and MGM (Metro-Goldwyn-Mayer). The films produced at the Disney studio were still of the highest technical standard, but the ability to connect directly with contemporary mores had gone.

UPA (United Productions of America), formed after World War II by ex-strikers dismissed by Disney, seemed more relevant to the post-war world and its post-bomb insecurities, as did Warners, who had been developing their stable of characters since the mid-1930s. The UPA films, with Mr Magoo and McBoing-Boing, established 'real' characters who were significantly flawed and found the world around them mainly hostile. Warners were tuned in through Tex Avery, Chuck Jones and Fritz Freeling. They used new graphic styles and deliberately broke the conventions. They re-established the animator at the centre of the text and drew the audience into a knowing and playful conspiracy of parody and satire. *Bad Luck Blackie*, one of the Avery contributions to the general mayhem, ranks with any contemporary work as a comment on the inconsistencies of fate, and his *Red Hot Riding Hood* (1945) parodies the preoccupation with the pin-up and male voyeurism. Bugs Bunny and Daffy Duck were developed over the years into complex characters with a wide range of potential interaction. At MGM the films depended less on the characters and more on relentless action.

Meanwhile the rest of the world was preparing to compete with Disney. In Britain, *Animal Farm* (1954), made by John Halas and based on the book by George Orwell, was a unique attempt to use animation for the presentation of serious contemporary ideas. In France Paul Grimault made *The King and Mr Bird* (the first version shown in 1967), a visually rich and eloquent statement about oppression, with a script by Jacques Prévert. But none could match the Disney technique. British and French animators admired it and attempted to emulate it, while the audiences in the cartoon theatres watched Road Runner and Daffy Duck.

French film critics then discovered that, in the same way that directors like Hitchcock were the 'authors' of live-action films, behind

Above: Animal Farm, John Halas and Joy Batchelor, Educational Film Centre Ltd
The farmyard animals look on as the workhorse and moral guide, Boxer, lies dying. The serious themes of the film called for an avoidance of the sentimentality found in other anthropomorphic animation.

Below: Hopalong Casualty, Chuck Jones, © 1960 Warner Bros Inc, all rights reserved
The coyote pounces – the whiz lines around the back legs ease the large difference in the positions in the two frames.

Havoc in Heaven, Wan Lai-ming, Shanghai Animation Film Studio

The popular folk hero, the disrespectful Monkey King, uses his great magic power to oppose the forces of heaven who are trying to destroy him. Top: The great white planet comes to the mountain of flowers and fruit with an invitation from the Jade Emperor.

Above: The monkey goes with the great white planet to visit heaven. When the guards refuse to let him pass through the southern gate, the Monkey King loses his temper.

animated films there were also 'authors' – animators, writers, a team as well as a studio. The films were after all not made entirely by Mr Warner himself. It has taken time for the many artists who had a significant hand in the massive output of films from the studio system to gain recognition, and it is a process that still goes on. Recognizing the great skill of many of the studio artists and animators helps animation see its own true history, rather than the public relations exercise of a studio.

Animation in the East

Industrial reconstruction after World War II saw animation production grow rapidly on an international scale. Many national animation industries that had existed before the war were resurrected; others were quite new endeavours. Japan became a major producer of animated film through the TOEI studio, now one of the world's largest animation plants, producing a massive amount of animation every year – cartoon series and feature films, as well as co-productions.

China, through the long-established Shanghai studios, had an industry dating back to the 1920s. It was in 1930 that the Wan Brothers had produced China's first sound animated film, *Camels Dance*. Although during the years of the war with Japan and the civil war little was produced, the studios blossomed again in the 1950s after the communist victory. It was *Havoc in Heaven*, made in 1962, that caused the world outside China to take notice that Chinese animation was flourishing once more. The film, made by Wan Lai-ming, shows the struggle of the wise and courageous King of the Monkeys against the heavenly authorities. It makes use of Chinese traditions both in the artwork and in the staging. *Havoc in Heaven* also served as a training ground for a fresh generation of animators in China, who were soon producing films themselves. *The Red Army Brigade* (1965) used the cut-out technique and a large cast of cut-out characters to show the events surrounding the agrarian revolution in China. In fact, 1965 marked the beginning of the political and satirical use of animation in China. Films were made at an incredible rate with a very short production time – just a few weeks in many cases.

It was not until the Cultural Revolution came to an end in the 1970s that large-scale feature-length films and entertainment films once more began to be produced at the Shanghai studios, most using low-budget cut-out techniques, though gradually other techniques were also explored. The folk tales and legends of China gradually became the favoured content. The figure of the Monkey

King has featured in a number of films, such as *The Monkey King Conquers the Demon* made by Te Wai and Yan Ding-Yai in 1986. Chinese animation remains an important example of the way in which a strong national industry can develop, making use of its own styles and evolving techniques which are appropriate to its own methods of production. It indicates the power of Asian and other Third World production.

Mainstream decline and independent revival

By the 1950s the growth of television was having an enormous influence on animation. An animated film was an expensive product if it was produced in the 'full animation' style as practised by Disney. Warners had ceased the production of animated shorts by the late 1950s and although MGM continued high-quality production, television rather than the cinema had become the site of the audience. Production for television inevitably meant a great reduction in the budget and production values. But television gave animation a much wider audience for its products.

But in the 1950s there were also signs of a fresh surge of experimental work. The experimental animation tradition of the 1920s and 1930s was finding a response among a new generation of artists and film-makers. New Zealander Len Lye, the Scotsman Norman McLaren and the German animator Oskar Fischinger, all important innovators, were now working in North America. Their work, as well as that of their contemporaries, was being shown in exhibitions and on campuses, demonstrating that there was an alternative way in which animation could be used. Sponsors such as the Guggenheim Museum, which had funded McLaren's first films after he left Britain for North America in 1939, began to support this new phenomenon of experimental animation. These film-makers stressed the individual and personal nature of their production in opposition to the studio system. Some, like Harry Smith, created a complex impenetrable language in which animation functioned as a kind of magic, transforming images into a highly personal meaning. His major film (or series of films) is called *The Magic Feature* (c. 1958).

Robert Breer, one of the most significant experimental film-makers, took the exploration of the single frame as his theme, using filing cards to draw on as a very flexible method of production. Like Len Lye, he has worked in many forms, including kinetic sculpture and the production of mutascopes – the 'what the butler saw' machines. The preoccupation with the single frame led to some remarkable work. *A Man and his Dog out for Air* (1958), using a very simple style of line drawing, stretches the perceptions of the viewer to the limits. This completely abstract film only reveals the man and the dog of the title in the last frames, yet the viewer feels forced to examine the swirling lines for any sign of figuration.

The nature of the single frame and the material of the film itself have occupied a number of the American experimentalists. Another tradition has been the exploration of new technologies. John and James Whitney were the pioneers in this field, involved as early as the 1940s in computer animation. Others like Stan Vanderbeek and Ed Emshwiller moved on from early experiments in free or 'expanded' cinema, using mixed

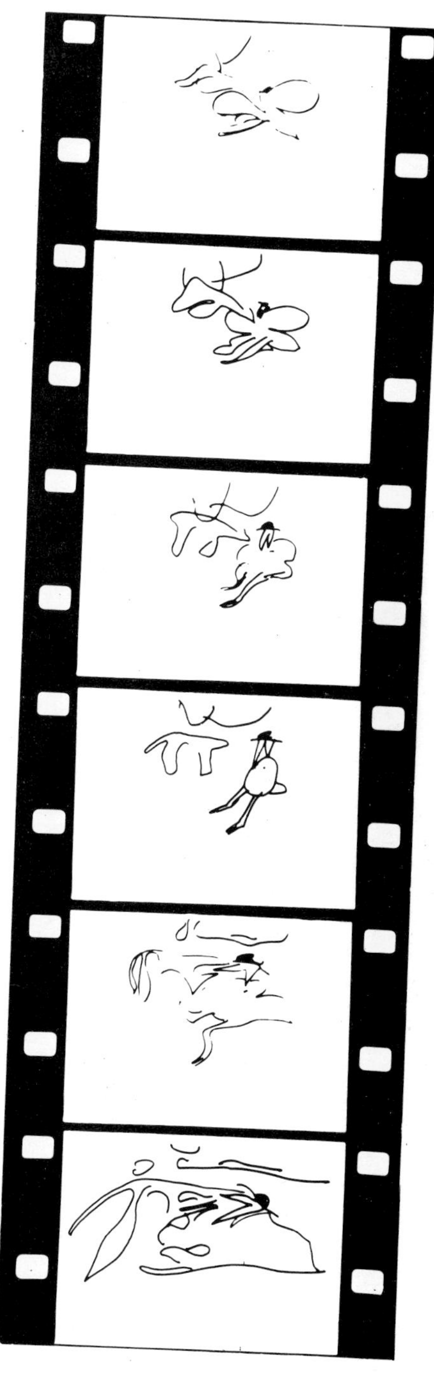

Above: A Man and a Dog out for Air, Robert Breer
The flowing lines, which move from abstraction to a glimpse of the figurative, give a tension to this early Breer film.

Left: Composition In Blue, Oskar Fischinger, © Fischinger Archive
In this shot, Fischinger used blocks of different sizes to achieve the illusion that they were growing – a typical example of his innovative techniques.

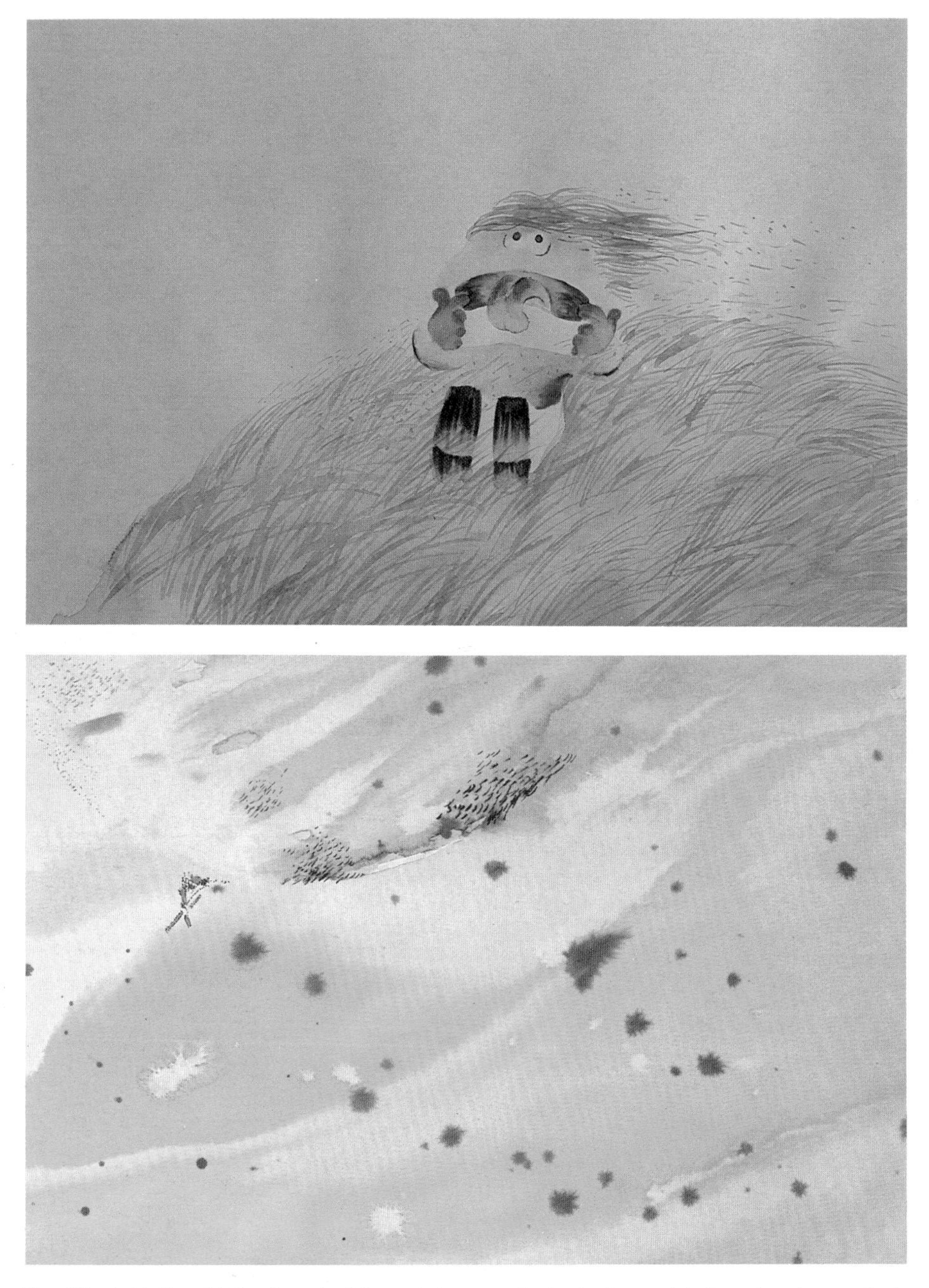

The Wind, National Film Board of Canada/ Ron Tunis
A film that exemplifies the National Film Board's innovative approach. The soundtrack is made from the improvised thoughts of children on the nature of wind, and the subtle pencil rendering and bold animation add to the unpatronizing but thought-provoking quality.

media including animation, to play a significant part in the development of computer animation.

The National Film Board of Canada (NFBC), with McLaren as its inspiration from the 1940s, became the model for a state-run nurturing institution, envied throughout the world. It attracted both native Canadian artists and film-makers and many from other countries. The animation produced by Colin Low and Robert Verral gained the NFBC a reputation for innovative if sometimes quiet work. From the board came films like the award-winning *The Street* (1976) by the American Caroline Leaf, *Pas de Deux* (1967) by McLaren himself, Ishu Patel's *Top Priority* (1981), Richard Condie's *Getting Started* (1983), Ron Tunis's *The Wind* (1975) and many others.

As well as this experimental and challenging approach to animation, the NFBC has managed to encourage the development of a different kind of cartoon animation, though with a very specific Film-Board style. Colin Low's own *Romance of Transportation in Canada* (1953) was both the first of these cartoon films and exemplary in its use of simple animation techniques and a humorous script to tell an important story. The film shows the way in which transport was used in Canada's progress towards unity. As with many of the best NFBC animations, it is not lacking in social comment, even though muted. The comedy of Zlatko Grigic's *Hot Stuff* (1971) and Richard Condie's *Getting Started* can be contrasted with the experimental films of McLaren and the work of Caroline Leaf and Lyn Smith in the 1980s.

The NFBC is not alone in producing animation in Canada. *Crac* (1981) was made for Société Radio Canada by Frédéric Back, an illustrator of exceptional ability who turned to animation late in his career, as was the feature film *The Man Who Planted Trees* (1987), with its rich style of rendered animation.

In Eastern Europe too, a new generation of film-makers was growing up in the 1950s. Czechoslovakia and Hungary both saw the development of national animation styles. Jíři Trnka in Prague gave a massive impetus to the development of three-dimensional puppet animation, and the older trickfilm traditions began to emerge from the shadows to which the domination of traditional cartoon animation had banished them. The Zagreb school in Yugoslavia was perhaps the most inventive of the emerging studios. From 1956 onwards, films such as the Oscar-winner *Ersatz* (1961) by Dusan Vukotić came to be seen as bringing something quite remarkable to animation. Zlatko Grigic made a number of films in Zagreb as well as at the NFBC, where *Hot Stuff* delivered a message about fire hazards in Canada with a truly East European smoke-black humour. In *Without Title* (1964), the famous animation by Borivoj Dovniković, the film never gets beyond the very long title sequence which keeps the hero off the screen. *Without Title* encapsulates the Zagreb approach of knowing humour coupled with strong contemporary graphics.

Advertising and independents

In the West, the effect of television on the cinema short, the main source for the production of the classic animated film, was terminal. But in other areas television had more positive results. The demand for ani-

Labyrinth, Jan Lenica
The collage technique, employed to portray sinister happenings in a strange city from which there is no escape, introduced a new freedom of expression. The black graphic style, one of the most instantly identifiable in all animation, reaffirmed the European tradition of the artist as film-maker.

mated commercials in Britain in the late 1950s made it possible for British animation 'authors' such as George Dunning, Richard Williams and Bob Godfrey to finance their own work. These film-makers ploughed back much of the profits from the production of commercials into films, which at the time had few outlets and little chance of reaching the TV screens. Films like *Alf, Bill and Fred* (1964) by Bob Godfrey, *The Little Island* (1958) by Richard Williams and *The Apple* (1961) by George Dunning, made with great courage against long odds, provided an inspiration for British animation. They proclaimed that there was the talent and skill waiting for its opportunity to reach a wider audience. These films also set a pattern for production which was later followed by others – contemporary animators Alison De Vere, Paul Vester and Geoff Dunbar all make films at least partly funded by their own commercial work.

By the late 1950s and early 1960s, independents were finding it slightly easier to survive. The Polish animators Walerien

Borowczyk and Jan Lenica (often working in France) and the Belgian Raoul Servais began to produce animation that found audiences on the art-house cinema circuits of Europe. *Les Jeux des Anges* (*The Games of Angels*, 1964) by Borowczyk created a world of dark secret chambers and sudden half-perceived acts of violence using stark images which drew on his background as a printmaker in Poland. In *Les Astronautes* (*The Astronauts*, 1959) made with the French director Chris Marker, Borowczyk demonstrated that his vision could be as penetrating even when it was lighter in mode. The film shows mankind creating progressively more ingenious machines for its own destruction.

Peter Foldes, one of the most interesting of this generation of film-makers, found it difficult to continue his animation after the highly successful film *A Short Vision*, made in 1956. He produced no animation for some years, until he eventually re-emerged with a series of films using metamorphosis to great effect, and finally moved into the production of computer animation. For the individual artist with a vision, unable to sustain production through commercial work, financing remained a problem. Raoul Servais is one of those animators who has nevertheless managed to maintain a regular output of strong individual films from the earliest *Operation X-70* (1971) to the stunning film *Harpya* (1979). Festivals such as Annecy gave these independent animators a showplace and revealed the worldwide spread of animation.

As the 1960s drew to a close, there were signs of an animation revival. George Dunning, a Canadian who had worked with Norman McLaren at the NFBC, made the Beatles film *Yellow Submarine* in 1968, which served as a training ground for many young animators and firmly established his production company TVC as a studio on the international stage. He was in the process of making a film based on Shakespeare's *The Tempest* when he died in 1974. Even in its unfinished state, this film still stands as one of the major achievements in animation. In America Ralph Bakshi produced *Fritz the Cat* in 1971 and audiences suddenly realized that animation could indeed be made for adults.

Important work was also being carried out in Poland, Czechoslovakia, Hungary and the Soviet Union. State-supported artists such as Yuri Norstein, Rein Raamat and Andrei Khrzhanovsky emerged as major figures. Jerzy Kucia in Poland and Jan Svankmajer in Czechoslovakia were developing individual styles. In Hungary the Pannonia studio was established, producing both cultural and commercial work of a very high standard and attracting talented animators such as Josef Gemes and Marcell Jankovics.

Top right: Harpya, Raoul Servais
In this production Servais uses a painstaking technique, which involves the photographing of the action, its treatment and subsequent re-photographing, to create a dramatic surreal atmosphere. The reassembly of realistic movements also allows him to produce some menacing effects.

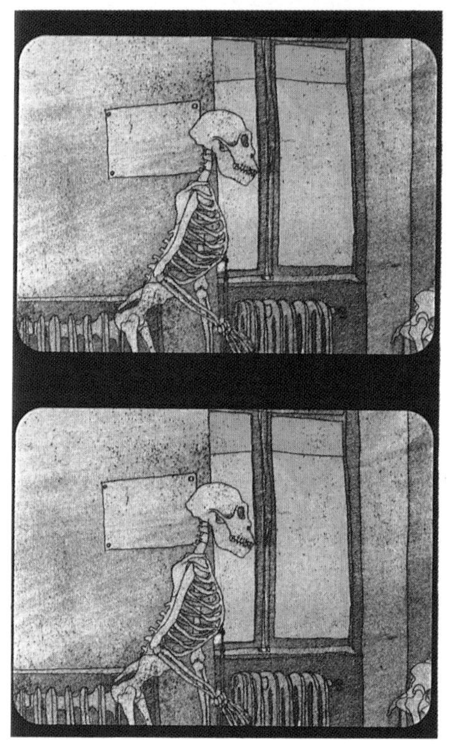

Right: Operation X-70, Raoul Servais
The Nosferatu-like skeleton, victim of the poisonous gas X-70, shows another of the wide range of styles employed by Servais. The location of the action is also crucial to the meaning, relating well to the more obvious concerns with the environment.

Television, new technology and the future
As the demand for cheap television output increased, many believed that the quality of film animation itself was suffering. Richard Williams Studio, which stood for quality pro-

Right: Fritz the Cat, Ralph Bakshi
Another orgy for Fritz. Its combination of economical production with contemporary adult subject-matter made *Fritz the Cat* one of the more successful animated features.

Below: An American Tail, Sullivan Bluth, © 1986 Universal City Studio Inc, and U-Drive Productions Inc, courtesy of MCA Publishing Rights
Don Bluth has sought to combine strong narrative with full high-quality animation. With the setting up of new studios in Ireland and the audience reception of *An American Tail*, he seems likely to continue to challenge the notion that the audience for quality animation has vanished.

duction throughout the 1970s, set about training animators in the old classic style, employing great Disney animators such as Art Babbet, and eventually began producing with Disney Studios. Ex-Disney director Don Bluth produced one feature film, *An American Tail*, which had considerable success and set very high standards for feature animation. It seemed to reveal a sustainable market for well-made features with the same kind of strong simple narrative that was once Disney's hallmark. Others like Richard Purdum have used the larger budgets provided by advertising to create animation of a high standard. This in its turn makes animation attractive to advertising agencies.

Television itself is unlikely to pay budgets of the magnitude required to deliver this kind of quality production values for its programmes. Even with co-production and merchandizing deals, the differences in funding are enormous. There are those who predict that development in computer animation will lessen or even obliterate this gap and make it feasible to produce full-length fully animated films with the sort of budgets available in television. Whether this will happen in the 1990s, or whether it is in reality even a desirable aim, is not yet clear. At the moment animation made for television must look for quality in areas other than production value – in concepts and characterization.

Channel Four in Britain has produced a number of the most interesting British animation films of recent years, and television programmes which are essentially public-service, such as *Sesame Street*, have also provided a space for a creative approach to animation. There are signs that the music-orientated television stations such as MTV and Sky Channel are also aware of the value of animation.

Innovative work still has difficulty finding a place on any screen apart from that of festivals, yet when they watch commercials and music videos audiences are accepting images which are as 'difficult' as any experimental animation. The use of new technology in animation is now accepted. It has so quickly become a part of the visual language of the media that we absorb without a thought images which a decade ago were simply astounding. The integration and manipulation of many different forms of image by electronics takes animation back to those early days of invention and illusion, back towards the edge of imagination and the immaterial.

There is, after all, nothing there. The great animator Alexandre Alexeieff once said: 'Isn't it strange! For much of the time an audience watches a film in the cinema, the screen is in fact blank while the film is moved through the projector. And yet they don't ask for half their money back.'

Animation is full of such questions that take us back to those early beginnings of cinema. What is it that we are watching when we see these drawings? And just why and how do such images of images hold us in so tight a grip, often from such an early age?

2
SCRIPT AND STORYBOARD

Getting started on an animated film takes a lot of careful preparation and hard thinking, from choosing a subject through to the creation of a detailed plan. Ever since the pioneering work of Walt Disney in the 1920s, the focus of this vital planning stage has been the script and its visual equivalent, the storyboard.

The storyboard is central to the process of producing an animated film. It can take many forms, from a rough sketch for a personal project to a highly finished presentation, and it may change as a project develops, but it always remains a unique point of reference for all those involved in working on the film.

The storyboard contains all the action, the dialogue, and indications of where sound effects and music may be needed. It provides a system in which the elements of the language of film can be defined before the production begins, and this calls for an understanding of the conventions of film construction that have become established – the use of shots, sequences and scenes, and the way in which transitions are made between them.

Storyboard techniques are as varied as approaches to subjects and narrative. But the

Heroic Times, Josef Gemes, Pannonia Film Vallalat
This feature film set in medieval Hungary makes use of an essentially discursive epic structure. The open form allows for an interweaving of character and plot, as well as for the development of visual set-pieces.

Above: Great, Bob Godfrey Films
***Great*, based on the life of Isambard Kingdom Brunel, concentrates most of the spectacle into musical numbers, justifying the very open structure of the narrative.**

Left: On Land, at Sea and in the Air, Paul Driessen
Part of the working storyboard for Driessen's film. Three parallel stories unfold on three separate screens.

essential element of storyboard production is accuracy and clarity both in the concept and in its final visualization.

Choosing a subject

People often say that something is 'not a suitable subject for animation'. This usually means simply that no one has ever tried it, or that it lies outside the traditions and conventions associated with certain kinds of animated film.

Nevertheless, there are some important things to consider before committing yourself to a particular subject for an animation. If it is a personal film, you need to decide how much can be achieved with the time and resources available. If it is a commissioned project, you will need to check the production costs against the budget. It is surprising how often these two differ – the client may expect the sophistication of *An American Tail* with budgets tailored to *Sesame Street*. Be realistic about what you can do – other people certainly will be. Another question is: who are the audience for this film? Again, it is worth being specific – try to 'see' the audience. A producer can often be a great asset in this, helping to focus an idea and find a suitable style for the film.

Ideas come from the application of thought to research. Research itself need not mean long hours in the library – it may be purely visual. It may involve keeping an eye on news items and events, or meeting and talking to special interest groups. It will certainly involve recording the information you gather, whether it is formal or informal. The best way is to keep a notebook.

Projects can take a very long time to come to fruition. For instance, Bob Godfrey's film *Great* (1974), based on the life of the Victorian engineer Isambard Kingdom Brunel, took some years of research before it went into production. And even when research has reached the point at which the outlines of a project can be sketched out, there may still be more research to be done as the project develops. There is a danger of over-researching a project and losing sight of the main objective, but on the other hand one element of the research may fruitfully lead to another.

Research, like drawing, is not sacred. Even if it seems that you have lighted upon a wonderful undiscovered area, you may find that it lacks the potential for a film. If it does not seem to work, try something else. At all events, the research is never wasted.

Disney and the script

The first animator to make the script the central element of his production was Walt Disney. The script was vital both for estimating and controlling the costs of a film and for

A 15 minute 16mm budget

Script	£600	($1080)
Storyboard	£300	($540)
Layouts	£600	($1080)
Animation	£5340	($9600)
Trace and paint	£2160	($3890)
Materials	£1250	($2250)
Sound, effects and transfers	£550	($990)
Editing	£2000	($3600)
Camera (in-house)	£800	($1440)
Laboratories and transfers	£860	($1550)
Voice fee	£100	($180)
Recording and stock	£125	($230)
Dub and stock	£320	($580)
Video transfers	£150	($270)
Music, effects and composition (original)	£2000	($3600)
Overheads	£1500	($2700)
Courier/carriage	£150	($270)
Production co-ordination	£750	($1350)
TOTAL	£19555	($35200)

Above: The budget for a 15-minute episode of a British television series made on 16mm film. The budget excludes items seen as part of the overall costs of the series, such as legal fees and copyright, but the overheads – for example, the cost of studio – are included. The major cost is in the production of the animation, for both hire of artists and materials. Stock and processing costs are relatively low in animation.

raising the initial finance. In commercial animation, this continues to be the case today.

But cost control and finance were not the only reasons why Disney gave such prominence to the script. He also saw that the animated films being produced at that time, in the mid-1920s, were lacking something vital. They depended almost entirely on the loosely connected antics of a character or group of characters. Even where a series of gags was worked around a single incident or situation, the relationship of this to the ensuing action was usually slight. For instance, in one of the best films of the period, *Felix Goes to Hollywood*, the animation follows Felix as he unsuccessfully tries to find work in a Hollywood studio. This central situation provides a focus, but still gag follows gag and the film is propelled forwards by its animation energy rather than by any true narrative structure.

By this time, however, live-action films had adopted powerful techniques of storytelling. Some were based on traditions of literature and theatre; others had been developed slowly as film-makers struggled with problems of articulating space and time in this new medium. Even the comedy films of the silent era had moved away from slapstick routine. In the films of Charlie Chaplin, Harold Lloyd and Buster Keaton, comedy was carefully crafted into a structured form. Chaplin's *The Gold Rush* (1925) and Keaton's *The General* (1926) demonstrate a highly developed visual narrative technique and language, with a coherence that even the best animated films of the period lacked. The strength of the great animated films of the mid-1920s, such as the Felix and Koko series, lies in their graphic style and in the surrealist, dreamlike development of their plots. As conventional narrative structures they are poor.

Even before the coming of sound, which was temporarily to turn the tables and give animation an advantage over live-action, Disney had begun to apply his talents to the problem of tightening up the structure of his animated films. He elaborated the script, and went even further than contemporary live-action production by introducing the storyboard, a detailed and precise visualization of the film as it would appear on the screen, presented in the form of a comic strip. The storyboard not only gave a clear picture of the development of the plot, but also provided an efficient instrument for organizing the complex production process. It proved possible to assign tasks, establish schedules and check productivity against the storyboard in a very effective manner. The storyboard also helped achieve a coherent studio output with a recognizable house style, and, even more importantly, it allowed all of the key personnel, even those not directly involved in the production, to have an idea of what was going on in the studio and how they might be called upon to take part at a later stage – a vital focus as the studios grew in size.

As Disney productions grew more complex and numerous, the storyboard was eventually considered insufficiently detailed, since it lacked any indication of timing or the relationship of sound to image. Disney consequently began to use the Leica Reel, a filmed storyboard. This element of the production is now called the animatic and is often made using single-frame video.

Script and storyboard today

There are individual animators who prefer to work without a formal script, using a less literary and more visual approach. Even so, they normally draw up a plan, however general and personal in form. For the kind of production that takes some time, where involvement with the detail of animation can at some stages obscure long-term objectives, most animators find that even the detailed storyboards usually associated with studio 'mass-production' methods have their uses.

There are sometimes problems when a professional scriptwriter more familiar with live-action conventions is used to produce the script for an animation. The essentially visual storyboard is not a form with which most scriptwriters are familiar, coming as they do mainly from a literary background. Even if they have worked on live-action film, this will

not necessarily help, since the storyboard plays a much greater role in animated film. Scriptwriters sometimes fail to understand the full visual potential of animation, or to appreciate that if they write a wonderful line of dialogue, someone has to animate it. For their part animators, who usually come from a visual background, have a tendency to underrate (and underpay) scriptwriters. Among the very few writers who specialize in animation scripts and can move between the various film disciplines are Stan Hayward and Don Arioli. *The Apple* and *Hot Stuff*, written by Hayward and Arioli respectively, show the results of the use of professional writers. Both films have a tight narrative line, as well as providing ample opportunity for the directors to elaborate the animation action.

Animators do, of course, write their own original scripts, thinking that as they will have to execute the film they are best placed to write it. One possibility is to adapt existing material. This can seem an easier task than writing an original script, but it runs into the problem that there are few forms which precisely match the short animated film. The live-action narrative film has a congruence with the novel; film, after all, developed with the novel as a model. Animation has similar links with the comic strip and caricature, which go back to its earliest roots. That comic strip is the form which adapts most easily to animation can be seen from some very successful examples in the 1980s, such as *When the Wind Blows* (1986), made by TVC from the book by Raymond Briggs and directed by Jimmy Murkami, and *I'm Not a Feminist But . . .* by Marjut Rimminen from the book of illustrations by Christine Roche. But the comic strip is not the same as the storyboard, just as the novel is not the same as the film.

Above: I'm Not a Feminist But, Marjut Rimminen, Marjut Rimminen Animation
Facing page: I'm Not a Feminist But, Christine Roche, Virago Books
The two illustrations by Christine Roche (facing page) have been simplified by Rimminen for animated film. In the Eve picture, the leaf on the apple becomes less complicated and the detail on the fingers goes; the mouth is made into a single line, but the nose and eyes remain as the original to keep the expression. The hair is treated differently – the scribble ensures that each line of the hair need not be animated separately. In the other example, the lines on the face have gone and the characters are positioned in such a way that the woman's feet are out of shot.

The plot

Writer and film-maker David Mamet has said that when screenwriters cannot think of a plot, they resort to using more dialogue. In a similar way, it might be said of animators that when they are short of a plot they turn to excessively elaborate animation. The plot is one of those elements of film-making that seem to baffle comprehension by their very simplicity. Straightforwardly, the plot is the plan of the story, decided before any scripting or storyboarding takes place. The plot is also, in its other meaning, a conspiracy – a conspiracy between the film-maker and the audience to construct a story. Like a joke, the plot must be able to communicate effectively and quickly. It is not dependent on a worked-out script. The plot describes the story in relation to the audience. Although the plot is the plan of the story, it is also the way in which the story is perceived by others.

A plot can be told in many different ways, or rather it can be perceived in many different ways so that the actual telling will differ. If when you tell the plot the reaction that you get is glazed eyes, it may be that the story itself has potential but the way that you perceive it in relation to an audience is wrong.

Narration and description

If things do go wrong at the storyboard stage, many hours of work can be wasted. It is worth spending time and money on getting the initial plan right, rather than waiting for that terrible moment of audience incomprehension or loss of interest. Whatever approach you adopt – whether a scriptwriter is used or the script is adapted or created by the animators themselves – there are some simple steps that can be taken to ensure that the eventual storyboard is coherent.

Firstly, you must consider how the film will stand in relation to the two basic approaches to animation: narrating and describing. The distinction between these two approaches has been the subject of a good deal of argument and debate. They do not always appear as clear-cut choices – a film may contain elements of both narrative and description. But thinking in these terms can illuminate how, for practical purposes, an animator sets about handling a project.

Narration – traditional storytelling – aims to take an audience through events in a linear way. Classically, it consists of a series of statements or questions, which are in turn developed and resolved. As each statement is resolved, we learn more about the situation and the characters. There may be any number of plots and sub-plots, as well as false resolutions and plot twists. The point of view from which the story is presented may also change as the plot proceeds.

Description relies on accurate observation and the creation of atmosphere and character to portray an event or situation. Normally the audience and the central character have the same point of view – the aim is to put the viewer in the position of the character, in order to share and understand the character's experience.

Almost all films have an element of both narration and description. However, it is vital to decide from the outset which is the more important. The differences between these two methods, and the way in which this affects the meaning of a film, can be seen by comparing two animations, *Girls Night Out* (1986) by Joanna Quinn and *Second Class Mail* (1984) by Alison Snowden.

Joanna Quinn's film is an example of a predominantly descriptive approach. It is based on the visit of a Welsh housewife to a pub ladies-only night, where the main event is a routine by a male stripper. The woman leaves her drab but comfortable home, husband sitting in front of the TV, takes her hat and coat and leaves for the pub. This is a normal 'establishing scene', introducing character and situation. The only dialogue is a telephone conversation between the woman and her workfriends, who are trying to persuade her to go out for the evening. She agrees and announces the fact to her uninterested husband.

The impact of the scene depends on the carefully observed decor of the room and the details of the characters, who are presented not in a stylized way, but as real human beings. The pose and the movement of characters builds up the first scene, preparing the audience for the transformation of the heroine. In the pub we share the heroine's

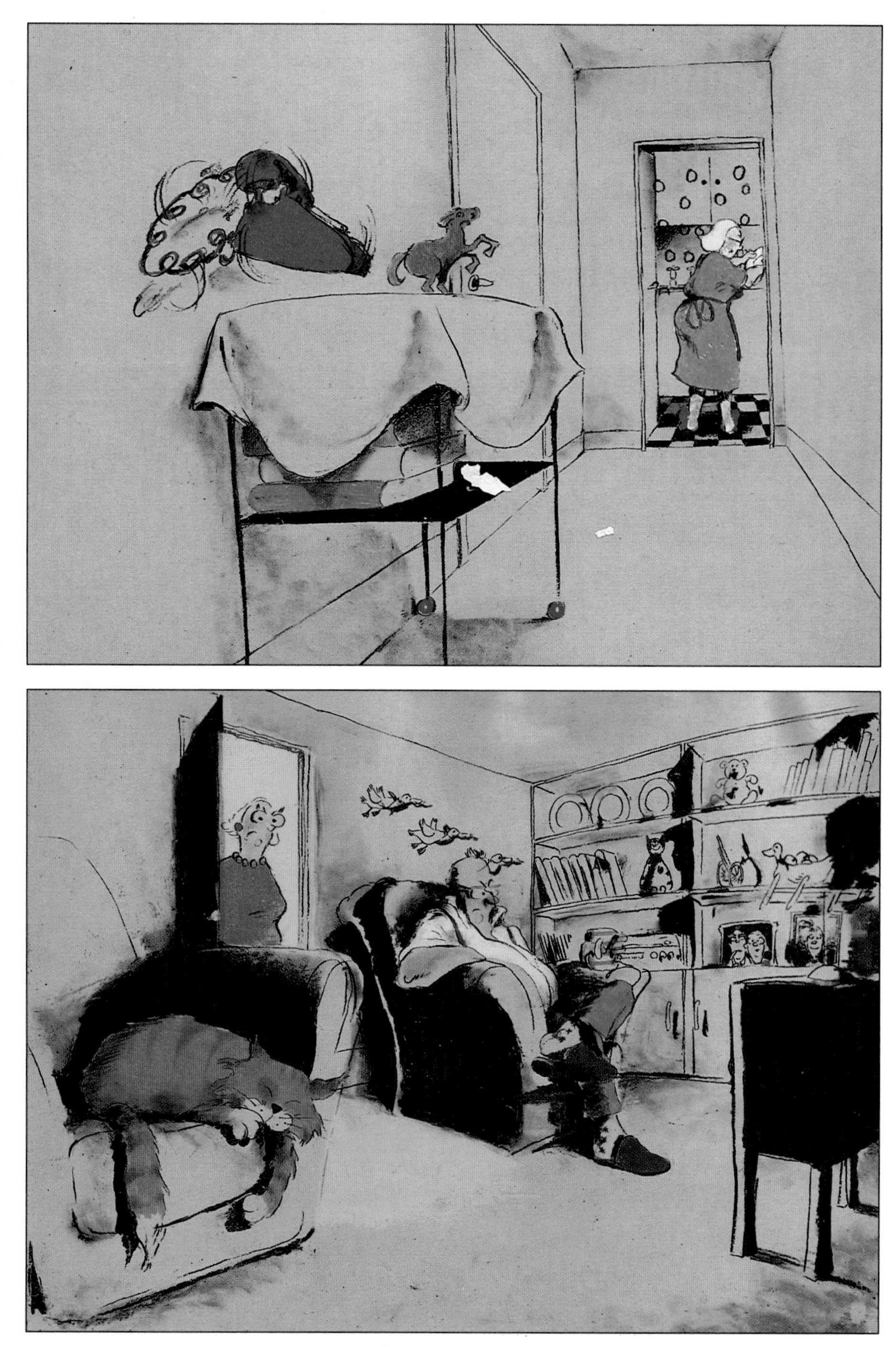

Above: *Girls Night Out,* Channel 4/Joanna Quinn

Top: Beryl is going about her business in the kitchen as the phone rings with a tempting invitation from her friends.
Bottom: Hubby sits with the cat watching the television as Beryl makes her plans. The detail of location and character is used to describe the situation economically and to set the scene for the ensuing action.

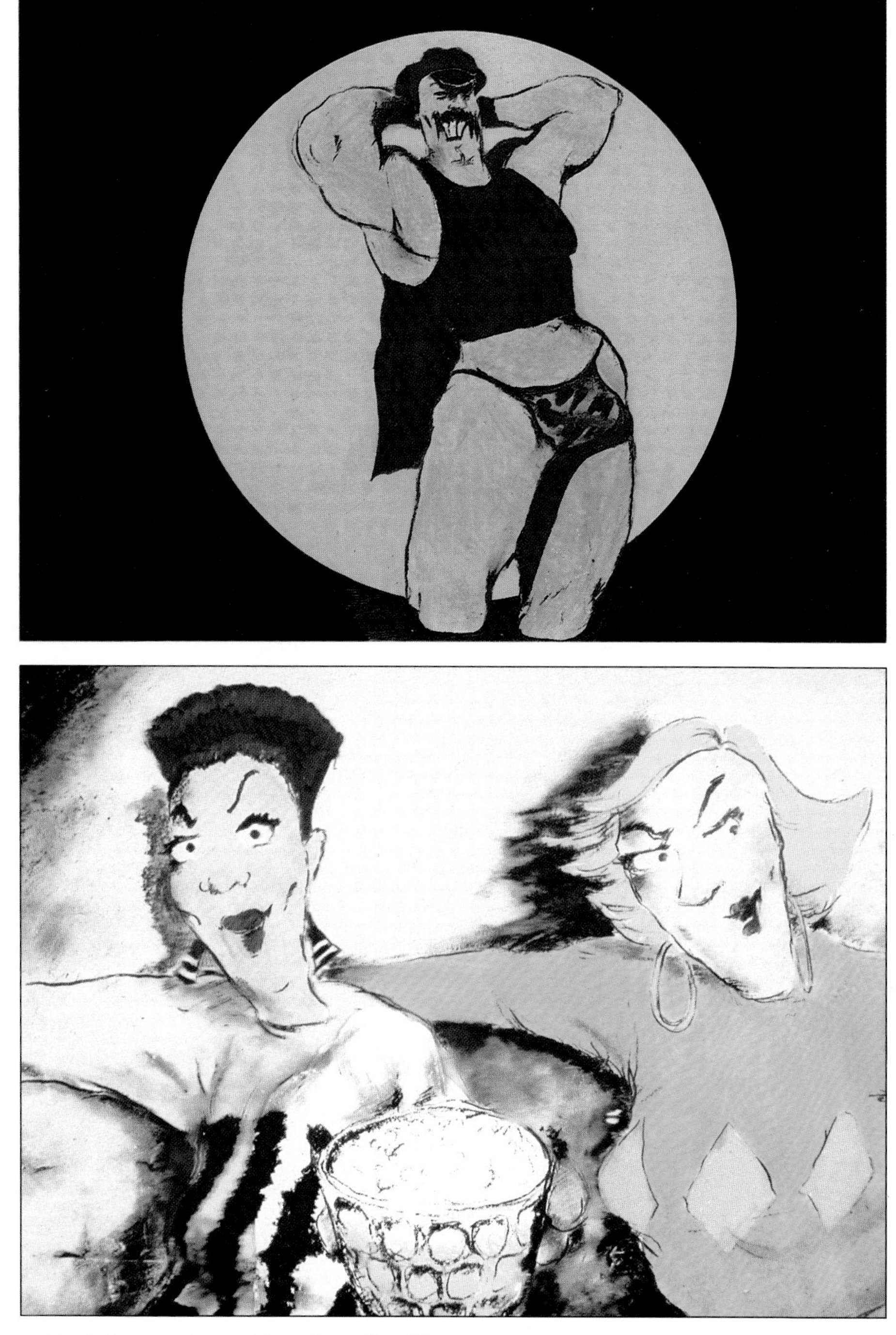

Girls Night Out, Channel 4/Joanna Quinn
Above left: The male stripper, for once the subject of the women's gaze.
Left: The reaction of the friends to the performance.
Above: Beryl lets herself go – her pleasure is unrestrained.
The point-of-view structure in these shots is used to position the viewer in relation to the action and to reinforce the identification with the heroine.

point of view as she watches the strip with growing enthusiasm. Her transformation from quiet housewife to wild joyful hooligan is shown entirely through her reactions in the company of the other women, as her real self is able to find expression. The film depends on the accuracy of its observation of location and character and on its ability to place the audience in a sympathetic relationship with the woman, who will later return inevitably to her dull routine.

Second Class Mail, by Alison Snowden, is predominantly narrative in approach. A plain brown-paper parcel drops through the door of a middle-aged woman's house; she pulls out an inflatable man, a 'husband' complete with a pipe, spectacles and a cup of tea. When the wife hugs the 'hubby', he explodes. Undaunted she sends for another model. The characterization is much more stylized in this film, closer to our idea of a caricature. The narrative is sustained by a series of questions which are posed and resolved: What is in the parcel? How will the rubber man handle his cup of tea? The main dramatic action is set against a sub-plot about a budgerigar in its cage, which is used to pace the narrative through parallel cutting. When the bird finally drops from its perch, the pay off in the main narrative can be unloaded. The film uses the proscenium-arch type of framing, as in traditional theatre, to establish clearly the viewer's detached position. The action is made primary, revealing the woman's loneliness and determination. The audience identifies with her predicament, rather than her character.

Halls, Animation City (agency: McCann-Erickson; client Lambert Confectionery)
This series of stills shows the use of live-action editing techniques in the making of a storyboard: the angled mid-shot to show the driver sounding the klaxon; the close-up of the face straight-on illuminated by the furnace; and, finally, the pack shot which shows the product. All these shots, which could be arrived at during shooting in live-action, must be thought out at the storyboard stage in animation.

These two films deal with similar subjects and characters. It is the way they are structured that differs. In the first there is little storyline; the action develops around the visit to the pub and is indicated through a very accurate description of the woman and the location. In the second there is a strong plot, with audience expectations carefully orchestrated and resolved. Both these films deal with the real world, one very directly, the other through references to other films and traditions of cartoon. But even if a film deals with fantasy, the same choice has to be made.

There are examples of both traditions in mainstream animation. Road Runner films are perhaps the most rigorous examples of narration. The characters of Wile E. Coyote and the Road Runner are predetermined and unchanging; it is the repertoire of the unfolding, ever more disastrous action which is predominant. Disney, especially in the earlier short films, used description quite freely. A film like *Flowers and Trees*, the studio's first colour film, as well as the winner of the first of many Academy Awards for Disney, is clearly almost as pure an example of description as Road Runner is of narration. In the film, nature is animated to the music of Mendelssohn and Schubert.

Even the thirty-second commercial has many examples of both narration and description. In the Halls Mentholyptus advertisement from Animation City, the short description of the locomotive driver is achieved using a hard-edge graphic style which makes explicit reference to the style of the American Realist painters such as Edward Hopper. The commercial seeks to evoke a mood rather than tell a story. A similar approach is shown in Russell Hall's famous commercial for Richard Williams Studio of a North Sea oil rig during a storm, animated in the style of the nineteenth-century Romantic artist Turner.

On the other hand, commercials can and do sometimes set out to tell a story, even in the very short duration allowed to them. Oscar Grillo, in his commercial for Heineken lager, parodies Disney's *Three Little Pigs*. In the space of thirty seconds, the commercial manages to tell the whole story of the original full-length version. In this case parody helps the audience fill in the gaps in the truncated narrative.

Narration and description, then, can take many forms. Although when thinking of mainstream American cartoons it is the narrative mode that comes most readily to mind, there are many examples of animated films where description is dominant. Of course, as with all rules, those for narrating and describing can be broken. But if the rules have been fully understood, deviations from the norm will be more effective. The non-narrative or anti-narrative film still operates with a structure, even if this structure is visual or thematic.

Elephant Theatre, Sabrina Schmid, Swinburne School of Film and Television

The idea for this film developed quite loosely, based on some improvised dialogue by Gregory Pryor, certain images of a house, a theatre and elephants, and pre-recorded sounds and music using a synthesizer and barrel organ. The structure of the film was arrived at as production progressed and all of the separate elements were brought together. The plot is described by Sabrina Schmid: 'One man has built a little theatre which he can hold in the palm of his hand. It reveals a world of its own. Yet there remains one dream to be fulfilled: that some day elephants will come to live in it.' The narrative is loose and the story appears and disappears during the telling. It is an open-ended structure which allows unexpected juxtaposition and detours both visual and verbal.

Above: Poligon, Anitolo Petrov

Written by the Soviet science fiction writer Ganovsky, the film concerns the development of a thinking tank which destroys anything or anyone showing fear – including the developers and testers themselves. The technique of photo-realism is further heightened by making the characters resemble well-known film stars. The stars' characteristics are used as a kind of mask to denote a type.

Classical narrative and alternatives

Classical narrative is often spoken of as having a beginning, a middle and an end. It derives from the three-act play and the form of the nineteenth-century novel. The beginning establishes location, character and the main plot points, then the middle produces variations on the plot points and sets questions for resolution in the final part. It is a formal structure that can provide a very clear framework for an animation, even a relatively short one.

There are, however, objections to classical narrative both formally and ideologically. The formal objection is that the last part, the resolution, causes problems. Because of the demand that all of the questions set up be resolved before the narrative concludes, the ending can become unwieldy, and implausible in terms of naturalism or realism. Difficulties sometimes occur even in terms of straightforward comprehension. There are great cinema classics where it would be difficult to describe the development of the action convincingly and where questions about how it all happened still linger.

The classical narrative comes in for criticism ideologically because it casts the audience in the role of passive observers and consumers. It does not allow for different kinds of understanding. By doing the work of the audience for it, the narrative arguably deprives the viewer of real pleasure, substituting an easy gratification. Classical narrative is also seen as irrevocably a part of the Western cultural tradition, distorting other non-Western cultural forms if they are adapted to its strict logic.

These are not questions that can be put aside with claims that animation is simply fun or entertainment and should not have to deal with such serious matters. It is precisely because of the power of animation to amuse that these serious questions do have to be considered.

A number of attempts have been made to avoid the negative aspects of classical narrative. In *Great* Bob Godfrey used the form of a musical to comment on the life of Brunel. This permitted movement between the past and present and between levels of humour and seriousness that could not easily have been achieved in classical narrative, which seeks to maintain a coherence of location in space and time. Some of the exciting achievements of pop video come about precisely because music allows the animator a much freer approach to imaging than even commercials which, though short, do tend to conform more closely to the classical model.

There are films that deliberately set out to challenge the norm, such as Vera Neubauer's work where narrative conventions are com-

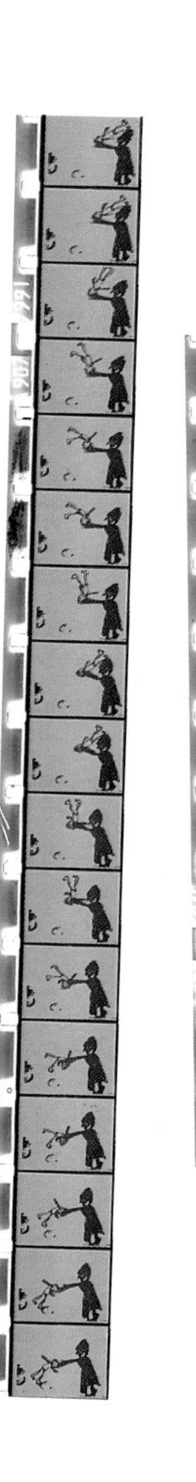

Left: The World of Children, Vera Neubauer
Different styles of film image can be combined to convey a powerful message. Drawings by children, images of children and documentary footage of children at play all serve to challenge adults' easy preconceptions of the child's world. It is more difficult to storyboard this kind of film thoroughly, as the documentary footage cannot always be predicted.

Below and bottom: Asparagus, Suzan Pitt
Animation films which draw on the imagery of the unconscious have usually been more successful than their live-action counterparts. In *Asparagus*, a totally convincing world of erotic and threatening objects is constructed. It can be useful for an animator to keep a dreambook on a regular basis.

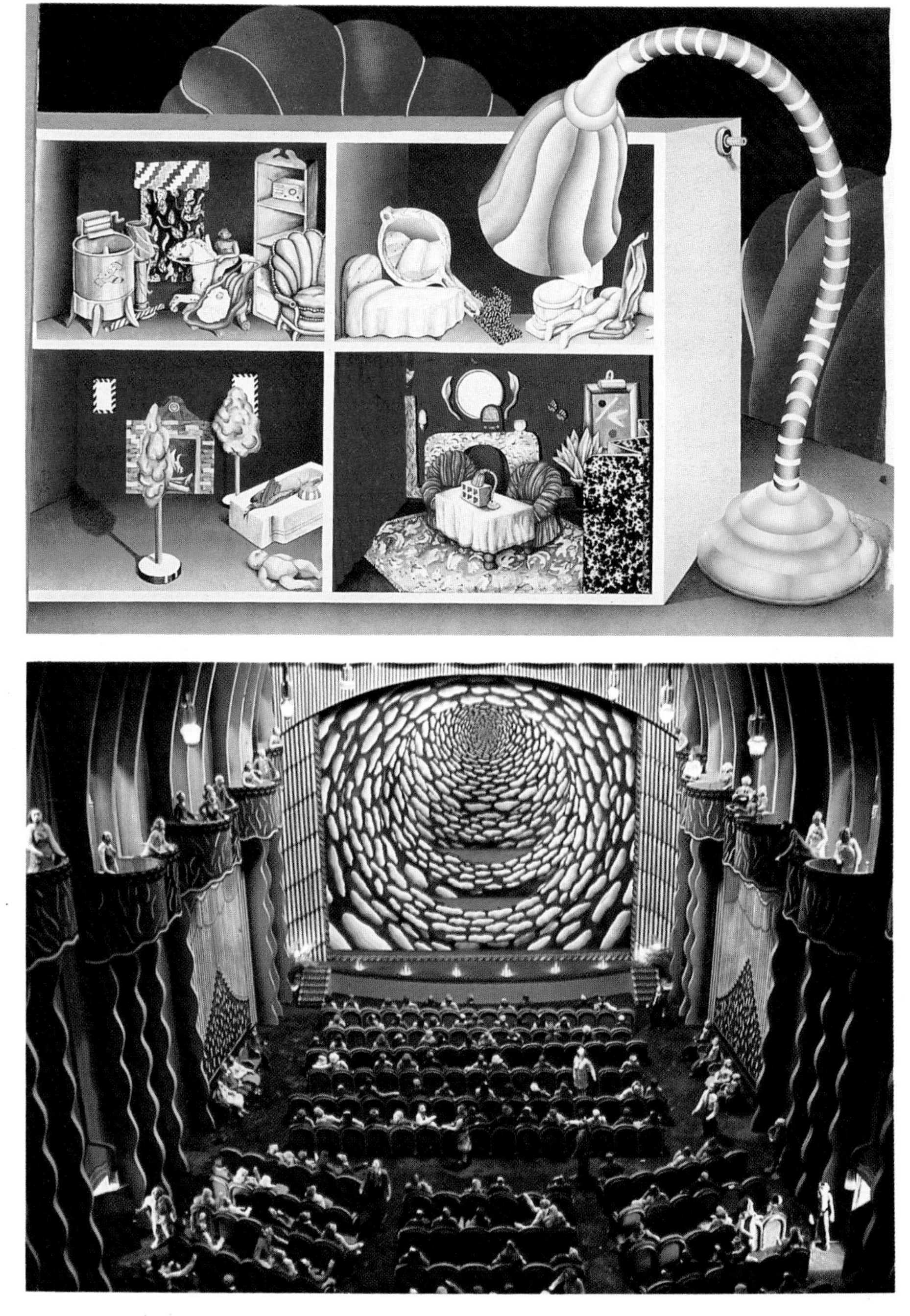

pletely rejected in favour of a structure that permits meanings to emerge through the juxtaposition of images. In her film *Decision* (1981), the old folk tale in which a young princess must decide which suitor she will choose to marry is juxtaposed with images from everyday family life seen from the woman's point of view. The princess, it is clear, has no choice – the decision is not real if she has to choose between husbands, rather than whether to marry at all.

The transition between the images carries a meaning and is open. There is no attempt to

Left: The Sinking of the Lusitania, Winsor McCay
The film's serious message and sustained sober mood remain impressive. In this shot, the liner is beginning to sink after the torpedoes have struck it. Passengers leap into the sea from the stern, almost in slow motion.

Below and below right: Pica Don, Renzo Kinoshita, Animation Studio Lotus
Below: A Hiroshima schoolchild peers into the bright sky, hearing the sound of the aircraft that will drop the atomic bomb. The threat about to be unleashed, and the vulnerability of humanity in the face of it, is emphasized by the high angle of this shot. Everyday images are carefully built up before the final impact and the horrific aftermath.

resolve the questions raised by a neat closing of the story and a completing of the narrative line. The style itself is also varied, so that the different 'voices' of various kinds of production contribute to the meaning. Live-action film is used in an almost documentary form, the animation of everyday life is presented using a harsh line and deliberately awkward movement, while the folk tale is seen as if it is an old movie, flickering and boiling like early animation.

Description and its variants

Description can be a very powerful means of using animated film. Perhaps the first and most famous was Winsor McCay's film *The Sinking of the Lusitania* (1918), a re-creation of the event based on news reports. Of course, no film cameras were present at the torpedoing of the passenger liner, and it is doubtful anyway whether they could have constructed so powerful a record. The film shows the German submarine firing torpedos at the American liner and the subsequent sinking of the ship. Figures are seen leaping into the water to escape. Everything is drawn in great detail, with the clear intention of making the animation as real as possible. The detail achieved, as well as the skill of the animation and the use of shots and angles drawn from the developing language of live-action film, vividly evoke the situation and place the audience as witnesses to the event.

In the same way, the film *Pica Don* (1978) by Renzo Kinoshita re-creates the events of 6 August 1945, when the first atomic bomb was dropped. It is as harrowing as *The Sinking of the Lusitania*, showing the terrible effects of the moment of the blast on the inhabitants of Hiroshima. It is the very fact that animation films can present a general description of such events from whatever point of view they choose that gives them this power.

These films were based on research after the event. Animator Susan Young actually made drawings during the Toxteth riots in Liverpool in 1981 and re-created the scenes in *Thin Blue Lines*, which shows what it was like to be there as an observer on the spot. Once more it is the placing of the viewer, through point of view, that gives these descriptive films their meaning.

But description can take other forms, moving towards documentary. Red Groome's *Fat Feet* (1966) tries to give a description of life in the Bronx which is both accurate and uniquely personal, using expressionist visuals with distortions in scale and proportion. The effect is both disturbing as a record, having an obvious relationship to the real, and as a challenge to ideas of representation. Jane Aaron, another American artist, inserts her animation into other spaces which are photographic. So a drawing of driving along a road is mounted on a real car windscreen as

Right: Thin Blue Lines, Susan Young, Liverpool Polytechnic
Taking as subject a real event does not mean that a realistic style has to be employed. The freely drawn figures of police and rioters in this film give the sensation of images torn from the real, of the moment itself.

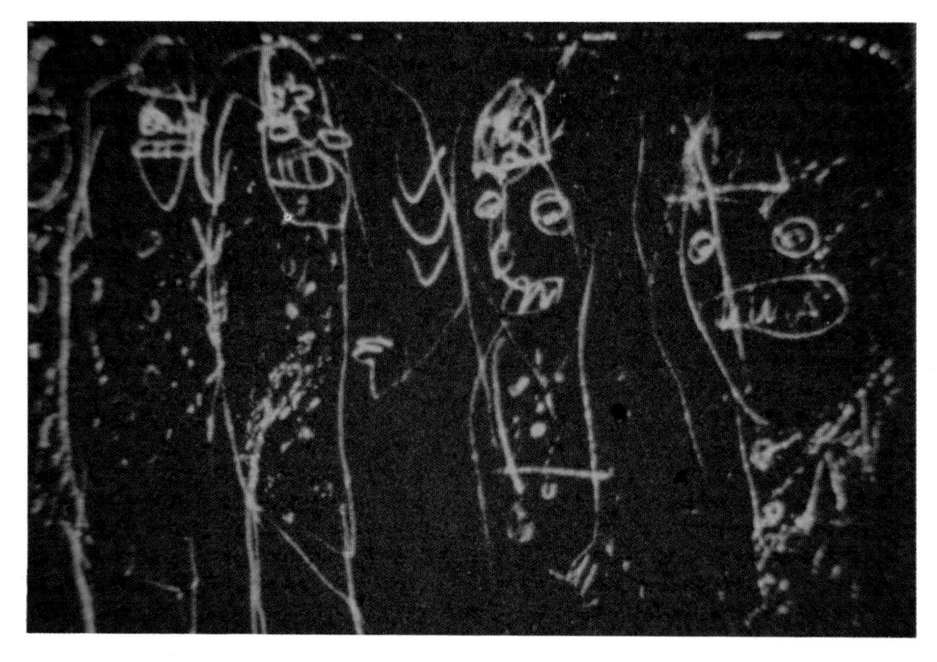

Below: The full force of the first shock wave from the bomb hits the victims' clothes and flesh is torn from the victims' bodies. The viewpoint is now level with the casualties, so that we are asked to share the event and experience the horror. Although the film is harrowing, it achieves catharsis.

the car drives along the same road. Or the drawn movement of sunlight in a room is set in the same space as a photographed room. There is clearly as much scope for challenging the way in which we describe things and the world around us as there is for examining the way in which we tell stories.

Putting it on paper

A subject has been chosen, a possible audience defined and the broad approach decided. What next? For the animator, the storyboard is the key. There may be a script, existing material, notes, character sketches, atmosphere sketches and so on, but it all has to come together in a storyboard.

The storyboard is the plan of the action and gives a clear idea of the timing and the transitions between the shots, scenes and sequences. 'Shot', 'scene' and 'sequence', by the way, are all terms which derive from live-action film-making. They are very useful for describing animation, but they can be discarded if they inhibit the flow of the film. The main thing to remember is that the storyboard is a map of transitions and timing.

The *shot* is the basic element in building up a storyboard, the basic unit of the film's construction. It corresponds to a single continuous take by a film camera in live-action. As an animation film has to be pre-planned, the storyboard artist must be able to think like a film editor. The full vocabulary of live-action film is available to the animator – the long shot, the close-up, establishing shots, point of view and cut-away. The animator must be able to visualize all of the shots and transitions, and the camera movements – or rather the animation copies of camera movements.

The simplest shot transition is the cut; it can also be the most effective. The precise point at which to make the cut may depend on the soundtrack as well as the action. Other transitions are the mix, where one shot dissolves into the next, the fade-in and fade-out, where a shot fades out to black or fades in from black, and various kinds of wipes, where one image (or a black screen) wipes across another and replaces it. New technology has also added a whole range of editing possibilities to the repertoire. All of this has to appear at the storyboard stage, so it is important to have a clear idea of what new techniques can offer.

In addition, animation has further scope for shot transitions making use of metamorphosis. Images changing into other images, and creating meaning by doing so, can bring animation close to techniques associated with poetry, rather than narrative traditions.

Shots are organized into *sequences*. A sequence may consist of any number of shots – or even of one continuous shot – but it usually defines one action, at the same location in time and place and with the same

Gwen, Jean-François Laguionie
Part of the working storyboard for *Gwen*. Throughout these shots, which make up a single sequence, the movement from long shot to close-up is carefully controlled. As the rhythm of the pursuit of the ostrich by the bedouin and hunters increases, the editing becomes more rapid and there are a greater number of close-ups. The change of direction of the running ostrich is carefully marked so that it does not suddenly run in the opposite direction but is seen to turn. Similarly, the positions of the hunters and the bedouin are consistent: although they are not seen in the same shot, their relative situations are made clear by the relationship of the ostrich to each of them.

characters. The exception to this is a so-called montage sequence, in which a rapid assembly of shots is used as a transition between scenes – in this case the space, time and character will change rapidly, often to demonstrate the passing of time.

Sequences are organized into *scenes*. A scene may consist of sequences depicting different locations and characters. It is often referred to as 'opening with . . .' and 'closing with . . .'. This act of opening and closing defines the scene's function in classical narrative – it is the unit in which the action and plot points are resolved.

If films were made strictly according to this logic they would be, as some are, dull and mechanical. It is the attacks on the conventions which all film-makers delight in, whether they are working in the classical tradition or experimental animation, that

Left: Duck Amuk, Chuck Jones, © 1953 Warner Bros Inc, all rights reserved
Duck Amuk represents one of the most sustained parodies on narrative in mainstream film. The Duck is subjected to a non-stop change of location and role by the mysterious director. Each time the location changes, the role of the character which Daffy is playing changes also, forcing him to try to adapt.

Below: Tale of Tales, Yuri Norstein
The narrative structure of _Tale of Tales_ has a relationship with the point of view and the act of repetition. Scenes are observed from different points of view throughout the narrative. This structure allows the theme of memory, personal and public, to be explored.

make for excitement and for a shared conspiracy between the film-maker and the audience. The departures from convention may be humorous, as in Chuck Jones's *Duck Amuk* (1953), where Daffy Duck suffers countless humiliations as set or role changes are forced on the perplexed bird by the hidden hand of the director – in the process revealing the way in which narrative itself is made. Or they can be designed to make the audience question their preconceived easy acceptance of a universe of cause and effect, as in the films of Robert Breer, where connections are made by the audience in a free association of images which cluster around a number of central concepts. Or they can disrupt the sense of time, collapsing the past and the present, as in Yuri Norstein's *Tale of Tales* (1979) where the repetition of images of events observed from different points of view are distributed throughout the film to create a sense of displacement and loss.

Animation is fortunate in having so many different conventions to engage with and therefore rules to break. Live-action, art, graphics and cartoon all have established sets of conventions to break, and more recently we have begun to see that the new technology itself cannot stand immune.

Storyboard techniques
The storyboard is the method by which shots, scenes and sequences are put down on paper. It may range from the roughest of sketches for the lone film-maker or the initial visualization stage of a commercial, through to actual working storyboards and presentations. There are special layout pads made for storyboarding, already marked out with

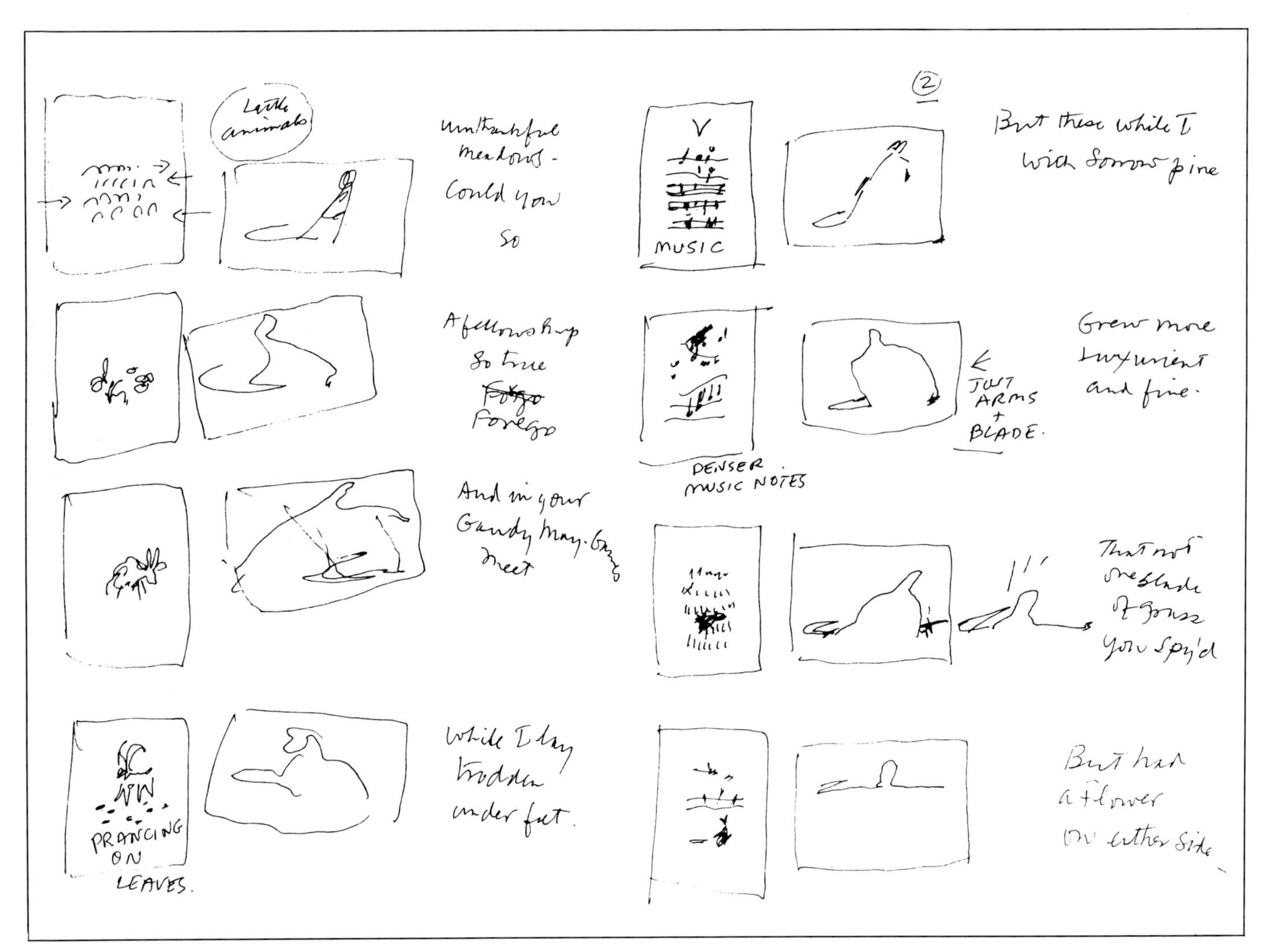

frames in the proportions of a TV screen (in TV ratio), and with spaces for indicating sound or dialogue. Any of the frames can be taken out and moved at will to a different position in the storyboard, if a TV format is what is required. If a different style or format is needed, then the animator has to make up a storyboard in the appropriate screen ratio. Whatever happens, the storyboard must be legible. If it is at a stage where there is still work left to be done and it cannot be finalized, the artwork should be made in a way that allows for further changes without having to remake the whole board.

The form of the initial *rough storyboard* may be quite schematic. There is no need at this stage for anything more than a basic indication of the development of the action. The level of drawing can be rudimentary – it is more important to communicate the broad concept as economically as possible. Many of the best story and concept artists have limited drawing skills; they are unhampered by concerns about the quality of their artwork or what others might think of their drawing ability. They can put an idea down on paper quickly and be ruthless about discarding elements that do not aid the process of communication. In fact, good drawing can be the enemy of a good storyboard in the early stages, if it makes the animator unwilling to carry out changes that necessitate the destruction of fine graphic work.

Once the basic decisions have been made and thoroughly discussed, the storyboard can be taken to the next stage – the working storyboard, and the presentation storyboard to be shown to clients, financial backers and so on.

The *working storyboard* should contain all the information needed to enable the layout artists to lay out the scenes. It indicates the action in each scene, as well as the general movement of the camera and characters. The dialogue and sound effects are also marked. As with all the stages of animation, the sheer amount of artwork, paper and cel produced means that things can easily get confused or lost, so a very precise system of logging is required. Scene numbers must be indicated clearly, though often rather than a reference to sequence numbers or shots, there is a brief description of the action itself. It is helpful to do this because there may be many different people working on a single production. If a sequence is marked with both a scene number and a sequence reference, together with a description of the action, this creates a useful safety margin.

Above: The Tempest, George Dunning/ A TVC Production

The rough storyboard for *The Tempest* was drawn in a small 6×4 notebook. It shows clearly the relationship of the text to the image, as well as indicating special sound or music effects. If the image needs clarification, this is also done in writing. The text is placed on the far right of each line related to the images. Even though these are rough notes, they are still cleared of any possible ambiguity.

Below: All the Best, Animation City, © MPL Communications Ltd/EMI Records Ltd
This is a presentation storyboard, and so carries a lot more information in the images, which are more highly finished. As well as the visuals there is a good deal of descriptive text. This defines the movement, the motivation and the captions which are to appear. The music is also detailed at this stage, as are any dialogue and voice-overs (v/o). The presentation storyboard is the communication link between the client, agency and production house in the first stages of production. No technical details are shown, only the main scenes which will appear in the film.

The *presentation storyboard* is normally not as fully worked out as the working board. It contains the main scenes and gives an idea of style and content, using relatively few images compared to the proposed length of the film – perhaps half a dozen for a thirty-second commercial. It does not have details of all the action, but only the main events. On the other hand, the artwork itself is usually worked up to a more finished state, and if an artist is being brought in as a designer, the board will reflect this style in some detail. Each frame is mounted on board and the artwork protected by an overlay.

The animatic

Developments in video technology have made preparing and presenting the storyboard as an animatic very easy. The old Leica Reel, or filmed storyboard, was both expensive and took time. The new technology has introduced single-frame video using low- or high-band video recorders, and sophisticated image digitizers and frame stores which provide for considerable manipulation of the image. All of these systems allow the shooting to be carried out to a soundtrack or for the sound to be added afterwards. A rough soundtrack and voice track can be laid and synchronized to the images with a high degree of accuracy. Camera movements can be made to show the effect to be achieved in the final production.

The animatic has great advantages over the storyboard. The real timing of the film can be gauged more accurately and adjustments can be made if necessary – indeed, substantial changes are often carried out at this stage. The animatic can be edited on video and additional video effects added. There are

The Snowman, Channel 4/A TVC Production
Based on a book by Raymond Briggs, *The Snowman* made full use of the range of animation in its adaptation from the still image. Point of view was used very effectively to involve the viewer with the child's fantasy of the snowman coming to life and befriending the child.

advantages both for animators, since they are able to eliminate errors at an early stage and save a great deal of work later, and for clients, who are in a position to judge what the final product will be like.

But the animatic can never be a substitute for the final film or video. Each stage of production makes a unique contribution to the final film. If the animatic is perceived as the final work with the animation to be added (a mistake that is not unknown), a quite false impression may be produced. The animatic needs to be read, like a storyboard, as a plan for the action and not a substitute for it.

Point and point of view

A question always worth asking at an early stage of planning is: 'What's the point?' When storyboarding, this question has quite a precise meaning. The point of a sequence and a scene will relate to plot points in the script. It is these plot points that move the narrative. Given the often laborious nature of animation production, any action which does not relate to these plot points or does not help in building atmosphere or character should be eliminated. This rigorous pre-selection is an important part of animation and makes it an excellent discipline for non-animators as well. Many live-action film-makers succumb to the temptation to put into their work a great shot that they have been thinking about for years, even if it does not contribute anything to the film.

Although many experimental animators choose to work without formal storyboards, their rigorous approach to film-making still shows. In *Free Radicals* (1958), Len Lye produced many thousands of feet of film which he had drawn on directly, and then edited this down to produce a film of great simplicity, one of the most precisely controlled and structured works of animated film.

Another question to ask when storyboarding is: 'What's the point of view?' Establishing the point-of-view structure may seem a strange preoccupation for animation. After all, there are rarely any actors in an animated film. But, of course, the concept of point of view can apply to any narrative form. It can include the point of view of the narrator, of the storyteller or of the characters themselves. And it can itself feature as an important part of the dramatic structure.

Point of view is established at a number of levels. The first is the point of view of the narrator. Is the narrator outside the action or one of the characters? Where are we, the audience, placed in relation to the action and the characters? Are we being asked to see what happens through the characters' eyes?

The second level of point of view is the positioning of the 'camera' and the spectator. Animation is particularly well-endowed with possibilities of shifting the point of view in this sense, as there are no physical limits to what the 'camera' can do. This can result in some spectacular sequences such as the flying section from *The Snowman* by TVC or the famous lighthouse sequence of *A Christmas Carol* (1971) by Richard Williams, in both of which the camera leaves the ground and we are carried along with the characters as they fly through space. Metamorphosis is another way of changing point of view in animation. This is used very effectively in the NFBC film *The Street*, an adaptation of a Mordecai Richler story by animator Caroline Leaf, in which sweeping transformations unexpectedly and suddenly shift the point of view from character to character.

Designing characters

Characters are another consideration in storyboarding. Character design is attempted by many and remains a mystery to many. The central task of the character designer is to produce character sheets – a series of illustrations showing a character from every possible aspect and in a range of moods and situations. These are then followed as a guide by the animators during the actual production of the film.

There are very few good character designers and all share one attribute – they observe the people around them very closely and analyse themselves more closely still. The notebook is an essential for character designers. Following the conventions of character design – how to make a 'dumb' or 'cute' character – can only produce stereotypes. Good strong characterization comes from understanding and observation carried out remorselessly. Even when designed, the character will often react differently when animated by different animators, so that even given the discipline of character sheets, there can still be room for an original approach. For the purposes of the storyboard, however, it is not the design itself which is most important, but the way in which the interrelationship of the characters can be used to refine the broad dimensions of the character.

Motivation, too, can be indicated in the storyboard. Perhaps the best example of this is the Road Runner series by Chuck Jones.

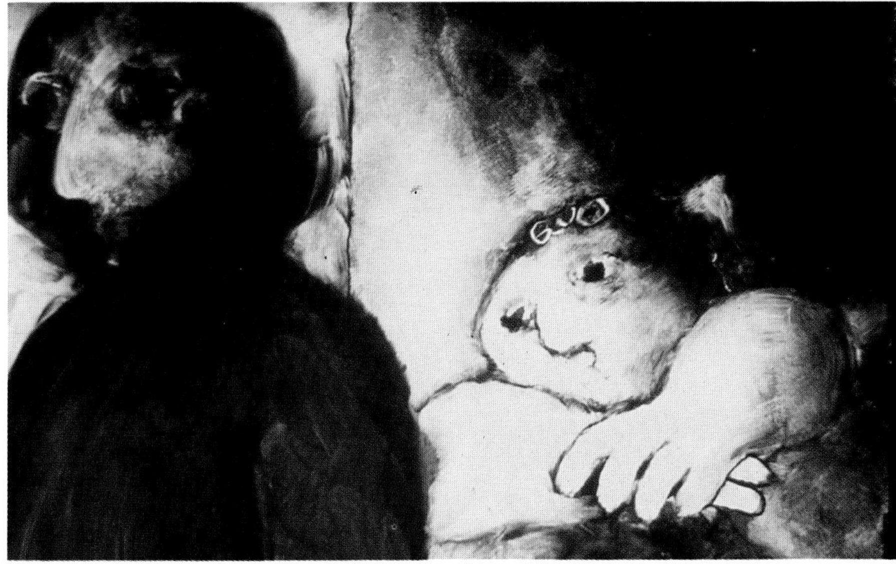

Left: The Street, National Film Board of Canada/Caroline Leaf
This adaptation from the Mordecai Richler story deals with a boy's view of the sickness and death of his grandmother. These two shots show the mother with the dying grandmother and the boy talking to his mother about the grandmother's bequests. Using the technique of painting on glass, Leaf achieves the transitions between scenes by metamorphosis rather than straight cuts.

Below: Granpa, Channel 4/A TVC Production
This character sheet for a new film from TVC, again based on a Raymond Briggs book, shows the detail of the character of granpa both in line and in colour. The character is presented from a number of angles, so that the animator knows the whole figure. This is one of a number of such sheets that will be used for each of the characters in the film, helping maintain consistency when the character is drawn by many different hands.

Wile E. Coyote is hungry; Road Runner represents food. There are no distractions, no other characters. It is a motivation of pure logic. But they need each other. It is in the relationship expressed through the action that Wile E. is defined.

The storyboard represents the first stage in the process of making animation. Other processes go on at the same time – the preparation of the sound begins, some key scenes start to be laid out and work is done on the character design. But it is the storyboard that holds all of this together; it makes it possible to examine more exciting ways of dealing with sound, for instance, or of making a transition between scenes. Because animation is a collaborative process, the storyboard is crucial, creating clear communication between all of those who may spend months or years working together on a single project.

THE STORYBOARD

This case history focuses on the storyboard for the film *Granpa*, based on an illustrated book by Raymond Briggs.

Right: The storyboard is pinned to the wall in a prominent position in the studios, so that the artists can become familiar with it. On the board, each of the different sequences and scenes is clearly noted with a name and number. Then names and numbers are used to keep control of the production processes and to enable the director and producer to see if any of the production is falling behind schedule. Below: The storyboard is also the centre for discussion, ranging from a chat between those artists involved in collaborating on a section to a full-scale storyboard conference with the senior members of the production team.

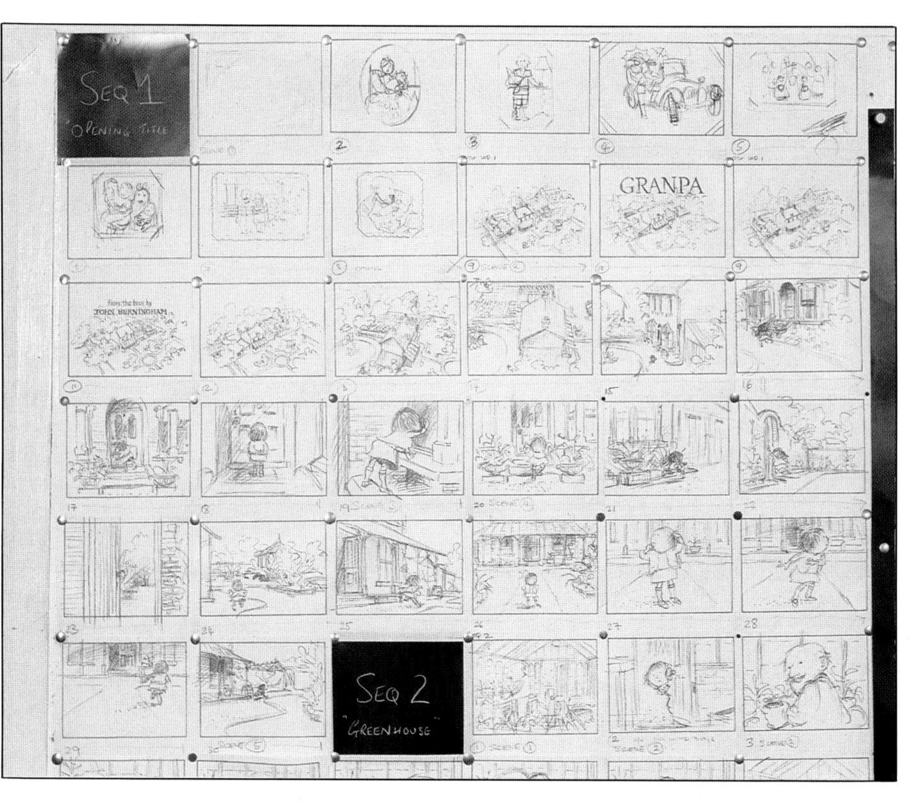

CASE HISTORY

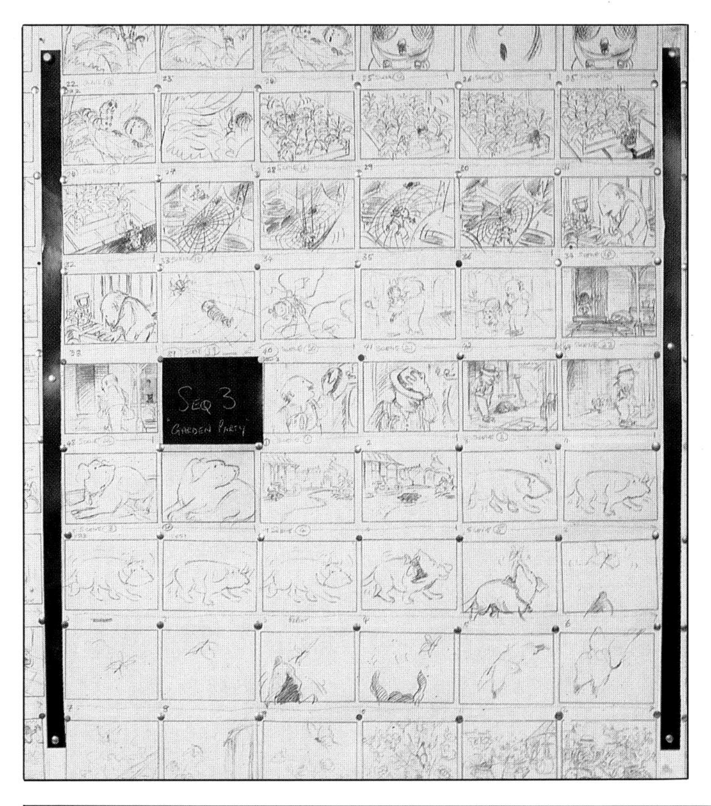

All illustrations in this case history from Granpa, Channel 4/A TVC Production

Left: The sequences are given titles so that they can be easily identified, in this case 'Garden Party' and 'Greenhouse'. There is a very clear break between the Garden Party and Greenhouse sequences. The location changes and there is a change in time. Below: The scenes which go to make up the Greenhouse sequence are mostly made up of a number of shots, but scenes 19–21 are one shot only. This is because there is a clear shift in point of view and angle between each shot, though they take place in the same location and follow each other in time.

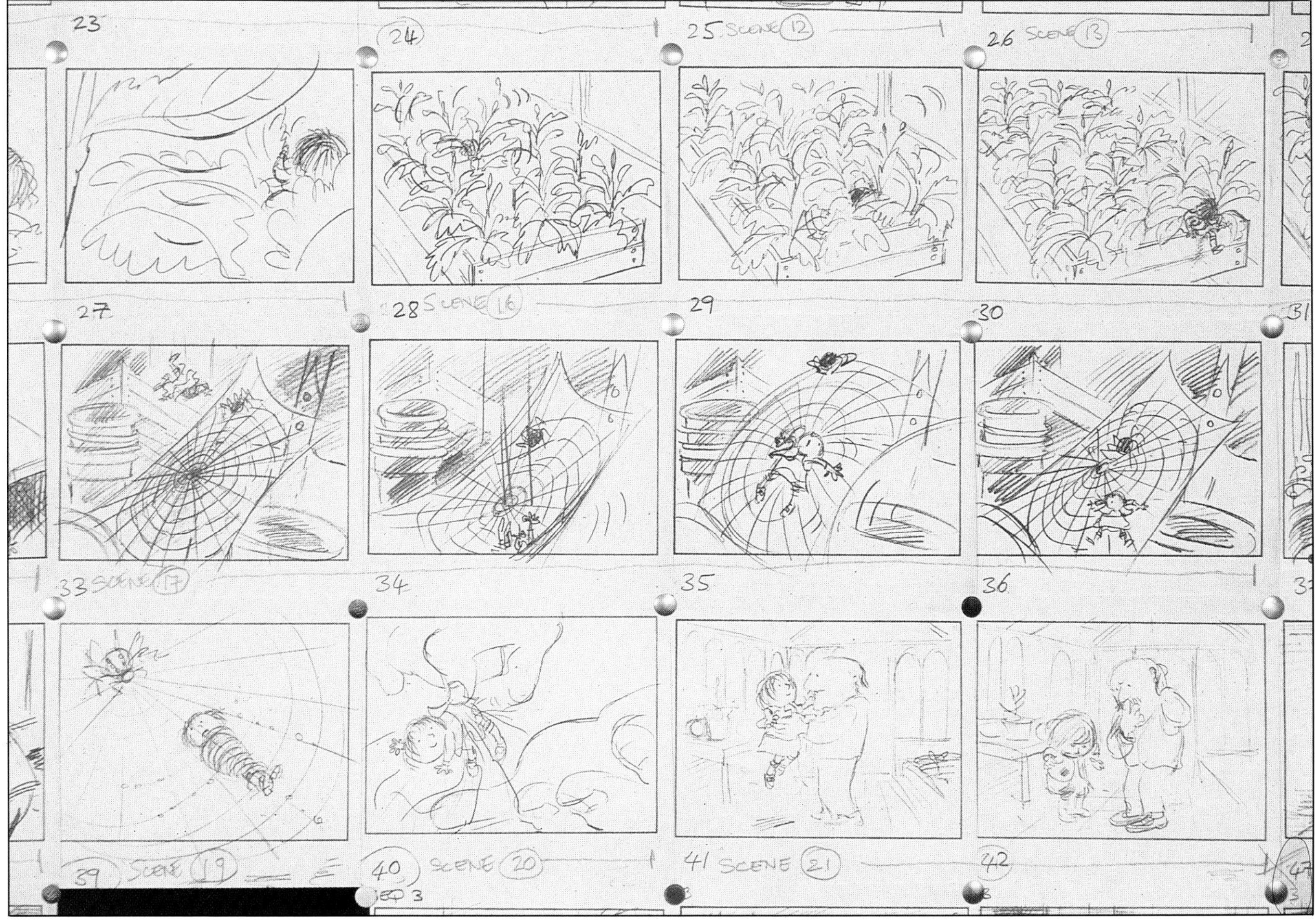

This sequence from the storyboard shows the little girl as she falls into the spider's web. Each of the key changes in the action is shown, although there is no change in point of view until Granpa appears. The second and third pictures show the movement of the spider's web as the figure hits it and bounces as if on a trampoline.

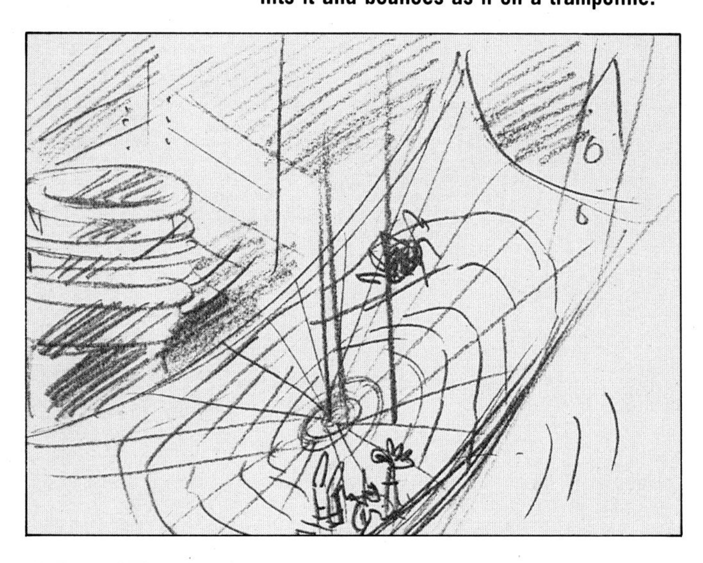

The different character sheets for *Granpa* show each character as it will appear in different scenes. All details of the changes in costume must be indicated, together with colour references. The final character sheet shows Granpa from different angles to enable the animators to maintain consistency in the treatment of the character.

3
SOUND AND IMAGE

The subtle and complex relationship between soundtrack and picture is one of the most potent sources of inspiration for the animator. But it also poses problems of technique – such as the synchronization of lip movements with speech – which demand a high level of skill and application.

Sound has a very special place in animated film. Often the soundtrack is prepared before the action and the animation is then carried out to match the sound. This gives a very precise degree of control over the relationship of sound and image and opens up rich possibilities of interpretation.

The use of sound has had a profound effect on the development of animation, from the early experiments of the 1920s through the introduction of sound to animated film in the 1930s to the rediscoveries of the 1960s and the current impact of pop promos and videos. Much of the impetus for the first experimental phase in the 1920s came from areas outside animation, especially music and painting. Some artists were searching for a new total art form that would encompass all others, and film was clearly a contender for this title. At the same time, attempts to apply scientific

Composition in Blue, Oskar Fischinger, © Fischinger Archive
Fischinger perfected his control over sound and image in this film. Realizing that colour would need the same detailed attention as sound, he collaborated on developing the first European colour film system, Gasparcolour. He also made use of the full potential of abstract animation movement, boldly mixing two- and three-dimensional images.

Above: Diagonal Symphony, Viking Eggeling
The relationship of curved and straight lines and their movement was intended to have the same function as music – Eggeling referred to the plan of the film as the 'score'. He had a clear vision of a new cinema which would develop its own non-representational language.

methods to art, demonstrated in the work of painters such as Kandinsky, gave credence to the notion that general scientific principles could be discovered which would be applicable to all art forms.

It was in Germany that there began the search for these principles in film. The painters Viking Eggeling (Swedish by birth), Walter Ruttmann and Hans Richter all turned to the medium of film, as did the young Oskar Fischinger, who was to have the most profound influence on animation. The titles of their films show how substantial the role of music and sound was in the approach of these film-makers. Eggeling's *Diagonal Symphony* (1921), Ruttmann's *Opus I-IV* (1921–25) and Richter's *Rhythms 21, 22, 25* (1923–25), all demonstrate a concern with the correspondence of the visual to the aural. But this was before the 'talkies', and there was no attempt actually to add sound to these mainly abstract films, or to produce a sound and light show, or even to have compositions specially written. Oskar Fischinger's early work was also based on establishing the dynamics of movement in relation to music, but he began to use records with his films. The *Film Studies 5–12* were made with reference to specific compositions – to jazz records or, in the case of *Study 7*, to one of Brahms's Hungarian Dances. Fischinger's studies, shown in cinemas as short films, gained a large following both in Europe and the United States. He continued to work in non-figurative animation after the introduction of sound film, making works such as *Composition in Blue* (1934) and *An Optical Poem* (1937). Like so many artists, Fischinger left Germany to work in the United States and was employed for a time on Disney's *Fantasia*. Later he concentrated once more on his own work which stimulated a new generation of American experimentalists, including the Whitneys.

When it became possible to join sound and image on a single strip of film, the experimentalists got even more enthusiastic about the idea of a synthesis – an idea which has never ceased to fascinate both artists and their audience. It reintroduced the concept, dear to the Romantics, of the total work of art. Finding and interpreting the hidden story in a chosen piece of music became the animator's preoccupation. Sometimes, musical classics were taken as a basis for interpretation, and many, like Alexandre Alexeieff's *Une Nuit sur le Mont Chauve* (*Night on a Bald Mountain*) using music by Mussorgsky, became animation classics in their own right. There was always a possibility that the interpretation would become too literal, however, and few achieved the powerful alignment of sound and image of Alexeieff's film, with its phantasmagoric swirling creatures and

Below: Night on a Bald Mountain, Alexandre Alexeieff and Claire Parker
In this film, Alexeieff made use of his pin-screen technique, in which small pins are pushed through a board and cast varying lengths and density of shadow to form the image. It enabled him to capture the dramatic and fantasmagorical aspect of Mussorgsky's music in a unique way.

78 Tours, Georges Schwizgebel, Studio GDS
The action of this film is played out on a revolving record. The disc changes its form to become a pool of light or a spinning carousel. The device of bringing the sound mechanism on to the screen in visual form has featured in a number of animation films. In *Fantasia*, the optical soundtrack itself becomes a part of the action.

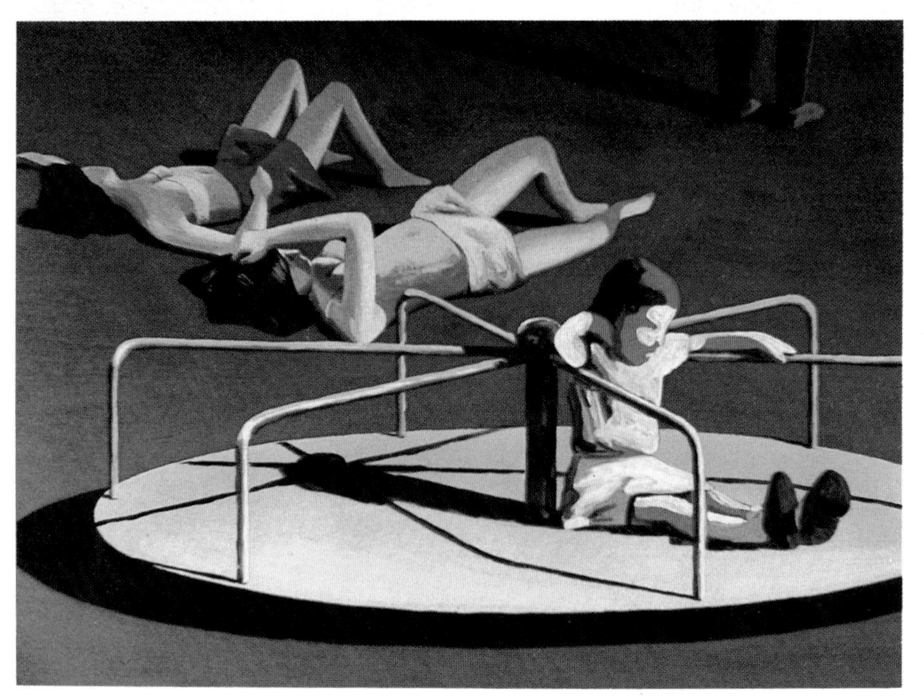

elusive atmosphere. Other attempts brought only criticism from the adherents of the composer, or even from the composer in person – as in the legendary confrontation between the giants Disney and Stravinsky over the reworking of the Rite of Spring in *Fantasia*.

Popular music was less contentious. More often than not the fans appreciated having their favourites set to images and appearing on the screen. Jazz provided a particularly rich vein for mining and some major works of animation grew out of this fusion. In the Fleischer film of *Snow White*, for instance, Cab Calloway performs the St James' Infirmary Blues in the form of Koko, while eerie ghosts and skeletons mimic from the background.

It was not the musical numbers Steamboat Bill and Turkey in the Straw, however, which startled the audience at the first showing of Disney's *Steamboat Willie* at the Colony Theatre in November 1928. It was the synchronization of the pots and pans accompaniment as Mickey Mouse improvised on the theme tune. At this stage of sound recording the music and effects had to be recorded live, so the early Disney films had a precise system of 'cues' marked on the film itself. Agreed between the animation director and the composer/arranger, these cues made for an exceptional degree of synchronization. The kind of very close synchronization found in these films, with sound and image coinciding exactly, even became known in the trade as 'Mickey Mousing'.

Synchronization

Synchronization is the bringing together of the sound and image, either on one single piece of film or video, as in the final print, or at the editing stage. During the editing many separate sections of sound are manipulated on different tracks. They are only brought together in the final mix. Whatever stage the production is at, however, the sound has to be kept in 'sync' with the picture by a system of 'sync marks' which can be matched.

There are two main forms of synchronization. The first, the one that concerns the animator directly, is *parallel sync* (level sync). This is where the sound and image run in parallel. The second is *printing sync*, where the sound is advanced to compensate for the different position of the sound head and the film gate on the projector. The 'neg' cutter, who is often part of the laboratory, advances the sound 'neg' as a matter of course, but he must know whether the film is in parallel sync to begin with. It is important to specify this, measuring from the first frame of the picture (FFP) to the position of the sync mark. When the film is being worked on, the relative positions of sound and image will need to be adjusted, so it is very important that there are sync marks at the head of each soundtrack, as well as on the picture cutting copy. There should be only one clear mark for each sound and picture track.

In animation it is now usual to prepare some of the soundtracks before beginning work on the picture, to function as guide tracks. The tracks containing the voice, which will need lip sync – the synchronization of

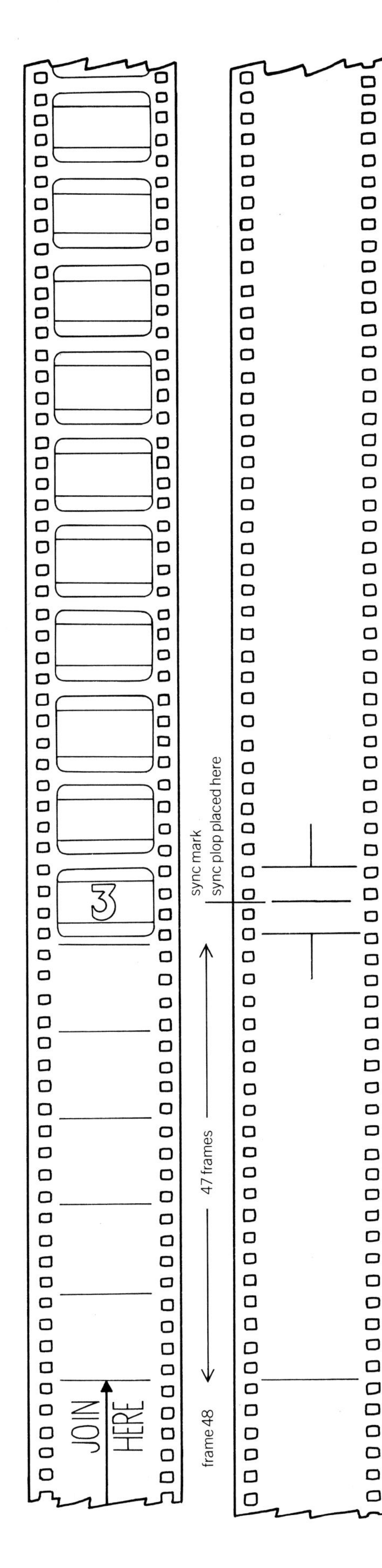

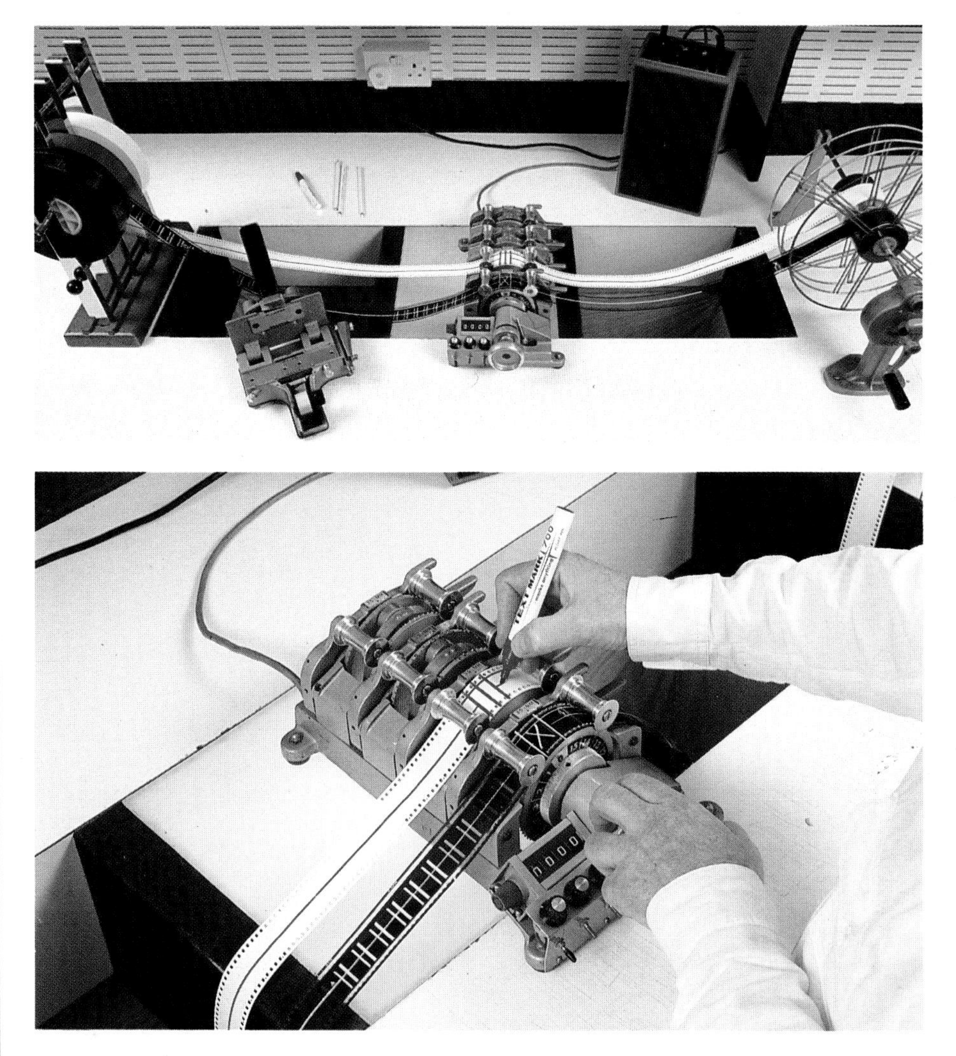

Top: The equipment used for synchronization is basic: synchronizer or track reader on which the sound and picture are placed; film horse, on the left, which holds the rolls of film on their cores; and a rewind, on the right. (Speedy Films Ltd, at Magmasters; agency: Collett Dickenson Pearce; client McEwans Best Scotch)

Above: The sync points are marked on the sound and picture – in this case 35mm film – with a felt pen or Chinagraph. The picture is nearest the editor. The sound and picture have a leader which is at the 'head' or start.

Left: The standard markings and positions for synchronization based on the Academy leader. The leader uses 35mm footage even on 16mm leader, so that the first frame of picture is 48FRMs from the sync mark. Once this is established, all of the positions of the sound relate accurately to each other and the picture.

speech to lip movements – when they are animated, also have to be prepared in advance. Other tracks may be added at a later stage, though any sound that needs to be linked closely to the animation action is usually prepared beforehand.

Marks are made on the film and the soundtrack to indicate the points for synchronization. It is very important that these marks are clear and unambiguous. If it proves necessary to work with more than one sync mark during the editing stage, any additional marks must be removed from the film before the final mix (the 'dub'). The tracks themselves will be on perforated magnetic film of various widths (35mm, 16mm, etc.). In the past, the soundtrack was on film and not tape, but nowadays the sound is only transferred onto the film after it has been mixed onto a master magnetic track.

Matching sound and image

There are many different ways of linking sound and image. Synchronization is much more than simply the joining of the on-screen

meaning is changed again. The sound chosen can increase or diminish the weight of the object and change our view of it and its relationship to the surface it strikes. For instance, we may see the object hit water, and yet hear it strike concrete. This counterpointing of sound and image has been used by animators across the whole spectrum of the animated film. It need not be limited to comic effects which are the equivalent of one-line jokes, but can be used to make us see an action in quite a different way.

At the wilder end, Tex Avery made great use of the unusual matching of sound to image in films like *Bad Luck Blackie*, in which he piles on the one-liners at all levels until the effect becomes painful. Another example, though, is the Cuban film *LBJ* by Santiago Alvarez, which at one point sets the speeches of various American politicians of the 1960s against images of the massacre of 'bad' Red

action to the sound of that action. The difference is analogous to that between cutting and editing. Cutting refers to the mechanical process of joining together segments of film. Editing is the process of decision-making which determines the precise placing of these segments and has a profound effect on the meaning of the film. Similarly, the synchronization of sound can be not just a mechanical process, but a way of altering the meaning of the image. In live-action, the decision about what sound to use may be left until quite late in the process. But in animation many of these choices must be made before the animation is begun. It is important to understand the choices and the way in which sound can be used creatively.

When the sound of an object hitting the ground is matched with exactly corresponding images of that object hitting the ground, it would seem to pose a straightforward problem of placing the sound accurately. Even if the points of impact can be established on the picture, however, a decision still has to be made. Matching the sound frame-to-frame can appear mechanical, although this may be the effect required – it is in fact an example of 'Mickey Mousing'. Usually instead, with this kind of very specific spot sound effect, an editor will slip the picture two, three or sometimes many more frames ahead of the sound. This supposedly compensates for the split second it takes for the sound to reach the listener. Even if the scientific basis of this reasoning is unproven, it works in practice.

But if the images of this same object hitting the ground are matched to, for example, the sound of a car crash, they take on a quite different meaning. Or again, if the images are matched to a sound of breaking eggs, the

Above: Ubu, Geoff Dunbar, Grand Slamm Partnership Ltd, © Arts Council of Great Britain

***Ubu* is a good example of director, editor and composer collaborating to ensure the maximum effectiveness of sound and image. The grunts and growls which the characters emit are presented visually in voice bubbles. The soundtrack, free of voice-overs, is used to create a brutal threatening atmosphere.**

Below: Black and White, Ivanov-Vano, Amalrik

A poem by the Russian revolutionary poet Mayakovsky is the basis of this early Soviet animation film. In a strong black-and-white style, it closely follows the text, which portrays the economic exploitation and racial oppression of black workers in Cuba.

Below: The Sound Collector, National Film Board of Canada/Lyn Smith

Lyn Smith's film tells the tale of a boy obsessed with sounds which others do not have the time or inclination to hear. He listens to a bee settling on a bowl of fruit, the sounds of wind and rain, and the sounds he himself can make. The film suggests that not only do we fail to listen to the world around us, but that we habitually take the soundtrack for granted as a background to the picture.

Indians by US cavalry, taken from an ordinary Hollywood Western and refilmed in slow motion. By such counterpoint of soundtrack and visuals, the film makes its meaning clear.

The choice of the appropriate sound is an important one, and it is not quite as simple as it might seem. It may not be the sound that appears the most obvious.

Music, voice, effects and atmosphere

Soundtracks are normally considered in four areas: music, voice, effects and atmosphere. These tracks are mixed together in the final dub. When a foreign-language version of the film is to be made, the music and effects are mixed separately onto a master (the M and E track). This simplifies the task of making separate dubs for foreign language versions.

Above: June Foray, one of the great unseen actresses in the history of animated film. She provided the voice for characters such as Cinderella, Peter Pan and Tweety Pie's Granny. (National Film Theatre)

If there is the opportunity to select the music to be used, the question of whether to commission a specially written work or to use existing music arises. Both have their advantages and drawbacks. Using existing music can (especially if funds are limited) give the tone and colour that comes from a larger group of performers and more sophisticated recording. But it does constrain the timing, though an editor (cutter) can make fine adjustments. It is also essential to clear copyright. If this is not looked into beforehand, not only the sale but the showing of the final film may well be jeopardized.

Commissioning music has the great advantage of bringing another creative mind to bear on the project; the music will be written specifically with the concept of the film in mind. It does mean, however, that it is necessary to go through the extra stage of music recording, though with the introduction of computer technology this task is becoming less daunting, as sampling and digital sound techniques become standard. When looking for the right musical material, it is important to listen to as many kinds of music as possible, including 'demo tapes'.

There is a great deal of creative musical talent around, often very ready to produce music for film and video.

Preparing the voice track presents its own problems. Voices are either character voices or voice-overs. The character design will go a long way towards determining the choice of the kind of character voice to be used. Even so, it can be difficult to 'hear' the voice as it will sound on the film. It is useful to do a test at an early stage, as well as listening to tapes if they are available. The voice-over also needs careful selection, though the voice in this case is being used to tell a story or communicate information directly.

Although it has been the custom to use actors to perform the voice-overs, a documentary approach can be productive. A series of animated films made for the BBC,

Down and Out, Aardman Animations Ltd/ © BBC
This innovative film used documentary sound, recorded on location in a Salvation Army hostel and then edited to form the soundtrack for the Plasticine animation. The stills show the down-and-out trying to get a meal without having the correct papers, arguing with the officials and departing with a gesture of anger and despair. The movement of the characters is low-key and the characterization is based on the real unwitting protagonists. The film questions many assumptions about the differences between live-action and animation subject-matter.

Animated Conversations, used the technique of location recording to provide the raw material for the soundtracks. This was daring in its challenge to the cliché that animation is essentially non-realistic. The mass of sound recorded was edited down for the final soundtrack. The subjects of the films vary from simple observation of a visit to the dentist, to the even more harrowing portrayal of a breakdown of communication between an old vagrant and an officer of the Salvation Army, as the vagrant attempts to obtain a subsidized meal without the correct papers. This kind of approach depends on the skill of the film-maker in selecting the subject. It also calls for the documentary film-maker's eye for the significant moment, as well as the patient techniques of the animator.

In another television film, *Some Protection* (1987) by Marjut Rimminen, Josie O'Dwyer

Some Protection, Channel 4/Marjut Rimminen, Smoothcloud Production
Again, a film with a soundtrack taken from real life. The experiences of a woman ex-prisoner form the basis for the film, part of a series on women and the law made for television. Animation is used to counterpoint the harrowing images of prison life with fantasies of life beyond the bars.

recounts her experience of life in a women's prison and of the everyday violence and humiliation which leads to the cycle of repeated offence and imprisonment. The animation is able to compress this account into a short and powerful description. The fact that the woman is not seen reinforces the concept that she, as an offender, is deliberately kept hidden from society.

The effects track has great potential for enhancing an animation. Effects can be found – there are effects libraries and records – or they can be made. Most effects libraries are servicing the live-action film-maker, so the effects which are available may be too 'real' and lack the attack and energy required for animation, especially for 'spot effects' which signify a precise event. One solution to this is to combine a number of effects into one or to manipulate the effect. If the effect is intended for a general background atmosphere it should not have any strong individual sounds which can be easily identified, as it may need to be looped – repeated again and again – and a recurring distinctive sound will be noticeable.

When effects are made, a whole range of unlikely tricks can be employed; it is often the least likely sound that seems convincing, whereas the real sound may perversely sound artificial. The sound on the film is what matters, not the fact that it is authentic (unless of course authenticity forms part of the meaning of the film). If the effect required is complex, such as a machine operating with many moving parts, then it needs to be built up – sometimes twenty different effects or more may be combined to produce a few seconds of sound. They are pre-mixed to make one single effect which will be mixed again at the final dubbing session.

Whatever kinds of music, effects and voice are chosen, they will need to be analysed in detail if the animation is synchronized. This is not a problem encountered with the atmosphere track. Atmosphere is a special kind of sound effect laid throughout a scene; it represents the background or ambient noise of the location. Each kind of location has a different sort of ambient sound. A large space with hard uncovered stone walls, like a church, will give a different overall sound from a small room in a house packed with sound-absorbent objects and soft furnishings. In live-action film a wild (unsynchronized) recording is made in each location to provide the 'atmos' track. In animation this is usually not possible, but still an atmos track needs to be made. The detail will to some extent depend on the specific location.

If there is no sound covering the image whatever, this results in 'dead track'. Dead track is very obvious when it occurs and little can be done about it in the dub, so care must

'I got a warm reception in L.A., I got a warm reception all the way'

'Folks are so nice there in L.A., I got a warm reception all the way, Doors opened wide for me out in L.A.'

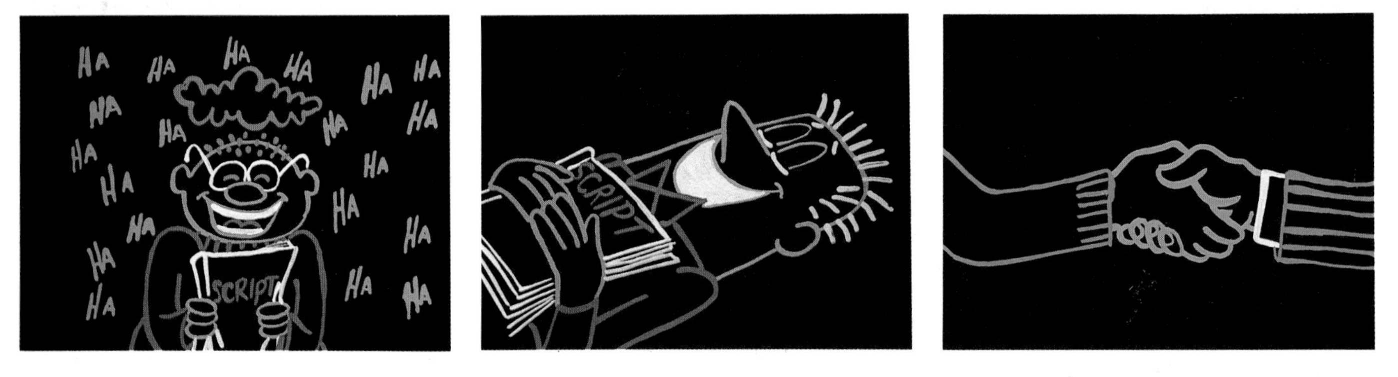

'They laughed and laughed out loud at my screen play, One laughed so hard he passed away, Folks are real fine, refined out in L.A.'

be taken to check that there is sound covering every image. If there is a mix or fade on the sound, be careful to allow at least three feet of overlap so that one track does not end before the other comes in, leaving a gap.

Timing

How you time a soundtrack and break it down depends on the amount of detail in the action. Lip sync has to be closely analysed, whereas a music track may only need an indication of rhythm or beat to serve as a guide to the animation action.

In order to time a soundtrack, you first establish the number of frames per second (FPS) at which the film will be viewed. This is normally 24 FPS for film and 25 FPS for television. Because of its divisibility by factors of two, many film-makers always prefer to work as if the film will be projected at 24 FPS. The FPS figure is the determining factor in the timing of the animation. It is the one element which will not change, so it gives the animator a constant with which to work.

Understanding the mechanics of the real relationship of the film to the concept of the single second of time is a skill which enables very complex movements and timings to be broken down into manageable parts. It allows for flexibility – criticism of computer-generated images often stems from the fact that the 'timing' established electronically imposes too strict a regime on the images in movement. If, as is more and more the case,

A Warm Reception in L.A., Vincent Cafarelli and Candy Kugel, © 1987 Buzzco Associates Inc, original song by Lanny Meyers and Vincent Cafarelli
The simple but robust graphic style used in the animation film relates well to the bouncy soundtrack. The line technique, pared down to a minimum, places a reliance on movement and speed of action. Scenes change rapidly as the music drives along. The tongue-in-cheek lyrics are also parodied in the images, as the hero strives for success in the film business with his great new irresistible property.

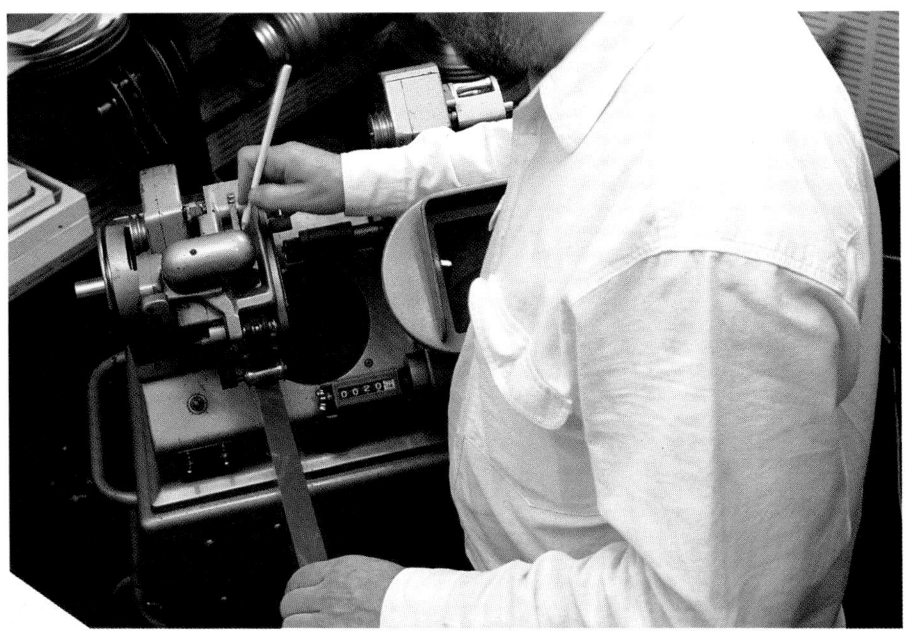

ove right: The beat is ' tapping it out with a ncil as the magnetic film runs head of the editing machine. n must be positioned the sound head and an machine gives easier access an a flat bed.

the electronic image is produced by people who have already found their own 'rhythm' through being trained in animation and who can impose this on the machine, then great works of computer animation will at last be produced, rather than work which looks like the product of a visual pianola.

The concept of 'frames per second' is used to organize and manipulate timing even where, as in electronically produced work, there is really no such thing as a frame. It is almost impossible to visualize even a simple sequence, such as a dance routine, without being able to break down the sound and movement into their constituent parts.

At an early stage it may be enough to establish a 'beat'. This can be done by running the music track through an editing machine and tapping out the beat of the music onto the shiny surface (not the emulsion which is dull) with a Chinagraph or grease pencil. Upright editing machines or motorized pic-syncs are best suited for this, as the animator can then work standing up over them. The number of frames between each beat can be determined in this way, though it is important to remember that music is seldom mechanical and that there will always be slight variations of beat. These subtle variations in timing and beat are what gives life to the work; human imperfection has the advantage over the machine's flawlessness. So the rough division by beats can be used to regulate the timing of the animation, but not too literally.

Breaking down the sound

If the sound needs to be closely analysed, it must be 'broken down'. That is, each separate element has to be isolated in order to determine the exact number of frames which each note or sound actually takes. To achieve this the film is read on a synchronizer or on a track reader (a synchronizer without a picture head). The magnetic track is placed over the sound head on the synchronizer and wound backwards and forwards to establish the exact starting point and end point of the particular sound. If the sound being analysed is a voice which is to be synchronized with lip movement, then each word spoken has to be broken down into its separate syllables. Although the animator or editor will have a script, this may not indicate what the word

Below: Sound is broken down one track at a time using a synchronizer. The magnetic track with the emulsion down is wound backwards and forwards and each sound located. The information is then transferred to a bar chart, which forms the basis for the animation.

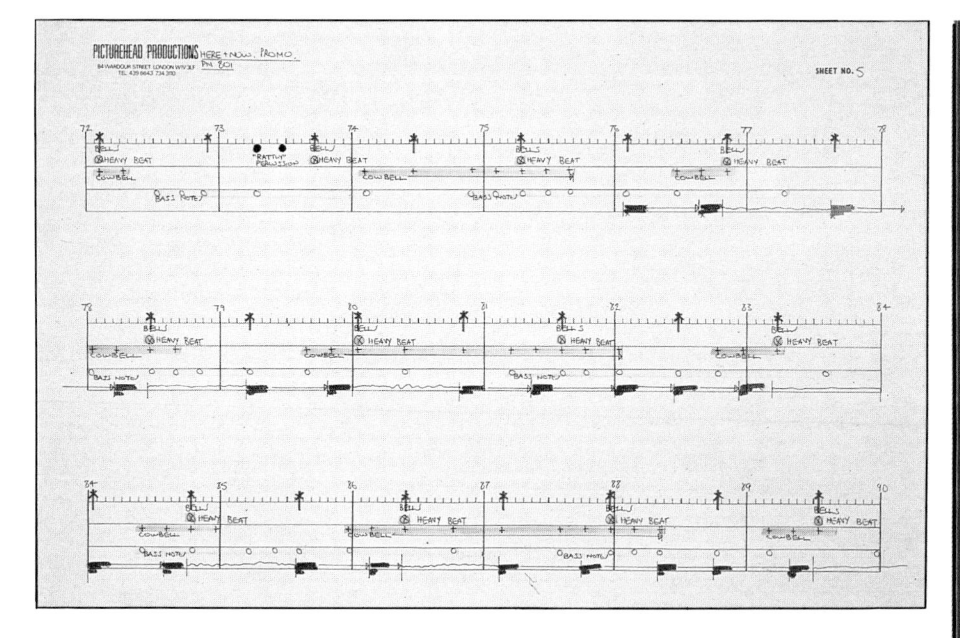

sounds like when spoken, and it is the sound of the word which counts. Even more care must be taken in locating sounds on the track if you are not using the standard professional 35mm.

Some sounds are more necessary than others. If there is an image of a gun being fired on the screen, it would be strange not to hear the appropriate gunshot – unless, of course, this is the effect you want. But if there is a flag flapping in the breeze, a general atmosphere soundtrack may well be adequate.

The way to approach the breaking down of a track is first to indicate where the sounds are and where there is an absence of sound. Once the section of track has the areas between the sounds marked as clear, the sounds themselves can be broken down in detail. If there is a need to synchronize with a certain frame, this can be marked accurately. Obviously there is no point in dealing with half frames. A decision has to be made on which frame the sound should be placed in, usually the first of two, given a choice. The sound can then be indicated by writing onto the track, at the same time showing any increase or decrease in volume. It is important to bear in mind that a single effect may be made up from several sounds.

There is something odd about a film in which every single event is greeted with a barrage of sound effects. They can easily be overdone. However, it is as well to record key effects in advance, so that they are at hand if needed.

Above: The bar chart has three sections, for dialogue, music and effects. If the sound is complex, one or more bar charts will be used for a single sequence. The sections each represent one track and are divided into feet and frames. (Picturehead)

Right and below: El Globo, Animation City for Nebraska Productions
Since lip-sync is carried out by phonetic analyses, the breaking down of foreign-language tracks does not present an insuperable problem. In this case, a commercial for the famous Spanish newspaper *El Globo* is animated by Animation City using a Spanish-language soundtrack, the main element being voices of famous world politicians.

Visualizing music

Putting images to music is far from easy, yet there is at present a large output of music videos which use animation, as well as a

Allegro Non Troppo, Bruno Bozzetto, Bruno Bozzetto Film
The pitfalls of visualizing well-known musical compositions are cleverly exploited in Bozzetto's parody of *Fantasia*. Above, a scene from 'L'Après-Midi d'un Faune', right 'Valse Triste'.

tradition going back to the earliest animated films in which sound plays an inspirational part. Music can serve merely as a prop to provide a formal structure for chaotic and muddled imagery. But the best work creates a real fusion of music and image into a new fresh work existing in its own right.

This kind of film calls for planning and for an understanding of what is involved in inventing a visual equivalent to music. Rhythm and beat are the elements which link closely to timing. The more elusive aspects of music – tone, timbre and space – are what can give a meaning at a more subtle level. All of these terms have an equivalent in the visual arts, yet even the most careful designer can easily forget that the care which is lavished on the rendering of light and shade, for instance, or on the weight of line perspective in the visual should also be considered in relation to the sound-quality of the music. If the film-maker does nothing but present his or her spontaneous vision of the 'feelings' which the piece evokes, then the images are merely interposed between the musical work and the audience, adding nothing. Films which transcend this problem, such as those of Fischinger and Alexeieff, as well as many of the pop videos produced recently, do so by respecting the musical forms with which they work, whether classical or popular.

As we have already said, the timing of animation to a soundtrack is mainly based on the relationship of the action to the beat and rhythm of the music. When the rough beat has been determined, cue marks are made onto a loop of clear film which is run in sync with the soundtrack. This serves as a test of the number of frames per beat and allows adjustment to be made easily (a complex rhythm may need a number of these loops). The timing of the animation action is then

Above: Satiemania, Zdenko Gasparovic, Zagreb Film
The music of Erik Satie inspired this scatological notebook film of the film-maker's journey through the United States. The music holds together the images which bombard the audience, as well as providing a rhythm and pacing for the work.

based upon this frame number or on multiples or divisions of it. Very intricate rhythms of animation can be carefully built up in this way by having different animation for on-beat and off-beat. For a short film it is possible to make a guide to the timing using a picture cutting copy marked with all of the sound cues, including the points where there are fades and mixes, and spot effects.

Lyp sync

Lip sync is a special kind of sound synchronization in which dialogue is spoken by a character in shot. In this case the sound needs to be broken down with very great care, as any mistakes in 'hearing' what has been said are very noticeable when translated into animation. This can be even more difficult if the dialogue is in a foreign language or there is a heavy regional accent. Normally an editor breaks down the soundtrack, marking the magnetic film on its shiny (acetate or polyester) surface and transferring this information to the bar chart. However, some animators prefer to break down the sound themselves, so that they can get the feel of the track they are going to work with.

It is often a problem deciding exactly where words and sounds begin and end. When the sound is run at the correct speed it is easy to hear the words, but the individual sounds cannot be isolated. When the soundtrack is wound through the synchronizer by hand, the sounds can be isolated but it is sometimes difficult to situate them. So first the individual words are defined and the beginning and end of each one is marked, so that when the breakdown becomes more detailed you do not have to halt constantly to find out what word or sentence you are dealing with. Then the breakdown of the precise phonetic detail of the word can be carried out. It is no use breaking the word down as it is written. This would be misleading. It is only the uttered sound which counts. It is useful to have a mirror and a cassette recorder if possible, so that you can check the lip movement and the expression by playing the voice to yourself on the cassette and mimicking it while looking in the mirror.

There is no need to animate every single letter which is articulated. This would in fact look very strange. It is important to pick out 'open' sounds – usually the vowels a, e, i, o, u, and the sounds b, f, m, l – so that 'Hello' will normally become 'Elo'. Because of our familiarity with seeing people speak with lip sync in live-action film, any mistakes or just straightforward misjudgements are likely to stand out embarrassingly clearly. A common mistake in animation is to over-animate if worried about movements or timing. This can cause real problems with lip sync, where it is thoughtful economy which almost always produces the best results.

Lip sync should be used sparingly, if possible. There is no way around having to break down the sound and animate it, once you have committed yourself to lip sync. But an audience will tend to notice if all of the characters speak from behind newspapers, with the back of their heads to camera or just out of shot.

At this stage any deficiencies in the script dialogue will be very clear – if the dialogue contains too many words, or if the script and the timing have constrained the actor, so the pacing and phrasing are awkward or just

Below: The editor, with the script in front of him, marks the start of a sound on the magnetic film. It is important that the sound of the words is put down and not simply what is written on the script, even if there are discrepancies in pronunciation.

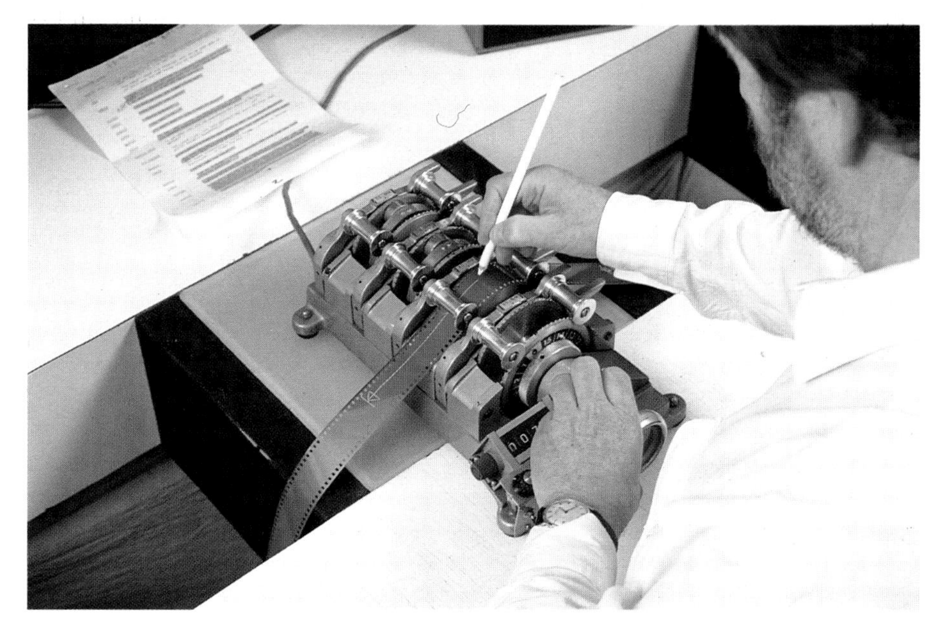

The bar chart

The main element in linking the soundtrack to the production of the animation is the bar chart. This is a chart on which all of the information the animator needs is entered, transferred from the soundtrack itself. It is calibrated in feet and frames, with three grids which are themselves divided into three. This represents the three major elements of the soundtrack – music, effects and dialogue. The chart is flexible enough for any information from the tracks to be entered there. It is the relationship of the footage and frames to the actual soundtrack which is most important, and this remains fixed. Every frame of sound is entered on the bar chart.

The bar chart relates directly to the animator's work sheet – the dope sheet – frame for frame. The information can be read off the bar chart to the dope sheet by laying both of them edge to edge. The notation used on the bar chart is determined by the kind of film being produced. If there is a large amount of lip sync, the dialogue will be entered together with the name of the character speaking and any other relevant notation. If the film consists mainly of music, on the other hand, this will be broken down. There may even be a kind of bouncing ball to show the structure of the music and how the sounds relate.

Below: The dialogue breakdown for *El Globo* shows the script reference in the top section and the breakdown of the script underneath this. Details of the general action are also included to aid the visualization of the lip sync.

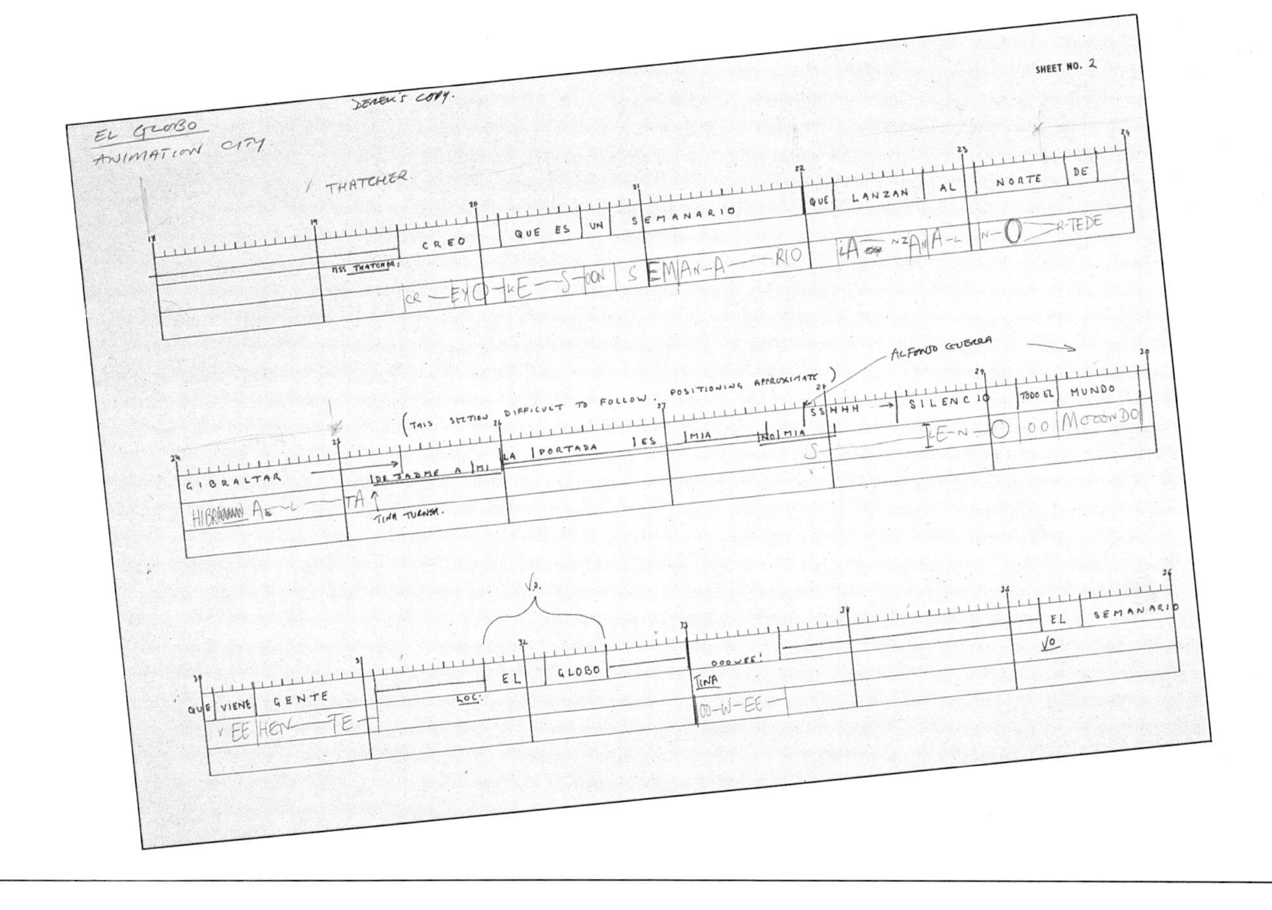

plain wrong. This is the last point at which a correction can be made without the costly and time-consuming production of the artwork being affected. If there are minor errors, the editor can usually correct them, but if things appear more seriously awry, the sound must be re-recorded. This is why lip sync track cannot be used as a guide track for the animation – the precise position of the sounds will alter in a new recording.

The editing process

The key to the effective use of sound lies in the editing, both during the preparation for the animation and at the post-production stage. The editing process in animation resembles the work of the live-action sound editor in certain senses, but it also calls for some special additional skills. The animation editor is involved at an early stage of production, working with the animator on breaking down the sound and preparing guide tracks.

Once this task has been completed and the bar sheets are ready, the editor begins to make up a test film based on the line tests of the picture and the guide soundtracks. Often there will only be tests of key drawings or tests of layouts to work with, but these have to be viewed in relation to the soundtrack so that adjustments can be made to the action track where necessary.

The animator will by now have transferred the bar chart to the dope sheet – the animator's work sheet. As the film begins to take shape it will be viewed many times, which can damage it, so the editor will work with a duplicate soundtrack. Duplicate pictures can be made if two cutting copies are required; these are called slash prints. As the animation is completed, the editor begins to make up the final soundtracks for dubbing (mixing). There may be many tracks, and if this is the

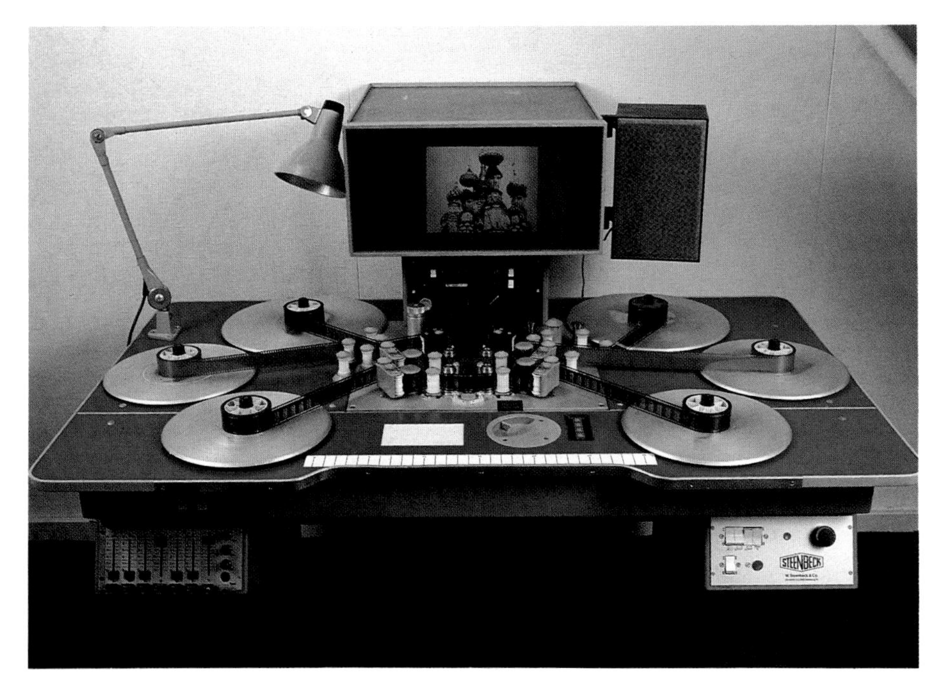

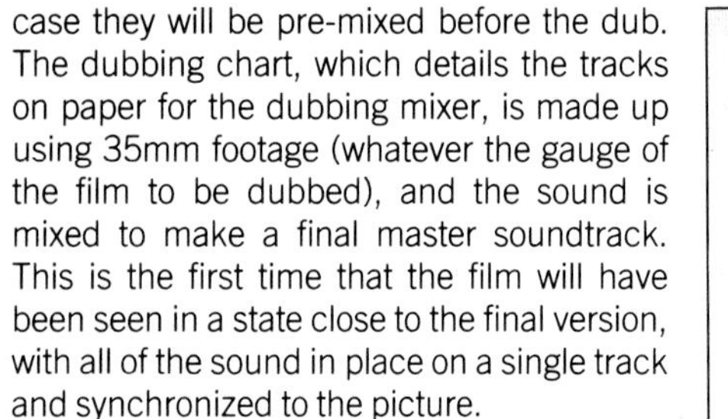

case they will be pre-mixed before the dub. The dubbing chart, which details the tracks on paper for the dubbing mixer, is made up using 35mm footage (whatever the gauge of the film to be dubbed), and the sound is mixed to make a final master soundtrack. This is the first time that the film will have been seen in a state close to the final version, with all of the sound in place on a single track and synchronized to the picture.

The dub

The dub is an important event in the life of a film. It finally determines the way in which the sound and image are joined together or 'married'. It is the closest the animator gets to the split-second decisions associated with a performance. The sound has been built up on its separate tracks and the dubbing chart is ready. All of the tracks and the sync marks have been finally checked and any extraneous marks removed. If there are cues for spot effects or voice-overs to be recorded during the dubbing session, these are marked carefully with a diagonal line which will move across the screen to provide a lead up to the cue – the cue point arrives when the line hits the edge of the screen. Any loops of sound which will be used continuously through a section are made up and kept separately. The tracks are clearly marked with the film title, the track number and type.

The spacing – the silent sections between sounds on each track – is checked to ensure that it has the shiny polyester side down (the magnetic track will be the other way round, with its shiny side up and the emulsion down). This is necessary as otherwise the emulsion on the spacing gets deposited onto the magnetic heads of the playback machines, causing a loss of quality and distortion over a certain period of time. All of the splices are checked and any splices which are taped on one side are double-joined on the picture. Tape is never placed on the emulsion side of the magnetic soundtrack as this causes sound drop-out.

The cans which contain the sound and the action must be clearly marked (black for picture and red for sound), as the hire of a dubbing theatre is expensive and the tracks will be loaded onto the machines while you are absent going through the dubbing chart with the dubbing mixer. If you are constantly having to go to identify the tracks, this can cause considerable delay and frustration.

The job of the dubbing mixer is to mix the tracks and to establish sound levels and quality. This is all done from a desk which also has facilities for enhancing the sound quality and adding effects such as echo. It is important that at some point previously you have been able to hear the sound on high-quality equipment, as the editing machines you will have been using give only a limited indication of the real sound quality. The dub is not the right place to discover that there are faults in the original recording or that the tracks have been damaged in the editing. Original sound should always be recorded at the optimum level and quality. There will be considerable degradations as the process goes on and by the time the married optical print is made there can be as much as a 20 per cent loss of quality from the original.

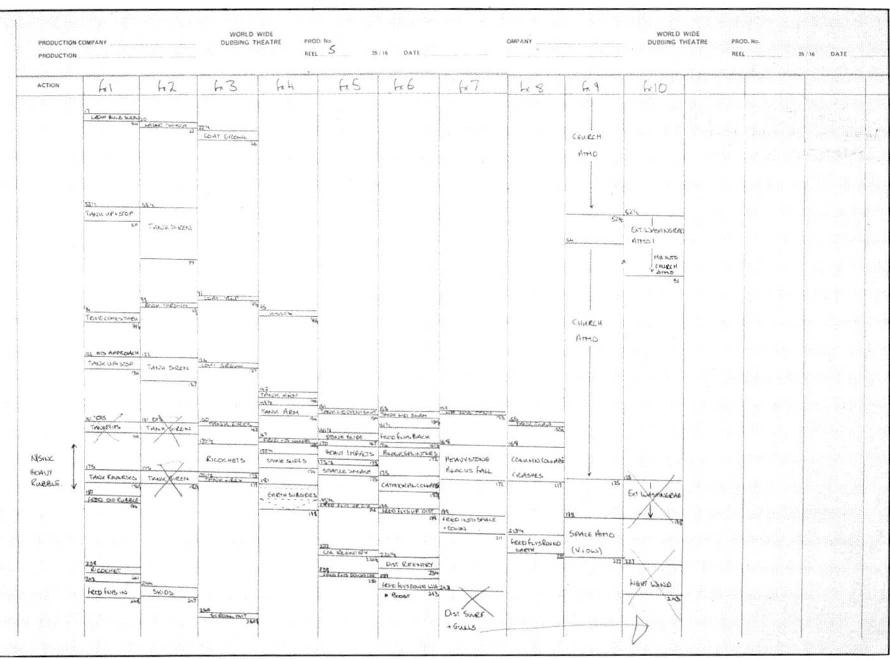

Top: The final editing is carried out on the flat-bed editing machine. Two tracks can be run simultaneously with the picture and synchronization accurately maintained.

Above: The dubbing chart is made up and checked on the flat bed. Each soundtrack has a separate column and each individual sound is entered. Fades and mixes between sounds are indicated. This complex example has a number of tracks and short sections of sound. (Picturehead and Magmasters Sound Studios [agency: Collett Dickenson Pearce; client McEwans Best Scotch])

The dub will usually be done using 'rock and roll' – which means that the sound and action can be stopped at any point during the session and rewound so that levels can be corrected. The length of the dubbing session will depend on the complexity of the sound – the number of tracks and mixes needed.

The films are now loaded and they begin to roll. It takes some time for the machines, which are locked in sync electronically, to reach full speed. This is why 15-foot leaders are needed. As the Academy leader flickers on the screen you wait for the first sync point. This is the 'sync plop', normally three feet from the leader (the neg cutter will assume this to be the case if it is not specified and will advance the sound accordingly). If the one frame of tone (1000 cycles per second) spliced into the soundtrack coincides with the three-foot mark on the screen, the film is in sync.

From this point the dubbing mixer operates the equipment in real time. He is helped by the fact that he has a clearly written dubbing chart and that you have not placed any effects which follow each other on the same track. It is also important that the footage which you have given is in 35mm, so that there is more control over the dub. The dubbing mixer watches a counter placed under the screen and uses this to judge when to bring up each of the tracks and when to bring in loops and other effects. Obviously, working in 35mm footage will greatly aid the judgement of the precise moment for an effect for a 16mm film. There will be two-and-a-half times more numbers indicated on the counter than there would be if the 16mm counter were to be used. Most editing machines have the footage indicated either in 35mm or in both 16mm and 35mm. When the dub is completed a final run through of the sound and action is carried out and the film is checked. It is difficult and expensive to make changes after this stage. Any serious changes would cause a costly re-dub.

This is the first time that sound and image have been assembled in their totality and for the first time the film is in a state close to its final manifestation. Since the master track – the final mix which has just been completed – is a vital element in making prints, a copy or dupe (duplicate) is run off at this stage. All of the further laboratory work is carried out using this dupe and not the master (called the 'mag' master). The name, production type and length of the new tracks must be clearly marked on the can and the film.

At this stage all of the camera negative which has been logged, the sound which has been transferred to an optical sound negative, and the cutting copy carefully marked with cutting points, mixes and fades, is sent for negative cutting. If the camera operator has allowed twelve frames either side of the shot for the 'neg' cut to be made, the cut negative and the sound negative (or 'mag' if the film is to have a magnetic soundtrack) is sent to the labs for the first graded print. Colour grading is a skilled job and for animation it can be especially difficult. The grader working with live-action uses the skin tone of characters to judge the accuracy of the grading, but as there are not usually real skin tones in animation, it helps if the labs have a reference in the form of a camera test (a 'wedge' test) and a colour chart exposed at the start of each roll. The camera report sheets received with the camera rushes will have been recorded by the laboratory, so they will have a record of any difficult changes in exposure of stock which need compensating. It is advisable to achieve a consistent exposure through using wedge tests and keeping, if at all possible, to the same batch of film stock for one production.

Although film has in the past been the main form for the final print, video and the growth of computer effects and editing have changed this process considerably. The integration of film and video images is now becoming commonplace, especially in those areas where computers are used. The potential of broadcast standard video production now means that computer-controlled video editing and other effects which would be time-consuming and expensive using film alone are widely available to the animator using a combination of tape and film. In turn this extends the expressive power and the competitiveness of the medium.

Above: The soundtracks are run in synchronization on playback machines. These machines are also locked in sync with the picture.

Below: Dubbing (mixing), the moment at which all of the sounds and the image are brought together by the dubbing mixer using the dubbing chart. The mixer is seated at the desk with the controls for each of the tracks. As the film runs, the mixer is able to balance the sound levels and make adjustments to enhance the quality. (Speedy Films Ltd at Magmasters Sound Studios [agency: Collett Dickenson Pearce; client McEwans Best Scotch])

CASE HISTORY

POP PROMOS

The award-winning *Sledgehammer*, directed by Steve R. Johnstone with the collaboration of a variety of film-makers from different traditions, shows many of the features of the best work in music videos. Johnstone welds together disparate images which are drawn from art and film history as well as his own imagination. The method of working is closer to that of the musicians who commission the work – in this case, with a limited shooting schedule of six days, the filming itself took on the nature of a performance. Each of the sections of the film was animated separately by film-makers Peter Lord, David Sproxton, Richard Colesowski and the Brothers Quay, each controlling their own animation within the central concept provided. The film mixes pixillation and three-dimensional animation techniques as well as the pixillated lip sync used by Johnstone on his earlier *Talking Heads* video. These techniques are as demanding of the performers as they are of the animators, but the resulting energy justifies the creative risk-taking of the enterprise.

All illustrations in this case history from Sledgehammer, Aardman Animations Ltd and the Brothers Quay, © Real World (Productions) Ltd

Above: The set-up for the 'Furniture Room' scene. Peter Gabriel in the centre of the stage holds a pose, while around him the animators move objects. This kind of single-frame shooting using actors calls for great concentration and attention to detail.

Below: The train is animated on single frames around the head of Peter Gabriel. In situations like this, the animator can use the sleepers as a guide to the positioning of the animation. Once the animation is started it cannot be halted until the shoot is completed – any mistake calls for a total reshoot.

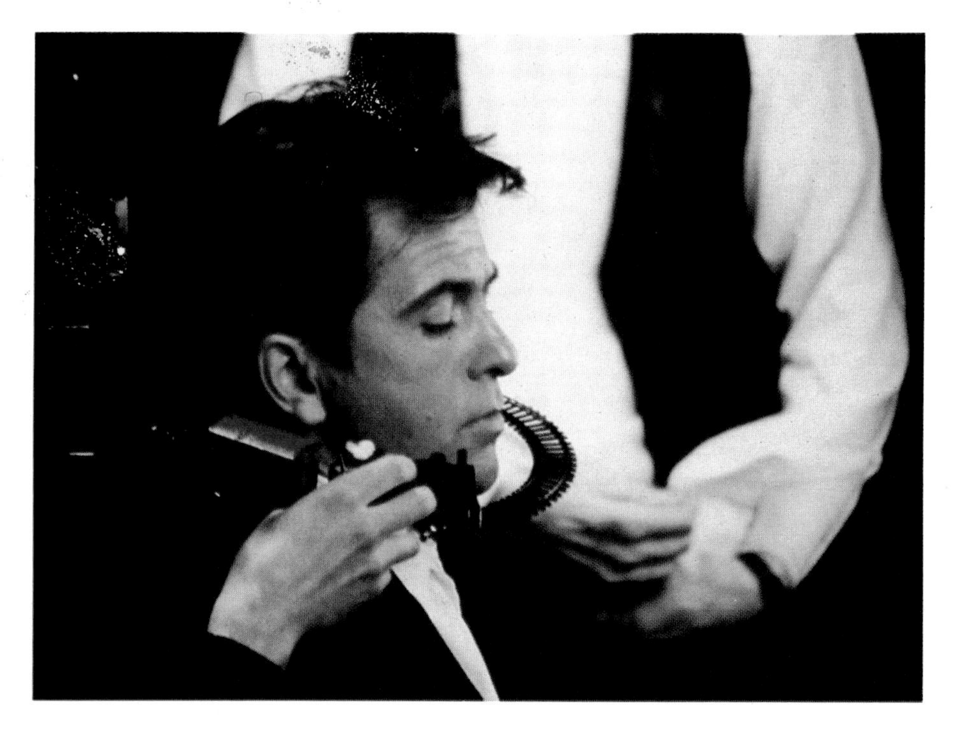

Above: The television monitor showing Peter Gabriel's head under the glass. Above it is the fruit being animated by the Brothers Quay. The monitor is marked with camera tape to show the safe-action area. It can also be used to mark the increments of the animation, so that accurate timing can be achieved even in less controllable situations.

Above and right: The 'Fruit Cake' sequence: one of the Brothers Quay starts to build up the animation sequence, placing the fruit in position. Again, the use of a monitor permits a very precise control of the movement. The sequence, a homage to Jan Svankmajer, took many hours to complete. The fruit was placed on a sheet of glass with Peter Gabriel's face only inches from it. The length of time such a shoot can take, and the necessary breaks for the performer, mean that either accurate marks must be made for taking up the position or cutting points allowed for in the action.

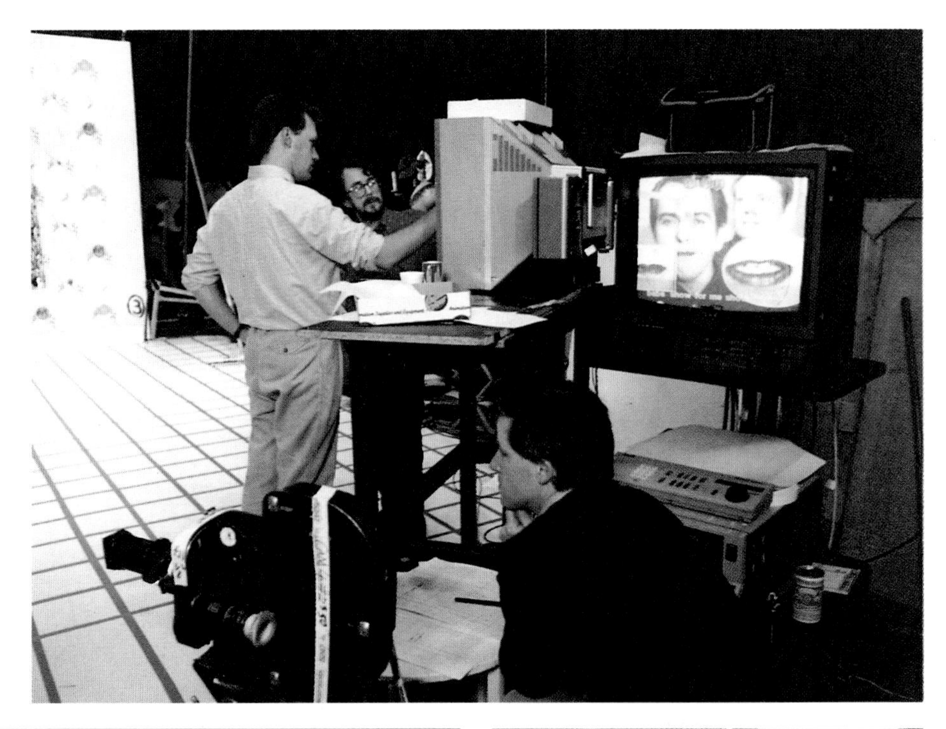

Right: Peter Lord and Richard Coleszowski marking the position of Peter Gabriel's face with a Chinagraph pencil directly on to a video screen. The control unit for the single-frame video unit can be seen underneath the monitor. One of the five cameras used on the 'Furniture Room' scene, a Newman Sinclair P400 with a single-frame motor, is in the foreground.

Above: Using the single-frame technique calls for careful positioning of performers. Peter Gabriel watches the monitor to line up the exact lip position for the next shot. He is able to see the previous shot and to judge the distance to be moved.

Left: Peter Gabriel holds the megaphone as one of the Quay Brothers checks the alignment using the monitor.

CASE HISTORY

Left: The Plasticine animation technique, sometimes called claymation, is one of the specialities of Aardman studios. It is used for this short sequence in which the Plasticine figure of Peter Gabriel is struck from either side by sledgehammer hands. Though animation is normally thought to be a time-consuming medium, techniques such as this can be carried out relatively quickly.

Below: Video technology and computerized editing allow the rapid mixing of styles and techniques. Here one of the oldest forms of trickfilm, the animating of inanimate objects, is used, as two dead chickens form a chorus line while being roasted on a spit.

4
STAGING THE ACTION

Successfully transforming a static storyboard into a moving film demands a high level of creative and technical skills. Animators may not get to direct a cast of thousands on set, but nonetheless they have to bring their picture to life through their staging of the action.

Henry's Cat, Bob Godfrey Films/Stan Hayward
Henry's Cat prepares for action in his new career as director. In animation the megaphone is metaphorical – the role of an animation director differs from that of the live-action counterpart in that much of the direction is done at the planning stages.

Staging the action in an animated film is very roughly equivalent to directing a live-action film. It involves translating the script and storyboard into detailed animation action, expressing the meaning of the film through choices about timing, framing and camera movements.

As with most aspects of animation, staging the action requires a great deal of careful planning. If the film includes character animation, character and colour sheets are prepared and linked to the scene layouts, while backgrounds are specified and matched to the animation action. All of this action has one goal – to translate the ideas and concepts present in the storyboard into a clear working plan, where all the dimensions of film act together. The plan of the action gives the animator final details on framing and timing, as well as providing essential

Left: Un Point C'est Tout, Claude Rocher
A complex staging problem involving the movement of ship, sea and character, with the added complication of a false perspective. Claude Rocher calls his film an irrational tribute to Filippo Brunelleschi (1377–1446), the inventor of linear perspective.

Below: Dreams of Toyland, Arthur Melbourne-Cooper
This early trickfilm shows many different actions taking place in the same space, as well as in foreground and background, as the toys take on a life of their own. Such films offer the creative film-maker insights into alternative developments of staging.

information for the layout artist. Whatever the category of animation – classic cel, experimental or computer – it is essential to have a clear plan or procedure to follow. Animation, perhaps more than any other variety of film, calls for an organization of resources early in the process. Animation cannot be saved in the editing.

There are two aspects to staging the action. One is the production of meaning through the use of a film language – manipulating the conventions or codes which, often unconsciously, govern the way we make or see films. But no less important is the practical side of the process, demanding both skilful visualization and film sense. The organization of action in animation has some factors in common with live-action film. But other elements are unique to animation, and as the impact of new technologies on mainstream animation increases, new ways of establishing an order are beginning to emerge.

Film codes, space and time

When the new medium of film first started to develop sets of codes and methods of organizing time and space, animation continued to rely on the older forms of the graphic and fine arts to accomplish this structuring. The live-action film-makers and their audiences quickly learned to read the articulations of space and time produced by close-ups, long shots and cut-aways. Parallel action, in which two events are presumed to be taking place simultaneously, though on the film they develop in a linear manner, was demonstrated in Edwin Porter's *The Great Train Robbery* (1903). D. W. Griffith mastered the shifting location to such an extent that different centuries and continents could be portrayed in a single film, *Intolerance* (1916). At the same time, the meaning of this formal language became inscribed in the new medium.

Animation film-makers eventually adopted many of the formal devices of live-action as a part of their own attempts to structure film and to communicate with their audience. One of the main arguments of those who take an 'essentialist' position in evaluating animation is that these formal elements were imported from another medium, and that they in some way diverted animation from its true path. This is to ignore the fact that early animation borrowed its codes from many different areas, as did live-action. There was never an essential, innocent, primitive state to pervert.

Still, there is no doubt that what has been seen as 'primitive animation' does have a power and a fascination, arising from its position outside the dominant tradition. Film-makers working with trickfilm in the early years of the twentieth century were faced with a medium without rules and set about bring-

ing a meaning to the new medium in exceptional ways. Some, such as Birt Acres and Walter Booth, extended the music-hall act to trickfilm. They used a form of speeded-up action to produce lightning-sketch routines. *Tom Merry*, made by Acres in 1895, demonstrates this technique at its simplest. The camera is just set up in front of the artist who then does his rapid drawings. Walter Booth's *The Hand of the Artist* (1906) is slightly more elaborate. In this short film the drawings rendered by Booth come to life on the easel.

An exceptional maker of trickfilm, Arthur Melbourne-Cooper, at one time Acres's assistant, made a series of short films using toys and models. In *Dreams of Toyland* (1908) he animated toys, shot straight on. Rather than isolate one action and make it primary, Melbourne-Cooper has many separate actions taking place at the same time and in the same space. Not until *Tango* by Zbigniew Rybczynski in 1980 was this kind of technique attempted again in animation, so dominant had the prevailing codes of film language become.

Rybczynski is a film-maker acutely aware of the history of film, as his *Odessa Steps* video (1987) shows, and his work indicates the importance of examining the past to learn why film is structured in the way it is. Why was it, indeed, that one set of codes came to be dominant while others were marginalized? The answer to this is complex. There was clearly a response to the commercial success which live-action films by the newly formed independents such as United Artists were achieving. There was also an awareness of the flexibility which montage techniques could bring to the narrative. Yet the move to

Tango, Zbigniew Rybczynski, British Film Institute

***Tango* begins with a ball being thrown through a window into an empty room. A boy climbs into the room, picks up the ball and jumps out of the window. Then a ball is thrown into the room again and the cycle recommences. More characters enter and exit, going through their routines as if unaware of the actions of the others. The space of the room fills to a logically impossible degree, challenging our perceptions of screen space. Each movement is precisely choreographed and exposed separately on to the film. *Tango* won a Hollywood Oscar in 1983.**

Left: The Tender Tale of Cinderella Penguin, National Film Board of Canada/ Janet Perlman

Space can be controlled in different ways. In this shot the prince and princess penguins stare into each other's eyes, effectively closing the off-screen space to left and right.

adopt these techniques was slow. It may well be that the nature of animation as an illusion of an illusion determined how fast these techniques could be assimilated.

Screen space is, of course, an illusion both photographically and graphically. Conventions have become established which allow viewers to understand the space – to know where they are. In fact, there are two kinds of space involved: on-screen space and off-screen space. In Melbourne-Cooper's trick-films, only on-screen space is defined. All the action takes place within this proscenium; all the objects in the film are either situated within the space from the start or else appear from nowhere as if by magic. In *Tango*, Rybczynski exploits this concept of the single on-screen space by filling it with a plethora of actions. It soon becomes obvious that such a small space, that of a small room, could not possibly contain all the actions taking place.

Rybczynski also makes critical use of off-screen space, exposing it for the artifice it is. Off-screen space is the imaginary area beyond the edge of the screen, and in front of or behind the camera. There are a number of ways through to off-screen space in *Tango* – a window and a door in the back wall, doors on either side of the room, and a cupboard which also has its uses. Rybczynski orchestrates his entrances and exits with great precision. There are thirty separate acts, both ordinary and obsessional, being performed in the room at one point, and many more exits and entrances than this. The film serves as a kind of critical metaphor for the spatial relationships within the film space.

The edges of the screen – sides, top and bottom – are crucial in defining off-screen space. The top and bottom of the screen often have a very positive role to play in a film. As Road Runner protagonist Wile E. Coyote plunges once more into the canyon, or is catapulted by his own device high into the air, the space above and below the frame comes into its own. Or again, as Wile E. suddenly appears from the bottom of the screen, pauses for a moment as his expression slowly changes, and then plunges from sight leaving only the machine which has propelled him there to hang for a few frames before it too plunges down on the inevitable collision course with the resourceful coyote.

The edges of screen, despite not having the

Below: The Scarlet Pumpernickel, Chuck Jones, © 1950 Warner Bros Inc, all rights reserved

Daffy Duck is about to make a heroic leap off screen. All of our experience of the character leads us to expect fate will be unkind. How is it that the Duck cannot see it as clearly? In this case, the edge of frame is used to conceal the cause of his imminent downfall.

dramatic impact of top and bottom, do have potential for meaning. There may be a threatening object or character just out of shot. The main character may be heading rapidly towards an impending impact unseen. In Borivoj Dovniković's astute parody on the elaborate graphic titles of the 1950s *Without Title*, the main character is trying to get onto the screen, thwarted at every attempt by a seemingly endless title sequence that blocks his every attempt to appear. In this film, it is the conflict between the two-dimensional space of the screen and what we perceive as three-dimensional dramatic space which provides the core of the action.

There are film-makers who use two-dimensional screen space as the norm and try to avoid illusionism. Two examples of this are George Dunning's *Flying Man* (1961) and Robert Breer's *Man and his Dog out for Air*. Both take the flat surface of the screen and use it to suggest an endless and indefinable imaginary space. Both films use a loose drawing style that is constantly shifting – Dunning more consistently figurative than Breer. Since no spatial clues are given, the freely applied paint that makes up the man, the dog and the hat in the Dunning film can take on any form, defined by their relation to the edge of the screen. It is clear at some points where the 'ground' is, but when the man takes off into the air these assumptions are questioned. Breer's mainly abstract linear shapes also have a freedom of movement within a white space and, again, create tension by their relationship with an undefined floating space beyond the edge of the screen.

In the cinema, the screen on which the film is projected can be adjusted to give very precise control over the framing essential to accurate description of space. Television, on the other hand, is open to numerous vagaries. Not only is the frame ratio different, but both the transmitted area of film and its reception can vary. Some film-makers accept that their elegantly constructed shots will simply be transformed by a conspiracy of engineers and viewers bent on distorting their work. Others fight back. Paul Driessen, the Dutch film-maker, had seen his work transformed in this way and decided to act. He propelled the off-screen space onto the screen by the simple expedient of drawing it, using framing within the frame. In *The Killing of an Egg* (1977), the internal framing is the normal 3–4 of Academy ratio film, close to that of television. In *On Land, at Sea and in the Air* (1980), the screen is divided into three equal areas as in a triptych. Both films make use of the on-screen off-screen space.

In *The Killing of an Egg*, sound is used to

Above: The Killing of an Egg, Paul Driessen
The frame within the frame affords great control of the off-screen space. Here the use of colour also gives a strong visual clue to the relationship of the interior and exterior space.

suggest an external space. A figure sits at a table cracking an egg before eating it. At each tap of his spoon, a protesting voice emerges from inside the egg. The shouts and screams are finally silenced. Then, from outside the room, the tapping begins again. This time it is the character who begins to protest at this intrusion into his space, until finally a giant spoon breaks through the ceiling. In *On Land, at Sea and in the Air*, the triptych similarly emphasizes the interdependence of apparently separate spaces. The inescapable sensation that these are three films running independently, though with a strong relationship, is reinforced by the fact that the frames of the triptych were exposed separately. An ark full of animals appears in the land section, passes on to the sea section, then overturns and sinks. Characters reach from one section to another to satisfy their desires.

Framing can become the central element of the meaning of a film. In *Bitzbutz* (1984) by the Israeli animator Gil Alkabetz, high-contrast black-and-white images show a huge black animal pursuing a bird. The animal consumes the bird, which then appears as a white shape inside the black animal. The bird begins to peck at the animal from the inside until, finally, the black disappears and the bird, now black, remains on the screen. Using high-contrast black-and-white images is an effective technique for the manipulation of the screen space, also used in the West German film *Rope Dance* (1986). Made by Almund Krumme, the film shows a tug-of-war between two figures positioned either side of a rectangle. Depending on the posture of the figures, this rectangle becomes a chasm, a room, a carpet, a floor and a ceiling. Both *Bitzbutz* and *Rope Dance* use the frame to examine the ideas of border, the internal and the external.

Below left and below: On Land, at Sea, and in the Air, Paul Driessen
The frame can be divided into separate sections to give a number of internal frames. These two examples demonstrate the way in which the same elements can be shown in different relationships within the frames. The different ways the saw is 'thought of' in each frame and the rain falling in different locations are only related through the use of the triptych.

Right: Bitzbutz, Gil Alkabetz (consultant: I. Yoresh), Animation Unit of Bezalel, Academy of Arts and Design, Jerusalem
Framing becomes a part of the action. The beast pursues the bird and eats away its habitat, eventually devouring the bird itself. The bird then begins to peck away at the beast's inside. The technique used is sand on glass.

Left: Le Théâtre de M et Mme Kabal, Walerian Borowczyk
The use of line to define the space and draw attention to the frame is an essential part of Borowczyk's work. He makes the frame itself an active part of the meaning, drawing attention to the audience's position as spectator of the gruesome acts portrayed on screen.

Space can also be used to hide and to reveal. Borowczyk in particular used this technique very effectively. In his film *Jeux des Anges*, the labyrinth of passages connected by dark portals can suddenly produce a half-seen threat. In *Le Théâtre de M et Mme Kabal* (*Mr and Mrs Kabal's Theatre*, 1968), he introduces the idea of revealing through the use of devices such as binoculars.

Framing

The space is inscribed in the film through the framing. The projected or transmitted image relates directly to the image as it is filmed and to the initial framing of the artwork. The most common dimensions for a film frame are the 1:33 aspect ratio, often referred to as 'Academy'. This is the aspect ratio used for television, 16mm production and educational purposes. Other aspect ratios are referred to as 'wide screen'; these usually vary from 1:66 to 1:85, although there are larger film formats, such as CinemaScope, with different aspect ratios. Whatever the final destination of the film, cinema release or television, it is as well to use the 1:33 of television as a guide to the framing. On 16mm film, the camera aperture of .404mm × .295mm becomes .379mm × .284mm on projection and .368mm × .276mm for transmission. So the tolerances are extremely small and a slight error in framing could be catastrophic. To reduce the possible harmful consequences of a framing error, the action is usually staged within the 'safe action' and 'safe title' areas – in effect, frames within the frame – avoiding the outer edges of the frame proper.

The viewfinder of the camera being used will usually have these safe areas inscribed on it. If the camera is reflex, that is the image that can be viewed through the lens directly. There is a temptation to use the viewfinder to align the images accurately, but because of the small distance from the film plane to the artwork being photographed on the animation stand – 5 feet with a 50mm lens for a 12-inch field – the viewfinder should not be used until after the correct alignment has been achieved.

Specialized rostrum cameras provide a far more accurate method of alignment, known as 'light through'. A lamp is fixed firmly to the side of the camera and shone directly through the lens. This gives a very accurate gauge for the lining up. Further, if the lens centre needs to be established the light through can be carried out with film in the camera gate (this film needs to be accurate and can be obtained from camera manufacturers). The lens centre can then be aligned with the centre of the table. When the camera tracks in or out, the lens centre must remain in the same position relative to the artwork – any drift will be evident. If you have no choice but to use a non-specialized camera, at least shoot a test to determine the accuracy of the viewfinder.

The relationship of the artwork to the film is held constant through the use of a graticule. The graticule is marked out in fields in Academy ratio. The fields normally range from 2 inches wide up to 12 or 15 inches. Field sizes greater than this can, of course, be made. The graticule is printed onto acetate so that artwork can be viewed through it. There are also guides which give a very accurate

Below: Within the standard Academy frame for 16mm and 35mm there are safe areas for titles and for action. Animation is often shot 'open gate' – that is, without the masking for the optical soundtrack, which is only masked at the printing stage.

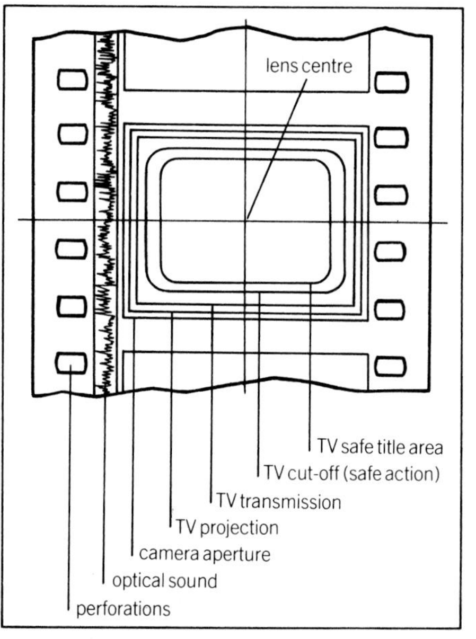

positioning for television safe action and safe title areas, as well as the various aspect ratios for film. These are made to fit specified fields, but they can be drawn up or down if the artwork does not correspond precisely to a given field size. The relationship of graticule to film is maintained by positioning the field centre. Field centres are determined by whether the travelling pegs on the table top are 12-inch or 15-inch; many rostrums have provision for both field sizes. The field centre is always specified on the dope sheet as well as the layout. A field position may be at any point on the 12-inch graticule – four fields east for instance – but it will still have a 12-inch field centre.

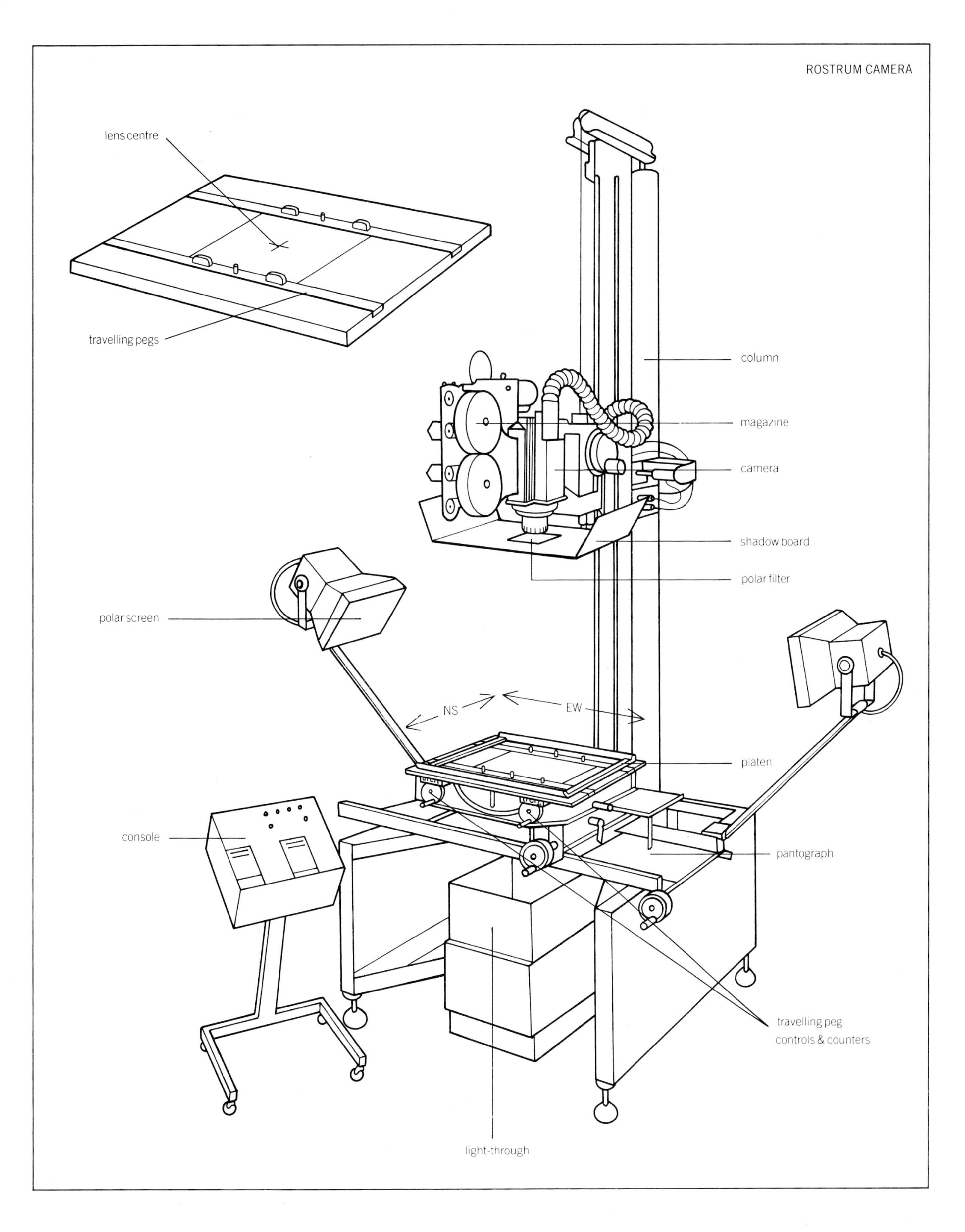
ROSTRUM CAMERA
lens centre
travelling pegs
column
magazine
camera
shadow board
polar filter
polar screen
NS
EW
platen
console
pantograph
travelling peg
controls & counters
light-through

Above: Life and Death, Joost Roelofsz, Rogier Proper/Delphine de Pury
***Life and Death* is made up of a continuous zoom. What appear to be the bald heads of observers become cacti; a saw and a pot of paint are suddenly revealed, transforming the meaning of the scene. As the camera pulls back further, the pattern of the curtain begins to dominate the whole room and the strange activities of the boy scouts take over. A continuous zoom calls for very careful calculations, as well as precision at the takeover points where the artwork is changed.**

Camera movements

In rostrum camera work, the camera itself is limited to tracking in or out, but to simulate other camera movements, the compound table holding the artwork can move north, south, east and west, and it can be rotated. The calibrations can be set to an accuracy of .001 inch and modern rostrums are often equipped with computer-controlled stepping motors to exploit this. A high level of accuracy is particularly important for optical or special-effects work, where there may be many separate exposures. The artwork is also moved using sliding pegs. The grooves on the table allow the pegs to move parallel to each other top and bottom, while there may also be an additional floating peg, not fixed to the table top, which can be used to mount artwork independently of the table.

Zooming or tracking in, like all camera movements, must be carried out frame by frame. It cannot be shot on double frames as some animation can. The effect of a zoom in animation is different from a zoom in live-action, since the fields are flat. What is actually being achieved is an enlargement or reduction of the field; there is no corresponding change in the focal length. This means that a zoom into the distance does not flatten out as a live-action zoom would. Since the viewer's understanding of this film code is to an extent based on live-action, you should be careful not to make excessive use of a straightforward zoom. The zoom will also not function effectively if even calibrations are used, because the speed of the movement will appear faster as the field gets smaller. To correct this, an exponential zoom must be calibrated.

As has been said, artwork can be panned on travelling pegs or by moving the compound table. Either kind of pan calls for careful calibration and it is likely that a buffer will be needed. The speed at which you pan will depend on the action, but if the pan is too fast or if the artwork contains a number of regularly spaced verticals, strobing will cause an unpleasant flicker effect. As a rule it is best to pan as slowly as is compatible with the action, and always on single frame. If a fast pan is really essential, then use a zip pan, which allows calibrations above .25 inch. A zip pan is good for creating dramatic effect or for showing impact.

Given that camera movements in animation are artificial copies of the equivalent live-action techniques, a combination of tracks and pans is usually more effective than a single obvious camera movement. When using a combination of movements, care should be taken with the frames between the start and finish position. It is easy to overlook the fact that in the mid-position of a track and pan unwanted elements are creeping into shot. In particular, if you are using table rotation, parts of the camera not in shot in the landscape position may suddenly appear in shot as the table rotates. A carefully prepared layout will stop this happening.

Other kinds of space

In two-dimensional animation, the multiplane camera was developed to create the potential for movement into the frame. On a conventional camera there is only one plane for the artwork; this is placed in the optimum focusing range of the camera lens. The camera's 'follow focus' will keep this plane in focus until it is disconnected. The multiplane camera was developed by Ub Iwerks at Disney's in the 1930s to increase the realism of the Disney films, particularly the feature productions. The camera had several different planes for artwork, instead of just one. The planes were

positioned one below the other and had independent movement. Artwork was placed on them to create the illusion of depth, with separate action in the foreground, middle and background. In addition, planes could move in and out of focus, thus creating an effect almost identical to live-action films.

The technique was not widely taken up, but the principles of multiplane have been exploited by Yuri Norstein in films like *Tale of Tales* and *The Overcoat*. It is not surprising that one of the great exponents of the spatial potential of film should see the multiplane as providing another element in his quest. Norstein's quest, however, is not for Disney's photographic realism. Rather, he seeks to challenge the Disney tradition and throw its spatial assumptions into disarray.

Norstein uses the frame not to propel the narrative forward by providing suspense, but to create meaning. In *Tale of Tales*, form and content combine to make a statement about memory. Images referring to the collective memory combine with images from other Norstein films and with the spectator's memory of previous scenes. Soldiers disappear into the mists leaving for the war, and the shot of a mother and child half-hidden by the angle of a ceiling is a space which is returned to a number of times in the film, as the point of view slides between the collective memory and the spectator's.

In *Tale of Tales*, Norstein uses the framing device of a blank sheet of paper. In his as yet

Below: I Fly to You in my Remembrance, Andrei Khrzhanovsky

In this work based on the drawings and manuscripts of the poet Pushkin, the flatness of the spatial plane is accentuated in order to bring attention to the fact that what we are looking at are, indeed, drawings. It is the tension between the paper and the screen which is central to the description of space.

Above: Tale of Tales, Yuri Norstein
In Norstein's work, space takes on an important meaning in relation to time and to memory. When figures move through planes, appearing for a moment only to recede and disappear into a misty background, they are lost in time as well as space. They have vanished from memory and must be consciously recalled.

unfinished adaptation of Gogol's *The Overcoat*, he elaborates another kind of frame within a frame. The main character enters his room, takes off his coat, sits at a table with a sheet of paper in front of him, and begins to write a letter with some difficulty. The positioning of the camera makes the painful expression on the character's face and the painful scratching of the quill pen mirror each other. Each movement is echoed – the paper could be the screen within the screen, but so could the face. More common framing devices include mirrors and windows, and reflecting surfaces like water.

Framing is essentially the antithesis of good composition, for framing is the act of giving meaning to the organization of film space. Composing this space according to graphic rules and conventions can destroy the attempt to create meaning through the organization of space and time.

Timing

Timing is the other major element in the structuring of meaning through the staging of the action. Timing relates an often specified duration, the running time, to the passage from scene to scene and sequence to sequence, and to the actual movement of the action.

The conventions of the running time for film developed slowly. The films which were the staple of the Nickelodeons were novelties of about 50 feet with a running time of four to five minutes maximum. As the industry developed, one-reelers which ran for 10 to 14 minutes became the primary form of production. Very few films of a longer length had been made before 1911. Then exhibitors realized that with the commercial success of longer films, the feature film was economically viable. Shortly before World War I, the live-action feature became standard.

Animation, however, remained firmly in the one-reel arena, with a conventional running time of five to eight minutes for each film. This is still very much the norm for the commercial entertainment short today and has translated into the television medium – with some detrimental effect on the funding viability of animation, since the rates paid by television companies are measured by the minute. Production of feature-length animation, on the other hand, although slow to get off the ground, has proved to be financially more attractive, even if relatively few features have in fact been produced. Series production also developed from the tradition of the one-reeler, so that each episode of a series would run for eight to ten minutes.

An important development more recently has been animated television commercials. Commercials are very tightly timed given the great expense of purchasing air time. They usually run for 15 seconds, 30 seconds or one minute, although very successful seven-second commercials have been produced. The animator working in a subsidized system or as an independent does not face such clear constraints and is limited by the resources available rather than by the requirements of exhibition. The medium itself imposes certain constraints on running time, since there is only so much work that can be done in a set time using the frame-by-frame techniques of animation.

Certain kinds of live-action film, in particular the classic narrative feature film, have been analysed to obtain a clear picture of the average number of shots and scenes which they contain. But there is no such clear evidence for an established structure in animated films. The statements of animators like Chuck Jones, working in the classic studio system, that a Warner's cartoon ran for seven or eight minutes and had to contain a set number of gags, give an insight into a particular kind of production process, rather than a fixed recipe for success. The storyboard or script will indicate the main elements of the film, forming the basis for the timing of the scenes. If an animatic has been made, this gives a very clear indication of the timing, and adjustments can be made as needed.

Timing the movement

The way in which the scenes, sequences and

Below: The Abominable Snowrabbit, Chuck Jones, © 1961 Warner Bros Inc, all rights reserved
Chuck Jones's Bugs, the master of the one-line throwaway gag and the impeccable timing. Within the rigid structure of these cartoons elaborate and wicked manipulations of space and time were perpetrated.

The Black Dog, Channel 4/story and direction Alison de Vere, producer Lee Stork

Timing and its application mark the unique voice of certain animators. In *Black Dog*, as in the earlier *Cafe Bar*, Alison De Vere transforms the story of a fantasy journey by the mesmeric movement of the figures. Even the moments of high drama have a dream quality to them. In these scenes, the heroine is faced with temptation and ridicule and then led to self-understanding and salvation as she follows the black dog.

shots are timed establishes the rhythm for the film. The timing of the movements in animation can cause initial problems. How long should a particular movement take? The basic unit is the frame – that is, one twenty-fourth or one twenty-fifth of a second. An understanding of this basic unit is vital, since it gives the animator a secure basis for timing the action. It also provides a system for breaking down the action into manageable sections.

The shot plan already indicates what action is to take place in a given time. If there is a single action in the shot, it can be broken down as a whole unit. A simple action, such as a character entering a room and crossing to a piano to start piano-practice, may appear limited in potential and could be timed in a very prosaic way. For instance: character opens door and enters room, five seconds; crosses to piano, five seconds; sits and opens the piano-lid, five seconds; and hold. But this

Left: Getting Started, National Film Board of Canada/Richard Condie
The pianist sits for a brief moment at the piano in Condie's film on the nature of procrastination. Fortunately, he is distracted once more from his piano practice by the paper cup, which has stuck to his nose when he attempted to pick it up without taking his hands from the keyboard. Timing has always played an important part in comedy – which, at its best, is always based firmly on observation.

regularity of timing would produce a film with little or no sense of pacing. If the same simple scene is timed using the full range of possibilities open to the animation director, it can take on a meaning and a character of its own. Richard Condie uses precisely this scene at the beginning of his film *Getting Started*. The first shot, even before the character enters, is on an open door. The character's voice is heard explaining to a friend that he cannot go out to a party because he has to stay home and practise for a concert. This shot, held for some thirty seconds, both establishes the drama and sets up an anticipation of the kind of action and timing that will follow. When the character does enter, the move to the piano, the action of sitting and the opening of the piano-lid are rapid. There then follows another long hold as the character stares blankly at the keys, before getting up and starting the quirky routines to postpone getting started which make up the film. This example shows clearly how an apparently ordinary sequence with a straightforward problem of timing can be transformed into a significant factor in a film.

The exaggerated pause, as used by Condie, has its roots in the work of the great Warner and MGM animators. Jones and Avery, in particular, were able to combine sequences of rapid action with a sudden halt of 24 frames or more which served to emphasize the preceding action. Tex Avery's *Bad Luck Blackie* (1947) is a classic of the fast and furious school of timing. The premise of the film is simple. A white cat being horribly tortured by a bulldog is saved by a black cat. The two cats make a pact to revenge this mistreatment: every time the white cat whis-

Above: Bad Luck Blackie, Tex Avery, © 1949 Loew's Inc, Ren 1976 Metro-Goldwyn-Mayer Inc
After the role-reversal in *Bad Luck Blackie*, brought about by pots of white and black paint, the bulldog is about to revenge himself on the white/black cat, while the black/white cat pretends it is invulnerable. Unfortunately for the dog, he has swallowed a whistle which causes objects to drop on him from the skies . . . and he has the hiccups.

Picnic, Paul Vester, Speedy Films Ltd
Paul Vester has brought together an understanding of both classic cartoon and experimental animation to create a quite original sense of timing at the limits of perception. In his non-commercial work this takes on a darker meaning, portraying a disordered and violent world gathering speed, possibly for its own destruction.

tles, the black cat crosses the dog's path and a heavy object falls on the unlucky canine. The objects include flowerpots, heavy trunks, bombs, cash registers, horseshoes – followed by the horse – a safe, an anvil and, finally, an ocean-liner. All of this action is packed into a seven-minute film. Avery achieves this compression by breaking the conventions of structuring and timing the action. Once the premise of the action is established, there are no further establishing shots. The framing concentrates wholly on the action. The action itself is timed so that there are no elaborate recovery shots – the longest is a fade of a few frames as the bulldog's head is replaced after being blown off. Once the first line of action is established, it is not necessary to re-establish that heavy objects will drop from the sky once a whistle is blown. When the dog swallows the whistle and has a coughing fit, whistling every few frames, the action reaches an almost subliminal pace. Pianos, steamrollers,

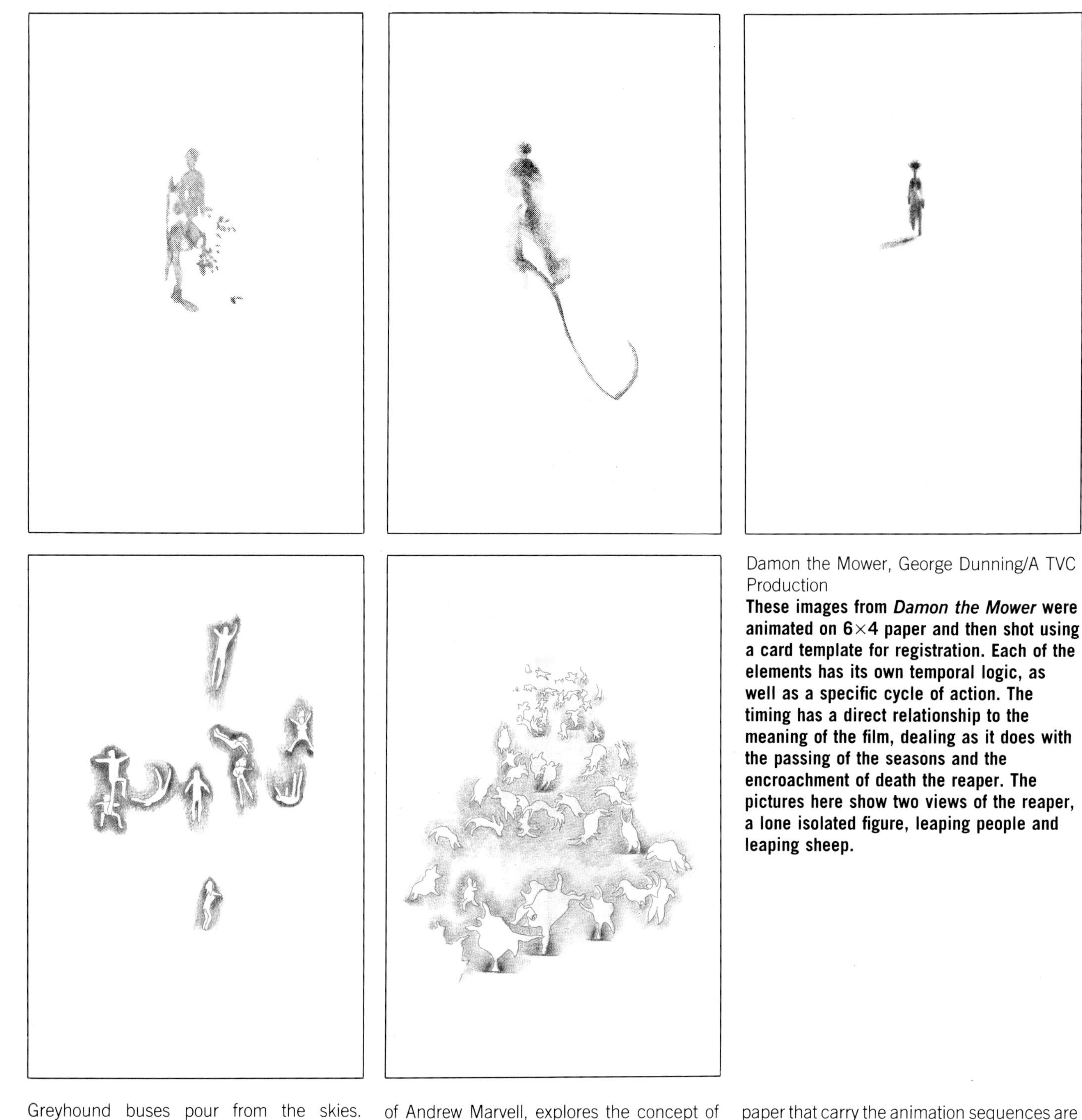

Damon the Mower, George Dunning/A TVC Production
These images from *Damon the Mower* were animated on 6×4 paper and then shot using a card template for registration. Each of the elements has its own temporal logic, as well as a specific cycle of action. The timing has a direct relationship to the meaning of the film, dealing as it does with the passing of the seasons and the encroachment of death the reaper. The pictures here show two views of the reaper, a lone isolated figure, leaping people and leaping sheep.

Greyhound buses pour from the skies. Although the pacing is frenetic and the action unremitting, in its cruelty the timing is carefully controlled. It builds skilfully to the climax when we realize that there has simply been a role-reversal, and that the cats' cruelty is as unforgivable as that of the bulldog.

It is not only the classic school of animation that can provide examples of the use of timing as a central device of communication in animation. George Dunning, in his film *Damon the Mower* (1971) based on the work of Andrew Marvell, explores the concept of time, a favoured theme of Marvell and other seventeenth-century Metaphysical poets. The film uses pastoral images – flocks of sheep, fields of wheat – the image of the reaper representing time and ultimately death, and finally a church tower which explodes almost in slow motion. These separate elements are positioned against a flat white background and are clearly marked as animation – they actually have the numbering of the animation left in. The small pieces of paper that carry the animation sequences are also permitted to move against the white background. The timing of the scenes depends once again on very clear lines of action being established at the outset. Once the main movements are in place, the various timings of the different elements are allowed to interact. The sequencing is complex – the close-ups of the scythe are related to the long shots of the reaper, the timing of the cycles coinciding at some points, while at others the images slide out of sync.

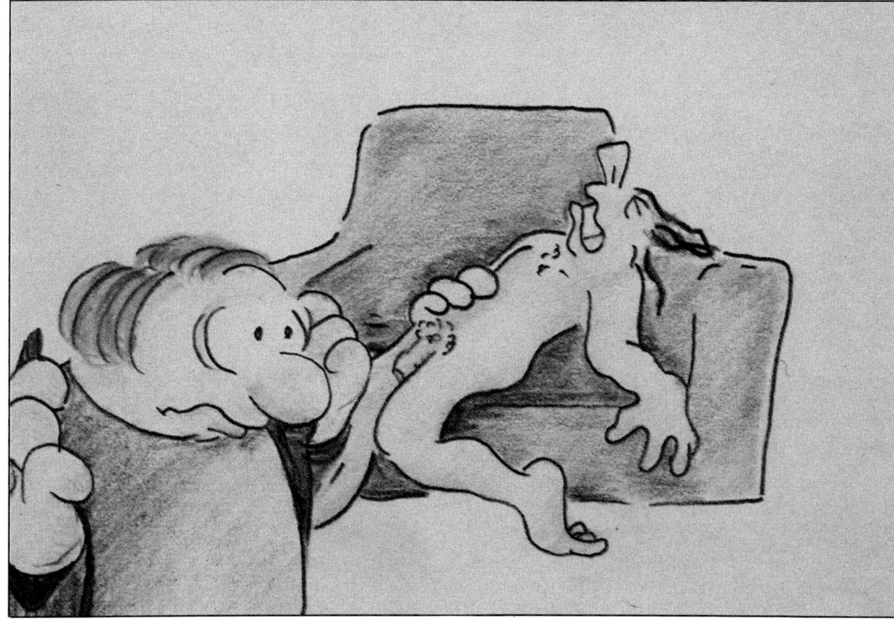

Special Delivery, National Film Board of Canada/John Weldon
Weldon's pacing can be described as laconic, in the best traditions of Canadian humour. Why does the hero's wife find a naked postman dead in her husband's armchair, and who will now deliver the neighbourhood mail? These are the central questions raised. Weldon uses sudden unexpected action, as in the final shot of the leaping angry husband, to contrast with the inevitable unfolding of the tale.

This kind of technique, where a number of actions with varied timings are counterpointed, can be used in many ways, including classic animation. Breaking the rule which states that one action only should be primary and that any other action in a sequence should be subordinate can be spectacular. The effect of many different actions taking place simultaneously, especially if they are synchronized to a strong soundtrack, is visually and aurally exciting. This will work for a short time only and is most suitable for a music promo or for a commercial. The use of overlapping animation action is also important with this sort of timing.

Many of the features of timing which apply to drawn or two-dimensional animation also apply to three-dimensional animation. Because of the nature of the materials used in three-dimensional animation, there can also be an interaction between the materials used

Above left and above: Dimensions of a Dialogue, Jan Svankmajer
It is the transformation of the material universe through violence and decay that makes the temporal so significant in Svankmajer's work. The violent conflict which turns the head made of vegetables and fruit into the head constructed from kitchen implements is at times so rapid it defies the eye.

Above: Street of Crocodiles, Brothers Quay, a British Film Institute Production in association with Channel 4
Based on a novel by Bruno Schulz, the film continues the Quays' quest for the exact position where disparate forms of material and matter take form and become something. The meaning of the film is located in the visual – the decor and the models – and the articulation of these elements – their alchemy – rather than in a straightforward narrative line.

and the kind of movement and timings employed. In one section of Jan Svankmajer's *Dimensions of a Dialogue*, this potential is exploited to particularly good effect. It is the section that makes use of the composite portraits of Giuseppe Arcimboldo, in which heads were constructed out of different objects and materials. In Svankmajer's film, two heads, one made of vegetables and the other of kitchen utensils, constantly devour and regurgitate each other. At each point the nature of the materials is both defied and made explicit by the movements chosen. The vegetables engulf the metal objects and grind them into misshapen lumps; the knives attack the vegetables, chopping and mutilating. In the middle section of this sequence, the nature of the materials becomes enigmatic – the vegetables now move with the aggression of knife-blades, while the kitchen knives take on an organic quality. Gradually, both heads are reduced to the same congealed material which moves with the same rhythm. The Brothers Quay, who also work in three-dimensional animation, have developed an approach to timing in which sudden sharp movements of camera or action are counterpointed with slow threatening changes in atmosphere and lighting.

Establishing the timing

Once the kind of timing needed to stage the action has been decided, the details can be established. All the timings must be broken down into their constituent elements, with only one timing for each discrete action. The actions can be combined again later.

The first thing to determine is the start and end position of each discrete action. A discrete action is one single line of action. This can be illustrated by the act of picking up a cup. The hand reaches for the cup, grasps the handle and lifts the cup. Three lines of action combine into the one movement – the hand moves forward and down, the fingers move together to take the handle, and the hand and forearm move upwards. Each of these movements will have a start and an end position.

The speed at which each of these discrete movements will be made is then established – for instance, one second for the first movement, half a second for the second movement, and the final movement one and a half seconds. Some of the movements will be buffed, so that the action will slow down as the point of contact of hand and cup is reached. This can be allowed for when the animation is being done. At this point only key positions are essential. There will also be holds on certain points of the action, which will be timed and entered in the dope sheets.

The Dope Sheet

The dope sheet carries all of the information needed for the camera operator to shoot the animation. It physically accompanies the animation scene as it progresses through the production process. At each stage additional information is added and finally, immediately before shooting, both dope sheets and animation are thoroughly scrutinized by a checker to see that they match.

The dope sheet is divided vertically into columns and horizontally into feet and frames. The frame lines may be numbered or blank, depending on the design of the sheets. Animators vary in their preferences, but sheets which do not have frames numbered are definitely more flexible.

Running from left to right, the vertical columns are:

1) A column for the animator to make notes on the action. It is used to describe what is taking place on the screen.
2) A column which has information on the sound entered from the bar chart. This may concern dialogue, music or the main effects.
3) The third column carries information on the animation. It is divided into six subdivisions, one for each level of the cel.

When using cel animation, it is important to specify a level of position for each cel. For the sake of efficiency during the shooting – always a laborious process – the top level of cel needs to be the level which is changed most, while the bottom level is changed least. If an object or character changes its position in the levels between scenes, there will be a change of colour caused by the density of the cel. Allowances have to be made for this when the paint is made up. It is also important that the number of cels remains the same, so if the number of cels needed changes in a sequence from four to three, a blank cel is inserted to compensate for any colour change. Level six is reserved for the background, always notated as BG. This indicates which background is to be used with the animation and when a background is to change. The background may be either 'static' or 'panning'.

4) The final vertical column carries the camera instructions. It details special camera effects – fades, mixes and so on and tells the camera operator the field size to be used and the position of the field centre. It may also carry the calibrated camera movements, if the film-maker is personally shooting the film.

Finally, at the top of the dope sheet there is space for the title of the production, the scene and sequence number, and the number of the dope sheet. The dope sheet is at all times kept in the same box or folder as the animation to which it refers. It is the vital link between the animator and the camera.

During the shooting, it is useful to have some kind of aid to mark the position reached on the dope sheet. A ruler is ideal for the purpose. Move it down one or two frames to the next position after the artwork has been exposed, and if for some reason you lose concentration, it remains absolutely clear which is the next exposure.

LAYOUT

Laying out a scene is an important and specialized part of the production process. Where the layouts are complex, calling for changes in perspective and point of view during a camera movement, it is normal for a layout artist to be employed specially. The layout artist works with the director and animator, creating rough sketches for the scene using the storyboard and character sheets. These are then drawn up in more detail with character and action shown. Next the position of the camera is indicated with the field centre and the field size defined. The final layout will have all of the information necessary to produce the background and the cels as well as the camera's dope sheet for the final shooting of the action. In this sequence John Challis, who has a reputation as a highly accomplished layout artist as well as an animator, lays out the main scene for a 30-second commercial.

All illustrations in this case history by John Challis, Eyeworks (agency: Saatchi & Saatchi; client: Reckitt & Coleman)

Top: Though it is possible to produce animation drawings on a light box without an animation disc, for laying out a disc is essential. The disc, which has sliding pegs on the top and the bottom, corresponding to those on the camera, is used to position accurately the various elements which will go to making up the scene.

Above: The position of the animation is checked against the layout in all of the key positions. These key layout positions are noted – in this case, the letter 'c' represents the particular set-up.

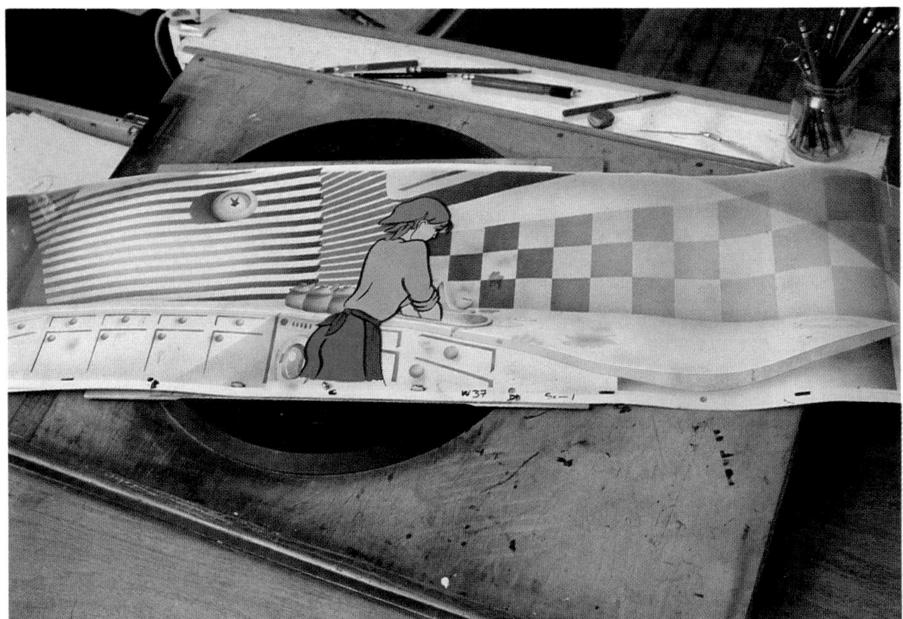

Above left: The detail in the layout is built up. As additional items, such as the kettle, are added, these must be checked in relation to the movement, to make sure the action will not be obscured by the background.

Left: The painted background with one of the final cels positioned over it. The planning of the colours is carried out when the colour models are designed so that the background and foreground are clearly defined.

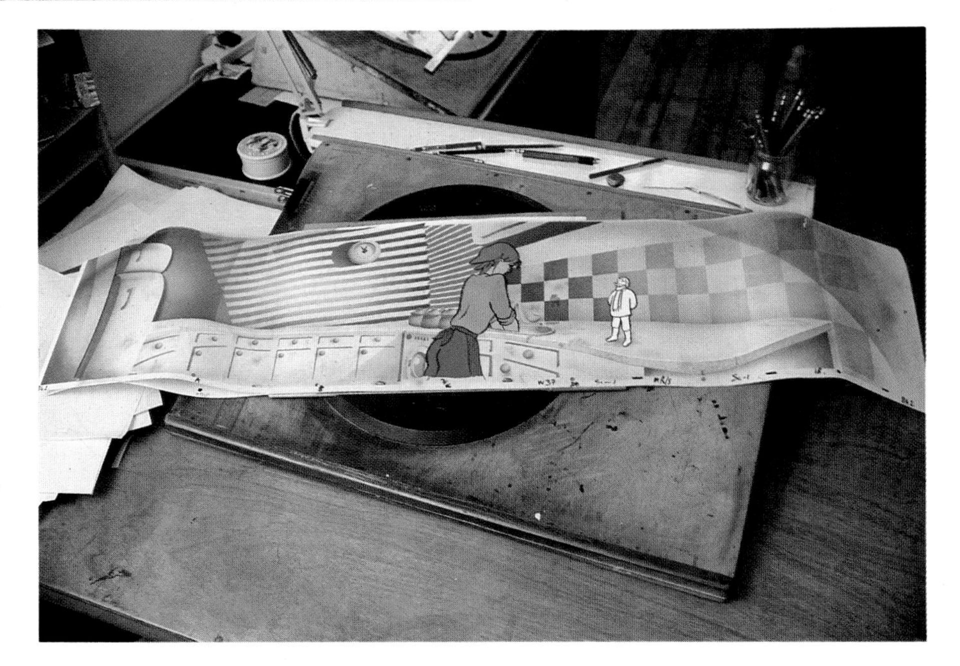

Right: The final position, with the cleaner-hero 'Mr Sheen' appearing to take care of all the kitchen surfaces. The importance of layout shows up in the way the character 'stands' on the surface of the kitchen unit. Any slight fault in the perspective would create the illusion of the character being above or below it.

The way in which the staging of the scene develops can be seen from these sketches. The initial sketch for the layout (top) is highly schematic. It only needs to indicate the point of view and the approximate relationship of character to background. As decisions are made about possible ways of staging the scene, the layout is cleaned up. In the third of the sketches (above), the background is drawn without the figure, so that the correct perspective can be worked out and the smaller details positioned. The final drawing (left) shows a sketch for another possible staging.

Referring to a rough sketch of the background (below top), a plan of the camera movement is made (below centre), which shows the precise position of the camera at the start and the end of a pan. It also indicates the normal field centre, so that the distance of the start and end positions from this can be seen. When the final layout is being shot, the camera operator will start to set up the movement from the centre position – that is, all of the counters will read zero and the field size will be set to 12 or 15 (whichever is the standard field size). The rostrum camera operator cannot see accurately through the viewfinder and so is working blind with the camera dope sheet, based on the layout, as the only guide. Before the final production the camera movements are checked against a more detailed background (bottom) so that animators and background artists are able to work accurately.

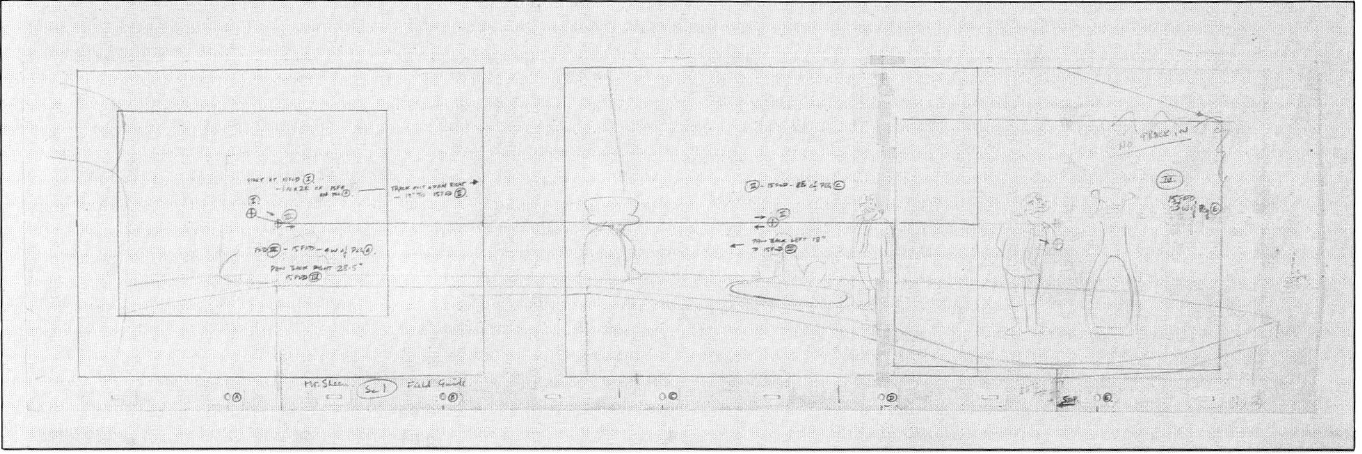

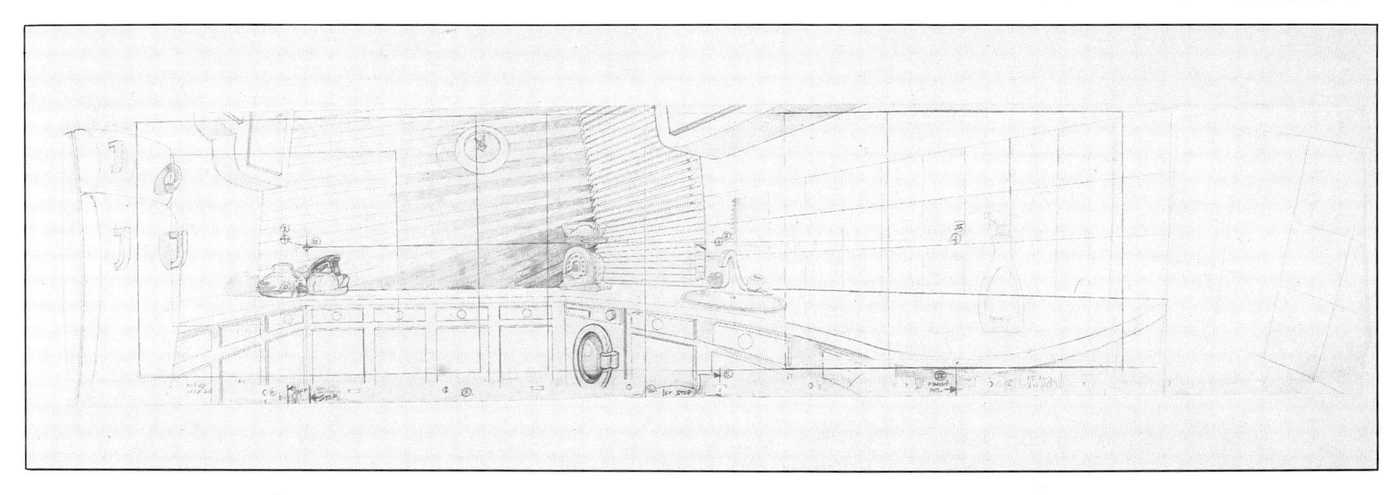

Below: The finished background without figures. The peg holes are reinforced with stiff paper or strips of punched film, as any wear on the holes could create movement and misalignment.

Below centre: The outline on cel is positioned on the background. The foreground and background must match exactly – for example, the point at which the woman's arms enter the washing bowl.

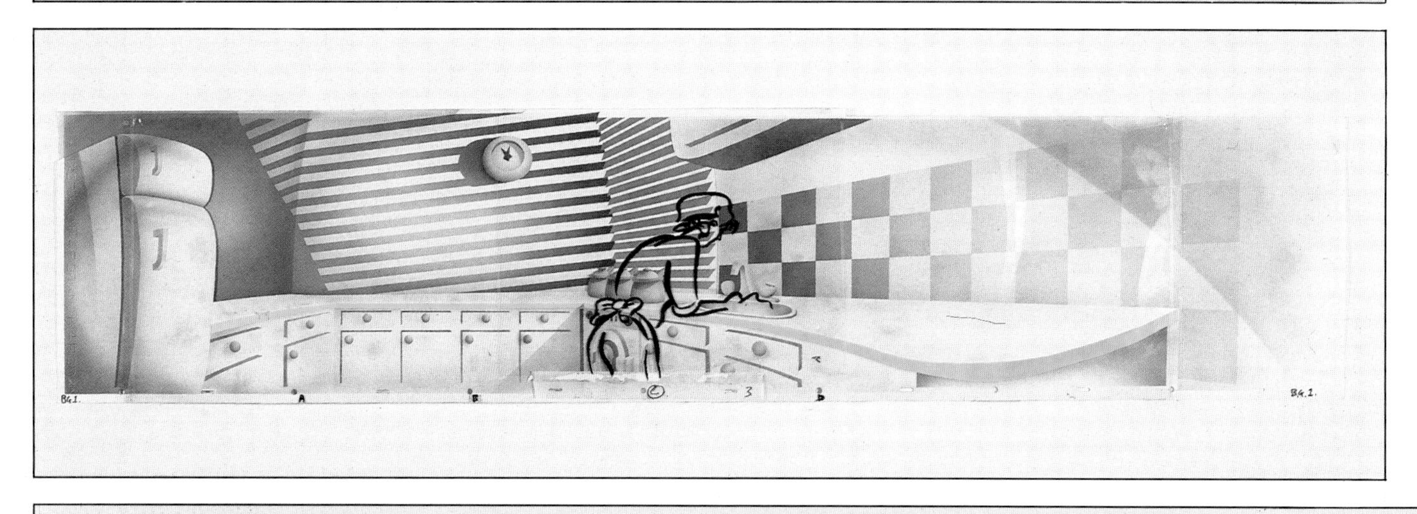

Below: Once the positioning has been established, the final cels can be painted and overlaid on the background.

Below centre: Not only one position, but a number of them must match throughout the sequence as the character moves.

Left: As the scene builds up, new characters appear on different levels of cel and react with each other's actions. The matching of movement and eyeline then needs to be taken into consideration. Panning cel, which is the same size or slightly longer than the background, is always used when the action takes place on a panning background. The peg holes on the cel should also be reinforced. The way the perspective curves as the camera moves in relation to the background is now clearly visible.

5
HANDMADE FILMS

Making traditional Disney-style animated films requires a large workforce and lots of money. But there are other forms of animation suitable for individuals working alone with a bare minimum of equipment – and the results can be extremely impressive.

Above: Monty Python's Flying Circus, Terry Gilliam

Terry Gilliam brought a new kind of animation to the attention of a wider television audience by utilizing the cut-out technique for the Monty Python series. The imaginative graphics and the speed of the production process created a new space for the use of animation.

A number of simple but effective techniques have developed for making animation without a studio team or expensive equipment, in some cases even dispensing with a camera by working directly onto the surface of the film itself. The reasons for avoiding the system of industrial production are numerous and often complex. There is the ideological objection to a rigid, mainly Western mode of production and the kind of stereotyped representation it is said to offer. There is the financial imperative to find cheaper means of production than the costly time-consuming procedures of the main commercial processes. The industrial system of production is also associated with the division of the workforce into different specialisms, which is seen as leading to a distancing of the creative artist from the

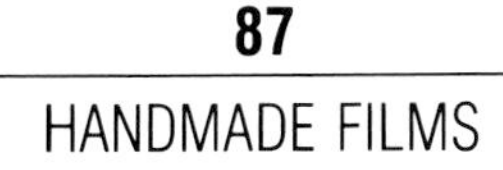

materials with which the work is carried out. Individual film-makers have sought a more direct approach, with closer control over the act of film-making and access to the whole production process.

Finally, there is the question of the freedom to experiment. The direct and handmade approaches have often been the test-bed for new techniques that have later found their way into the mainstream of production methods, enriching animation as a whole. It is unlikely, for instance, that computer animation would have developed as it has without the pioneering work of the Whitneys, who in turn learnt from the work of earlier experimental film-makers in Germany and the United States.

Experimentation is vital to the continued growth of animation, whether carried out by the committed artist or by the animation film-maker who merely seeks to develop the art and improve his or her personal skills. It is, of course, in the nature of experimentation that the future is yet to be discovered. Although it is possible to discern some trends, and there are clearly frontiers to be explored at the forefront of the new technologies, individuals can still make a unique contribution that may confound our expectations – if they are given the right encouragement and support.

The areas that are covered below do no more than indicate the main lines of thought in experimental and handmade animation. There are endless possible permutations of these techniques, and it is as well to look to the past as well as the future in order to find the suitable method for a new production.

Above: L'Idée, Berthold Bartosch
One of the masterpieces of animation, Bartosch's film employs cut-out and drawn animation, as well as a multiplane technique also used by Lotte Reiniger. The film's uncompromising imagery is combined with a soundtrack composed by Arthur Honegger which is thought to be the first use of electronic music in film.

Below: Cerridwen's Gift, Rose Bond
Drawing on film is often associated exclusively with abstract and experimental work, but even though the process is demanding, narrative film is possible. This film, an adaptation of a Welsh folk tale, makes effective use of the quality of line that can be achieved in this direct method.

Cut-out animation

It was Lotte Reiniger who first convincingly demonstrated that the simple technique of flat cut-out paper animated directly under the camera could sustain a major production. Drawing on her knowledge of the silhouette puppets of the Javanese and other long traditions of puppetry, in 1923–26 she produced a full-length feature film, *The Adventures of Prince Achmed*, using the cut-out technique. The first animated feature film, *Prince Achmed* also brought together many of the other artists experimenting with animation in Germany at the time, including Walter Ruttmann and Berthold Bartosch.

Reiniger persevered with the cut-out technique for the rest of her life, making films such as *Papageno* (1935) and *Aucassin and Nicolette* (1975). The techniques which she developed for her silhouette films were equally adaptable to the production of cut-out films in general and Bartosch elaborated on them in his film *L'Idée* (*The Idea*, 1932), based on the woodcuts of Frans Masereel. Using the cut-out technique to create an atmosphere faithful to the great Belgian artist, Bartosch spread a soap mixture on the surface of the glass plate which holds the artwork flat during shooting. The result is quite unlike any other cut-out film, as the images have soft edges, existing in a misty landscape.

Because the cut-out technique demanded the production of a relatively small amount of artwork compared with the cel animation techniques favoured by the studios, it was at first only individual animators and experimentalists who made use of it. The cut-out production process was difficult to adapt to the dominant studio system with its rigorous specification of roles. *Prince Achmed* had been made by individual artists working on their own sequences under Reiniger's overall direction. This was incompatible with the

Left: Labyrinth, Jan Lenica
Cut-out animation allows established artists to maintain their style – there is no need for the kinds of visual compromises which cel animation calls for. In *Labyrinth*, Lenica's graphic style creates a threatening and surreal environment.

Below: La Traversée de l'Atlantique à la Rame, Jean-François Laguionie
Although cut-out animation is associated with violence and destruction it can also be used to create mood and atmosphere. This film traces the journey of a couple as they row across the Atlantic and encounter the difficulties, hazards and ultimate joy of their shared quest.

production-line system, where the process was broken down so that many different individuals could work on one sequence, all undertaking separate tasks.

It was from the area of print-making that emerged the next generation of animators using cut-out. Jan Lenica and Walerian Borowczyk came from a background in Polish design, only later moving to the West and a closer involvement with animation. Lenica was an acknowledged master of the film poster and played an important part in its development in Poland. When he and Borowczyk turned to animation, working in collaboration at first, they quickly established a strong visual style, an extension of their graphic work. The subject-matter, too, was very different from the mainstay of animation in the 1950s; the humour was black and the themes obsessive. The style of the design was entirely suited to cut-out, providing Lenica with the opportunity to create spectacular collages. He used photo-montage and engravings as well, combined with a bold design in films such as *Labyrinth* (1962) and *Monsieur Tête* (1959). Borowczyk made use of a number of techniques, combining cut-out, pixillation (see below) and collage, as well as his own particular spiky style of line drawing.

Bob Godfrey and Jean-François Laguionie further extended the range of cut-out animation in the 1960s and 1970s. Bob Godfrey's eclectic style and frenzied rhythm, with objects combining in a loose stream-of-consciousness manner, is demonstrated in his early films *A Plain Man's Guide to Advertising* (1961) and *The Do-It-Yourself Cartoon Kit* (1961). Both films show how the cut-out technique can be used not only as a production method, but as an input into the meaning. The anarchic message of the Godfrey animation is supported by the spontaneous way in which the rapid assembly of images of consumerism is presented.

Jean-François Laguionie takes a more measured approach to cut-out. His first film, *La Demoiselle et le Violoncellist* (*The Young Lady and the Cellist*, 1964), used flat painted cardboard cut-outs, and he has continued to pursue the use of cut-outs with growing control and ambition ever since. The pace of Laguionie's cut-out animation is slow, although it is easier to use fast action in cut-out as this makes any mistakes easier to disguise. The surface of his cut-outs is rich and painterly. The advantage for Laguionie in using this technique is that he is able to concentrate on character and atmosphere. His films are often concerned with the theme of arriving in strange places, as in *Une Bombe par Hasard* (*A Bomb by Chance*, 1968) or undertaking journeys, as in *La Traversée de l'Atlantique à la Rame* (*Rowing across the Atlantic*, 1978).

Terry Gilliam brought a simple cut-out technique together with surrealist terrorism to produce a series of works for the Monty Python shows that broadened the audience for animation in general. His use of air-

Left: Monty Python's Flying Circus, Terry Gilliam
Terry Gilliam's cut-out technique grew more sophisticated, especially in the way that changes of scale and movement began to play an increasing part in the pieces. Unusually for animation, the soundtracks to the films were laid after the completion of the images, giving a spontaneity to both.

Right: Le Planète Sauvage, René Laloux
Although the first animated feature, *Prince Achmed*, had been made using cut-out, film-makers felt that cut-out could not sustain feature-length production. But Laloux, who had made a number of short cut-out films, demonstrated that high-quality cut-out and a strong concept could be successful with audiences, despite the lengthy production process.

brushed artwork also added a new dimension to the technique. More recently, a series of films made for Channel Four in Britain has returned to the roots of cut-out. *The New Decameron* (1987) goes back to the silhouette style first used by Lotte Reiniger in 1923.

Since *Prince Achmed* there have been few attempts at making feature-length films using cut-out techniques. One notable exception is the French film *Le Planète Sauvage* (*The Fantastic Planet*, 1969–73), made by René Laloux. He employed an unusual approach to cut-out: the film was first animated in the conventional way on paper, and only then were the characters cut out and coloured, using the paper animation as a template. The cut-out characters were then repositioned over the backgrounds. This technique provided the film-maker with a rich surface and a visual quality which could only have been achieved with difficulty using conventional cel animation. Nor did Laloux have to sacrifice the quality of the action, as his templates gave the accurate registration needed for subtle and expressive movement. By mixing the paper animation production process with the cut-out style, he was also able to bring the necessary organization of the work to the cut-out method operating on a large scale. As with Laguionie's works in the 1980s, such as *Gwen* (1985), it is becoming increasingly difficult to see these perfectly animated films in terms of the crudity or spontaneity usually associated with the cut-out technique. It has become clear that, as with so many animation techniques, the expressive range is limited only by the artist's imagination.

Cut-out animation techniques, although simple, still draw on the concepts of storyboard, sound and image, and careful staging of the action. There are some differences

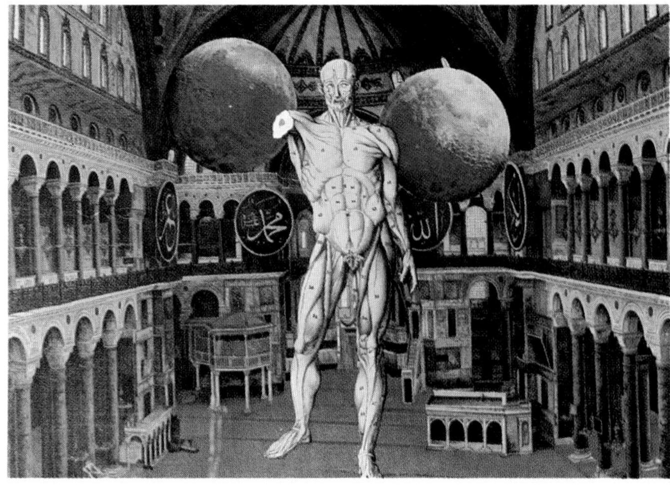

Above left: Sophie's Place, Larry Jordan;
Above: Moonlight Sonata, Larry Jordan;
Left: Gwen, Jean-François Laguionie
The use of collage as a technique in the fine arts is similar to the way in which cut-out techniques have been used in animation to achieve startling and unusual juxtapositions of images. Larry Jordan takes illustrations from anatomy and astrology books, nineteenth-century engravings and reproductions, to project very contemporary subjects. The still from *Gwen* shows the quality of images which can be produced using cut-out.

from other forms of animation – for instance, sound can be added at a later point, since it is not possible to achieve the very precise synchronization that is such a part of the cel technique. Cut-out technique involves the manipulation of artwork under the camera, and this in turn defines some of the approaches taken. The artwork will inevitably receive a good deal of wear and tear; there are no clear points of key animation to 'get back to' if there is an error; there is no precise relationship of timing to movement. But, at the same time, there is a degree of flexibility, a potential for improvization, and a graphic richness and variety which may be lacking in other forms of animation.

Cut-out artwork

Artwork can be prepared on thin flat card or paper, using any medium which does not cause it to buckle and distort. If the artwork is going to be used many times and is therefore likely to get damaged or worn, it is as well to re-photograph it and work with the photographic print. This also has the advantage that the surface of the print is easy to clean. The artwork should be cut out with a sharp scalpel blade (usually 10A or 11). The exposed edge of the paper is blacked using a grease pencil or felt marker to prevent the edge showing as a white outline when it is placed under the lights of the rostrum camera. The position of the lights at 45 degrees to the table top makes it imperative that the artwork is as thin and as flat as possible, to avoid shadows and reflections.

One great advantage of cut-out animation is that texture and rendering can be produced more easily than with cel techniques. This is because every line that makes up the texture in cel animation must itself be animated. This has been done with great effect, but the process is very time-consuming.

An animator using the cut-out technique, no less than the cel animator, is faced with the task of keeping track of the artwork. This is further complicated in the cut-out technique as artwork may be used a number of times in different contexts. It is often small and fiddly – and it is usually the small piece absolutely vital for a scene which gets lost. A system of filing and numbering is essential and artwork should be kept in envelopes when not being used.

Cut-out animation normally makes use of one plane only – it is in effect flat and at its best exploits this quality, emphasizing design and atmosphere rather than trying to create the illusion of a three-dimensional reality. If the animator needs to create a perspective movement, this can be achieved by animating the movement on paper and then remounting the artwork onto acetate cel, so that it can be accurately registered.

Cut-out animation can be made without jointing. If a long scene is required, however, or if the artwork or movement is intricate, it becomes necessary to make joints or at least register the artwork in some fashion. The most economical way of making joints for the artwork is by using thin wire (fuse wire is excellent for this purpose). The two pieces of artwork which are to be hinged have a small hole made in them, through which the wire is passed. This wire is then bent flat and held in place with a small piece of tape. The surface of the joint can either be painted over or masked with paper. Clearly, care must be taken to avoid protrusions which will show up when the artwork is lit – the kind of lighting used on a rostrum can unexpectedly reveal

Above: Working directly under the camera, the artwork is placed on a black velvet background to achieve maximum black.

Above: The glass must be placed very carefully over the artwork even though it is fixed.

Above: The images are changed under the glass, which has the edges masked with tape so that it can be moved more easily.

Above: The artwork itself is held in place with very small pieces of blue tack. Double-sided tape can also be used.

Above: The position of the image is marked on the glass with a Rotring pen; the black ink does not show against the background.

Above: White paper is then slid under the glass to give an accurate matching position; the ink is easily removed for the next position.

Above and above right: Three Inventors, Michel Ocelot, Ocelot AAA
In this technique, paper is used to make sculptural forms in bas-relief. The sharpness of the edges of the paper creates a style reminiscent of Reiniger's silhouettes. Ocelet also evokes a mood of period without using period artefacts.

Right: Gwen, Jean-François Laguionie
The desert in Laguionie's *Gwen* serves a similar function to the Atlantic in his earlier film. It is a place of mystery and the unexpected where the characters are adrift. In this film the cut-out technique is used to create a convincing atmosphere of the desert as well as to enable the director to use a narrative style suitable for the feature film length.

unseen lumps. Joints can also be made very effectively out of other materials, such as cotton. The choice will depend on the surface texture of the artwork and the degree to which it can support the material from which the joint is made.

Airbrushing, tinted photographs and highly textured surfaces, such as cross-hatching, can all be used in cut-out animation, whereas they are difficult to use in cel animation because of the surface detail which is required.

Shooting cut-out

The scale at which cut-out is best shot depends on the detail in the artwork. In general, however, it is best to shoot the largest scale possible – 15-inch field, 20-inch field, or even larger. This permits much greater control of the artwork, as well as making possible the introduction of camera movements and shifts in scale into the staging.

The registration of the artwork poses some problems. The glass platen, which is lowered onto the artwork to keep it absolutely flat when the shot is taken, tends to cause static and lift small pieces of artwork with it when it is raised to change positions and to move the cut-outs. Pieces of double-sided tape or even blue tack can be used to hold the artwork in place. Magnetic mats which can hold strips of magnetized paper are also employed, though they are expensive and difficult to obtain. If you are shooting a complicated scene, it is advisable to make a tracing on cel of the key movements of the cut-out artwork, so that the timing stays consistent. This tracing will also act as a guide if the artwork needs repositioning because of a shooting error. It can be used as a template – lowered onto the platen to check positioning and removed when the shot is taken. Templates can also be made out of card and the cut-out objects fitted to them as in a jigsaw. If a straightforward pan of a cut-out is required, a template is ideal for controlling the positioning and movement. The shooting of cut-out calls for a great deal of concentration, often over a long period, so as much organization and planning as possible should be carried out before going under the camera.

The timing of the movement in cut-out also requires some care. It is not possible to establish the precise timing before shooting, although there will usually be a breakdown of the rough timing. As the increments of movement are cruder than in drawn or cel animation, there is always the possibility that the movement will appear jerky and unpolished. This can either be put to use or it can be got rid of. René Laloux and Jean-François Laguionie have perhaps gone as far as is humanly possible in achieving uniform and steady movement using cut-out techniques. The staging and timing of their films *Le Planète Sauvage* and *Gwen* demonstrate all the control that can be achieved using conventional techniques, with the addition of finely rendered graphic style. These works were carried out with a large team of animators, but Laguionie has been able to achieve something of this quality as an individual animator, winning a Hollywood Oscar for *La Traversée de l'Atlantique à la Rame*.

When there is the kind of production schedule associated with television, however, the results appear less successful. Cut-out animation of a very high quality does require a long production schedule, as well as an extended shooting time. The costs of shooting can be offset by careful planning and preparation, but even so more time will inevitably be spent on the camera than is the case with cel animation.

Timing can also be important in the more frantic cut-out animation films. The very speed of the cut-out movement can be used to exaggerate the static and to undermine the statuesque. Both Bob Godfrey and Terry Gilliam have exploited the medium's potential for presenting a rapid disintegration of pomposity in sudden revelatory movements. The extent to which the movement is made smooth will also depend on the kind of product and the potential viewing environment. There is little point achieving classic movement in cut-out if the product is to be used only on video.

The potential in cut-out animation for collage and the use of existing material has been exploited to great effect by Bob Godfrey, using Victoriana and etchings in the manner of Max Ernst's collages. Gilliam has brought together the found image and the airbrushed artwork, as well as a vigorous technique in which the artwork is cut up and re-animated. Remember, though, that if the artwork is to be destroyed as part of the action, a number of duplicates must be made. It is always a good idea to ensure that the main elements are duplicated, or at least duplicable, when using cut-out techniques.

Cut-out animation can produce work of a quality equal to that of any other animation technique. It is no easier than cel animation, and certainly the shooting of it calls for great concentration, but it is more accessible to the graphic artist and to the film-maker. A number of those who used this medium for early works, such as Borowczyk, Terry Gilliam and David Lynch, later moved successfully into live-action films. Others, such as Jan Lenica, have pursued both graphic and animation work in almost equal proportions in their careers. Cut-out technique has brought many artists working in related fields into animation, enriching the medium, and it has given those who would like to experiment a relatively painless way of entering the discipline. It has provided a way in which the beginner can achieve acceptable results and is altogether suitable for use in schools and workshops, and for group production.

Drawing on film

The technique of drawing on film was developed in the early 1930s by Len Lye and Norman McLaren. It was a technique invented for the kind of production they were concerned with at the time – low-budget,

Below: Winter, Mar Elepano, University of Southern California

Almost any method of making marks on the film can be used. The photogramme technique in which parts of the film are exposed to the light and the film then developed is difficult to control but can be applied. A single light source can also be used as a light pen to draw on the unexposed film; for instance, a swinging light bulb in a darkened room, if shot repeatedly, will produce an abstract pattern of the type described by Alexeieff as an illusory solid.

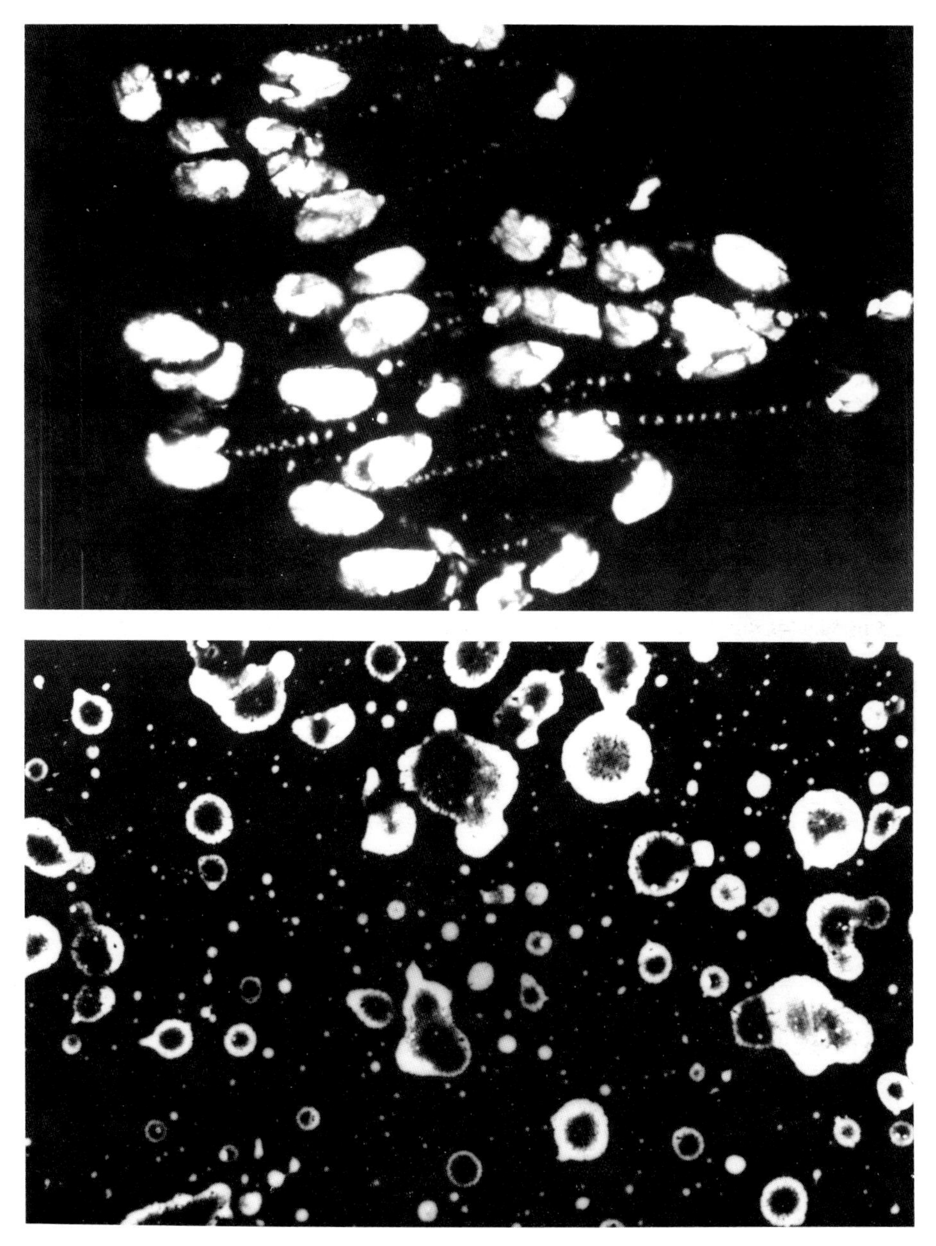

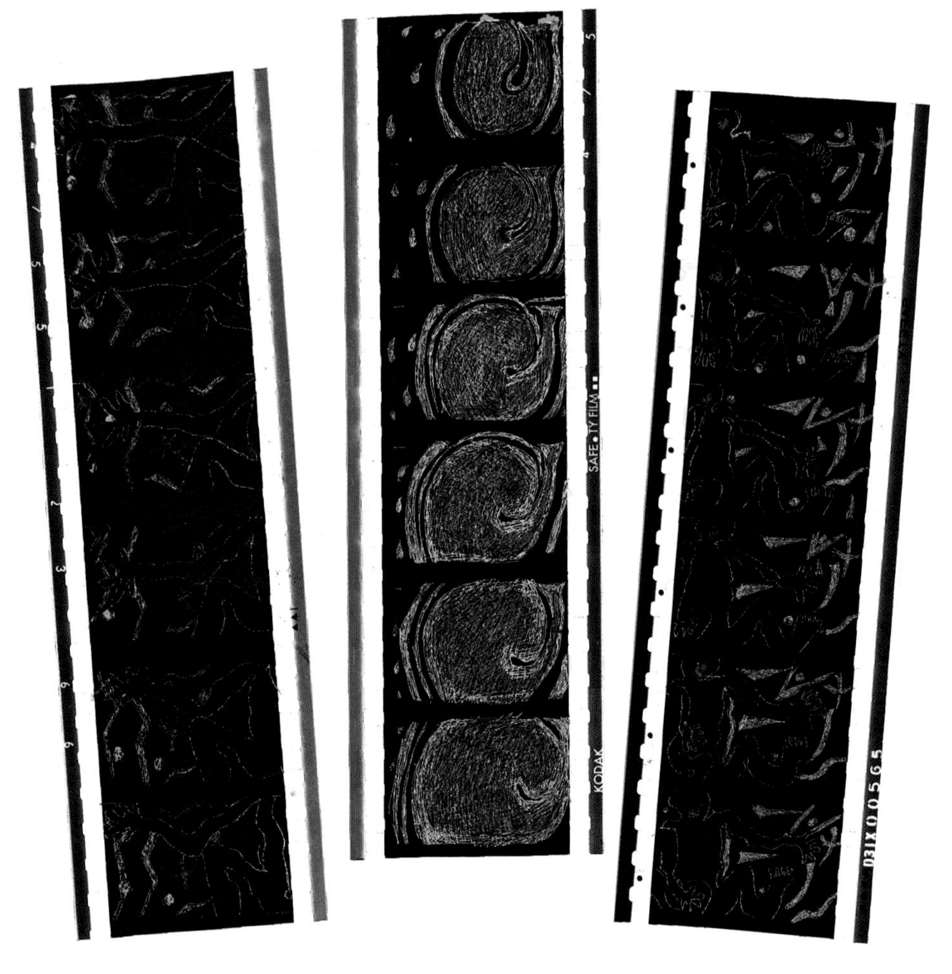

Above: Big Hands, Sarah Strickett, West Surrey College of Art and Design
The film is made by scratching through the black film emulsion of an exposed strip of 35mm film using an ordinary pin. The colour, which must be permanent, is then added using a lumicolour pen. Though drawing on black film is more difficult than using clear film for registration, the intensity of the coloured image against the black ground creates a powerful effect. In this case the film was registered simply by using a strip of tape on a light box.

mainly artisanal films, with a single person or a very small group producing the whole work. Lye brought to this technique a concern with the making of marks which grew out of his studies of Aboriginal and Samoan art. McLaren brought a belief in the primacy of the single frame, which he drew from his knowledge of the Russian montage films of Eisenstein and Vertov. The attention to the nature of the mark made on the surface of the film and the investigation of the nature of the single frame have remained at the heart of the technique ever since. Its application as a low-budget method of film-making, available to those who have no access to special equipment, has also been important.

Both McLaren and Lye continued to work intermittently with drawing on film, the two most uncompromising examples being *Dots* and *Loops* (1940) by McLaren and *Free Radicals* (1958) by Lye. Both films illustrate how an essentially simple procedure can, in the hands of experienced film-makers, be transformed into something which can compare with the most complex and expensive of film-making practices.

Some film-makers, such as Stan Brakhage, have developed approaches which foreground the essential nature of the material and of the projection process. Although Brakhage worked mainly in live-action film, the application of his experimentation to films such as *Mothlight* (1963), in which the wings of moths and other insects are affixed to the surface of the film, provides an additional expansion to the scope of the direct non-camera tradition of film-making. At the same time, the insight into the transformation of the image at the moment of projection, though quite formal in Brakhage's work, has implications for concerns about the way that meaning is conveyed and about our perception of the film image itself.

The non-camera direct technique has also become important as an introduction to film animation which can be carried out in schools and workshops, allowing the beginner access to film. It is a technique that is capable of very great refinement and it can be a powerful form of communication, simple as well as economical.

The means needed to get results are absolutely minimal. You can even use previously exposed and fogged film. By scratching on the emulsion of used film, beginners can start to get some feeling for the timing of animation and the length of a section of film. It is important to understand what can be achieved in one second of 24 or 25 frames, the basis for timing in animation. The direct technique is also an excellent way of understanding the changes which occur when the marks made on the film itself – whether through exposure or, in this case, through marking the film directly – are projected as an image on a screen. This change of scale and intensity sometimes plays an important part in animation. An apparently simple mark made on 16mm film can, when blown up onto the screen, reveal a remarkable subtlety and complexity. The same thing can be accomplished when materials are positioned on the film itself. Particularly striking is the effect when the film is scratched on and coloured

Below: Mothlight, Stan Brakhage
The wings of moths and other insects were collected by Brakhage over a period of time and then fixed to the surface of 16mm film. The effect when the film is projected is to reveal the complexity of this very small part of nature and the range of pattern and light which it possesses.

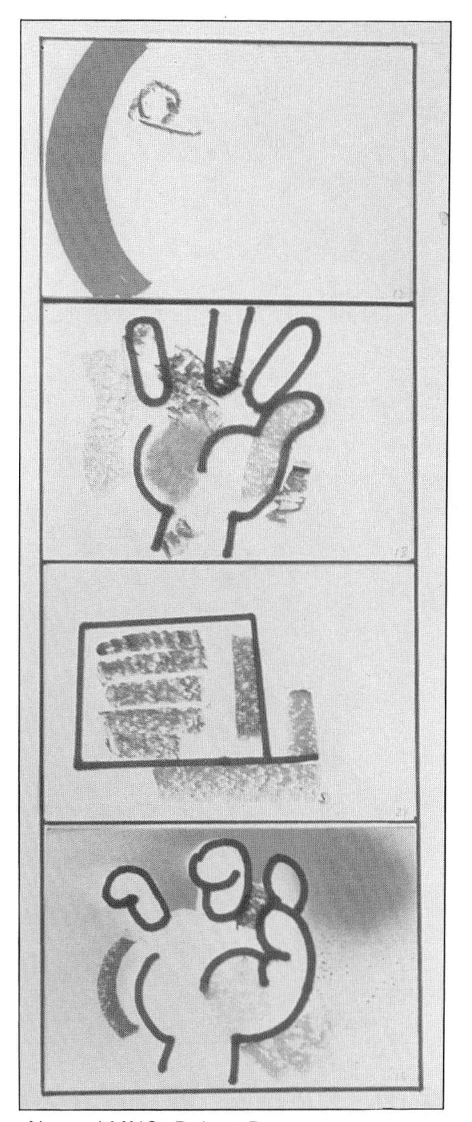

Above: LMNO, Robert Breer
Robert Breer uses small index cards to draw on. These are then shot in the conventional manner on 16mm film. The advantage of this method is its flexibility and portability, as well as the intimate feeling of a filmed notebook.

Below: Drawing on film can be a laborious process, as it entails the drawing of each frame in full. A very simple registration system can be made using card. This type of approach can, however, produce exciting effects: the movement boils; it is in continuous movement which gives great tension to the line; colour can be very intense and pacing bold. Though the short-cuts used in cel animation are not available and the process can be extremely time-consuming for the individual, when a group of animators work on a single strip of film a great deal can be achieved in a short time. There is really no limit to the numbers involved, only the length of the film and the space available, so this makes it an excellent technique for workshops.

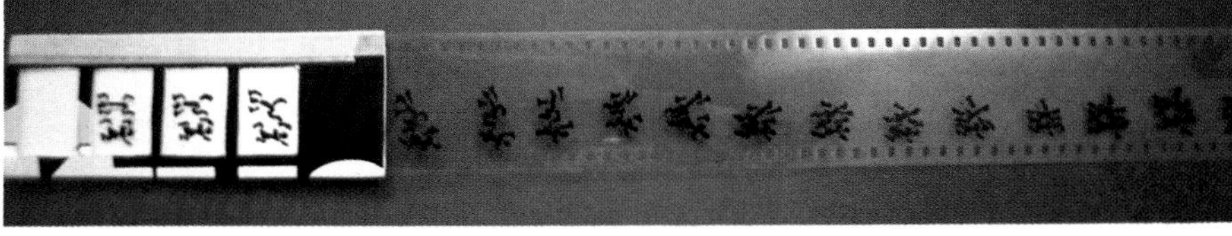

using audio-visual pens. The intensity of the colour produced by this very direct projection of pure light is almost impossible to obtain by any other method.

Selecting the film to draw on is important, though cost and practicality usually determine this choice in the end. It is possible to use any gauge of film from 8mm upwards to 35mm or even 70mm.

Obviously, when using the smaller gauges of film, the very small surface area available for making marks will to some extent determine the kind of marks which can be made. It is pointless to consider a long narrative fiction when the area available for marking is only .404mm × .295mm, the proportion of 16mm film. The selection of a subject and its treatment need careful thought. The advantages of the technique, however, lie in the very sharp quality of the projected image and the intense colours, as well as the potential for close synchronization with the soundtrack. This gives some indication of the kinds of project which are suitable for this direct and lively medium.

The film used can either be clear (leader or with emulsion removed) or black, or of course a mixture of the two. Clear film is either marked using ink or felt markers, or else has objects stuck onto it. It will show scratches much more easily than black, so it is advisable to wear animation gloves and to project the film as little as possible before making a copy. Black film can be marked by scratching through the emulsion with a sharp instrument such as a scalpel. This produces a very sharp, dynamic line when projected, which can be coloured by ink or felt pens. You cannot see through the black film, so in order to achieve some sense of timing, diagonal lines can be scratched at intervals, and other images positioned in relation to them. This method gives some guide to beginners, who may at first find it difficult to position images on film accurately.

It is important to remember that when the film is projected the image will be flipped – everything will be reversed, including the titles. If the images are complex or contain words, it is worth preparing an outline on paper which can be followed during production and placed under the film for registration.

Registration and timing

Norman McLaren devised a system for the registration of the film during production which actually enabled the artist to see the previous frame. But a much more simple device can be constructed to hold the film firmly and give a guide for the frame area. This consists of a block of wood or even card, with two grooved guides attached to the base, providing a channel through which the film passes. It helps with visualization if there is also a hole cut in the base, so that when the film is placed on a light-box the marks on it can be seen more easily.

A short section of clear film with frame lines will also help in positioning the animation. Even without a guide, it is possible to establish an approximate registration between the frame lines on 16mm film. If it is black film, this can be judged by estimating an imaginary line between the sprocket holes, or by drawing an actual line. On 35mm film there are four sprocket holes per frame, so it is important to keep a careful check – one sprocket out at any point will put the whole film out of sync.

The timing of animation drawn on film can be deceptive. It often seems that if a whole day has been spent drawing on film, the product must inevitably last a long time on the screen. But unfortunately this is not the case. While drawing on film is an excellent way of learning about timing and developing the skills of manipulating the material of film in a direct way, it can also prove to be a frustrating experience. It must be approached realistically. If a movement takes fewer than 12 frames it is unlikely to be read clearly by the eye when projected. If there are many movements that take even fewer frames, they will be confusing. This can be used as an effect – if a long slow movement is broken up with sudden rapid subliminal frames, the single frames will appear as flashes on the screen (in editing, a single fogged frame is called a 'flash frame'). This gives some idea of the effect of these kinds of frame groupings. One of the most exciting aspects of drawing directly onto film is unquestionably the ease with which experiments in formal timing can be carried out.

The tools

The quality and availability of felt-tip audio-visual pens is now such that they have become the main way of drawing on film. They are costly, but inks are more difficult to apply and control. Rapidograph and other draughting pens are also very useful for fine line work. The ink, though less adhesive than audio-visual pens, does adhere, and it can be scraped back in the same way that marks are made onto black or fogged film. There are many instruments for scratching on film. The scalpel is always useful and etching tools give a wide range of potential scratch marks.

There is really no limit to what you can use, as long as the medium remains attached to the film. Lye used stencils in his early work, so that he could repeat and overlay patterns and build rhythms. It is also possible to silk-screen onto film using normal inks. With this method, the animator can build up complex sequences and achieve fine shifts in colour.

When it is finished, the film will probably be in a brittle state. If it is not copied, it will become damaged over time and paint will peel off. Laboratories, however, are not enthusiastic about putting film with all kinds of foreign matter attached through their processors. It is important to talk to the laboratory if you want to have a print made. The best kind of print for copying drawn-on film material is a colour reversal internegative (CRI). This will usually give you a good copy of the original, though there is inevitably some degradation of the colour. Using the CRI as an original, more prints can be made and sound added. There are, however, more unusual ways of making copies. The film can, for instance, be copied using single-frame video or a quick-action recorder, which also makes it possible to manipulate the film further, adding loops and effects.

The results of drawing on film can be exciting, especially if it is practical to work

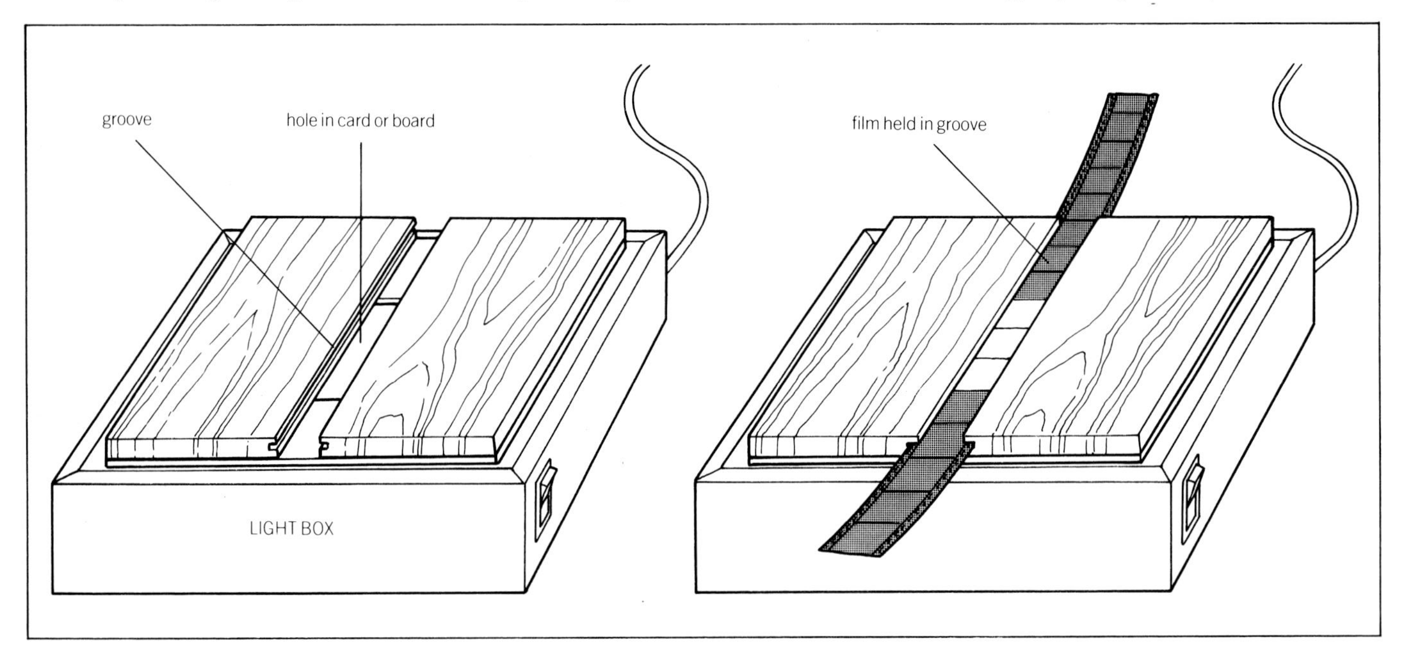

Below: This simple device for registering clear or black film for drawing on or for scratching can be made out of wood or stiff card. The base has a hole of 12 frames in it to allow for a light-through if the device is placed on a light box. Twelve frames is enough to give a clear indication of the movement which precedes the frame being worked on. The two strips either side of the black act as a guide for the film. The film is slid between the two blocks, maintaining accurate positioning and registration.

with sound. It is an excellent way to get a feeling for film as a material. Film can behave in unpredictable ways when handled and much unproductive time can be spent unravelling lengths of film which have become entangled. Working closely with the material, the beginner will find that the manipulation of long lengths of film becomes almost automatic. This is a skill that can be applied to many different situations.

Direct-camera animation

There are many different direct-camera techniques in animation, but they are usually a result of the application of new materials rather than new methods. So one outline description of direct-camera methods will apply to most techniques. In general, the camera used will either form a part of a rostrum stand, in which case the animation is performed on the table top, or the camera will be free-standing, giving an unlimited field of view.

One of the main characteristics of working directly under the camera is that you have to get it right first time. With materials such as sand or paint, a sequence simply cannot be repeated. If objects are being animated, returning to a start position is not impossible, but will still be very difficult. It is the usual human predicament that during this kind of animation, every conceivable camera fault will occur. So working directly calls for an even more careful checking of equipment, and the running of stock and exposure tests. It is also vital to check the camera mechanism at regular intervals and to clean the camera gate with dust-off.

When the film is to be made by one single

Interview, National Film Board of Canada/
Caroline Leaf

***Interview* was made working directly under the camera, manipulating the paint on glass. The field size was kept much smaller than the normal 12–18 inches, so that the movements could be more easily controlled. Though drawings can be placed under the glass as a guide, the essence of this kind of work lies in the immediacy and spontaneity of direct work.**

camera run with no cutting points, the pressure is even greater. If something does then go wrong during the shooting, there is no alternative but to go back to the start of the film and begin a complete re-shoot. Cutting points can be introduced by using fades to black or by clearing the screen of objects for a hold. It is then easy to start the next scene from the held position. The introduction of single-frame video has alleviated this problem, since the work can now be seen as it is shot and immediately replayed. Even so, if a section has to be repeated it can be difficult to match the positions of the artwork – and, of course, there is no light-through on a video camera.

The scale of the artwork should be as small as possible given the subject. Experimental animator Caroline Leaf works to a scale of four to five inches only, less than half what would be considered feasible in cel animation. The reason is that manipulating materials like sand calls for a high degree of control, which is easier to achieve over a small area than a large one. There is also a need for speed in the manipulation, to maintain the flow of movement. This rhythm can easily be lost when a large working area is involved.

The material is usually back-lit using a light table. The light must be flat and even. As well as sand, Plasticine back-lit can provide a powerful medium of expression. Ishu Patel used this technique in *Top Priority* (1981), a film of almost continuous movement which creates a powerful and realistic impression of the despair of an Indian family during a long drought. The film's quality results from the skill with which the Plasticine is manipulated and the sense of the presence of this 'hand' throughout. An earlier film of Patel's, *Bead-game* (1977), uses thousands of small decorative beads moved under the camera to produce the required effect. There is really no limit to the kind of materials that the animator can employ.

Another method is drawing directly under the camera, using normal drawing materials. This can be a very effective and vigorous approach, giving much more control of the image than drawing on film, while retaining some of the spontaneity of that technique.

The limiting factor is camera time. Most examples of this kind of production come from an institution such as the National Film Board of Canada, where the camera time is provided as an in-house facility, or from individual artists who have their own equipment or access to workshop facilities. It has always been difficult to adapt this direct-camera technique to commercial production – practitioners of the technique would say this was part of its strength.

Pixillation

There are a number of techniques associated with direct-camera animation staged in front of a free-standing camera. Some, such as pixillation, have a clear position within animation. Others are linked to experimental film and the challenge to illusionism. Others again, such as time-lapse, are related to specialized photographic techniques and the trickfilm tradition. They all share a very particular relationship to the 'real'.

Pixillation – the use of a stop-frame camera

Egged On, Charles Bowers

Trickfilm introduced a number of direct-camera techniques to animation. One of these was pixillation, the single-frame construction of movement, which was later greatly elaborated by Norman McLaren. At this stage, however, Bowers was using the technique simply as an aid to his comedy routines. Here the egg-laying machine he has invented begins to lay automobiles.

and live actors or real objects to create an animation effect – is perhaps the best-known of the in-front-of-camera techniques. Once again, Norman McLaren was central to its development. In his film *Neighbours* (1952), the pixillation technique was used for the first time to make a complete film, though there had been short sequences which made use of a similar technique in earlier trickfilm, such as Charles Bower's *Egged On* (1926). In *Neighbours*, each action is broken down and rephotographed. The actors, McLaren and his collaborator Grant Monro, move a little at a time and are photographed using single-frame exposure. In this way a totally new movement is created, constructed from the static positions assumed by the actors. Humans become like objects or automata in a mechanical process. In this film, the technique is used to demonstrate the way that conflict develops over a flower, destroying all involved, the innocent as well as the combatants.

Pixillation can also humanize the universe of inanimate objects. In McLaren's *A Chairy Tale* (1957), a chair refuses to be sat on until the sitter recognizes the rights of the chair to its own independent existence. There is no limit to animatable objects. In a film called *Thanksgiving*, for example, a turkey springs from the oven in which it is being cooked and tries in vain to escape – it is finally and brutally halted by the blow of an axe as it reaches the door at its moment of freedom.

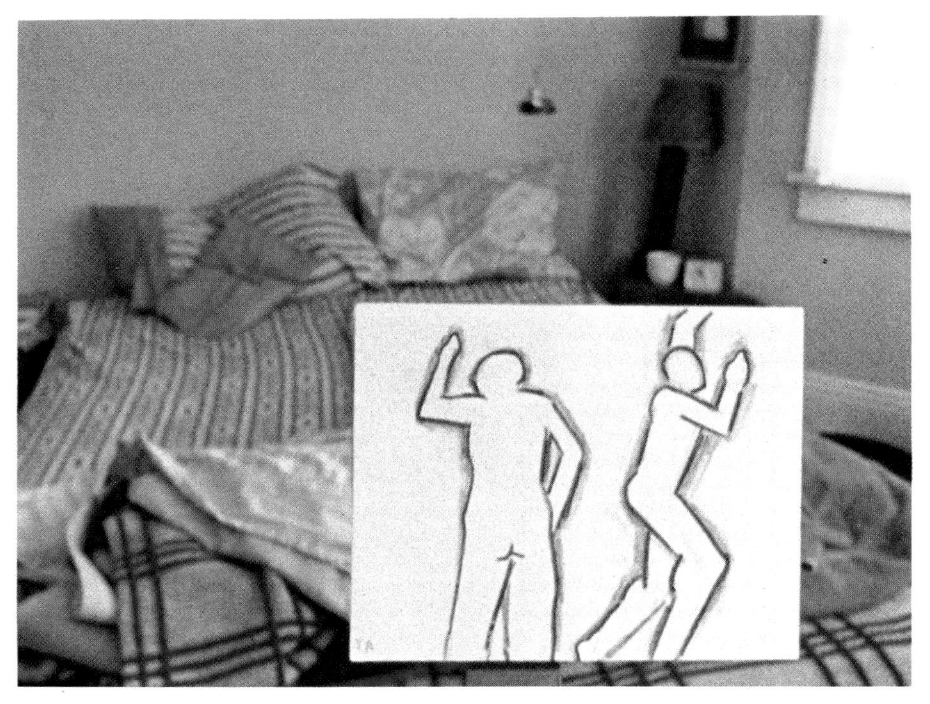

Above: Interior Design, Jane Aaron
One of the most innovative of the American independent film-makers, Jane Aaron locates her animation within real landscapes or interiors and then allows this world to interact with the drawn, or in some cases constructed, artefacts. The drawings are held in place in a variety of ways – stuck on to windscreens, placed on easels, attached to trees or simply placed on the floor.

Above: La Sève de la Terre, Alexandre Alexeieff and Claire Parker
In this film an oil derek sprouts from the ground and drops of oil fall from its 'branches'. In order to create the oil droplets, the drops were first filmed by a high-speed camera and then a glass blower recreated the droplets in glass to be shot frame by frame.

It is important when using the pixillation technique to lock off the head to stop accidental panning or tilting, and ensure that there is no movement whatsoever of the tripod. This can be achieved by securing the feet of the tripod with a spider, but it is also useful to suspend weights from the tripod. Obviously, a cable release is essential.

Pixillation lends itself to collective production and excellent results can be achieved quickly, but as with all direct techniques, it is very camera intensive. You can use natural or studio lighting for this kind of work. With natural lighting, there is always the possibility of sudden changes of light, but these impromptu effects may be acceptable. If you want absolute control of the light, studio lighting is essential.

The light source itself can be animated as a part of the action. In Jane Aaron's *Traveling Light* (1985), the movement of light cast by the sun through the window is integrated with the pixillation of objects moving in the room. In her *In Plain Sight* (1977), pixillation is used to animate life-sized cut-outs in relation to paper animation which is exposed at the same time and in the same space. The effect of both of these films is to demonstrate the relative nature of time and of our perception of it. The stop-frame technique is a good example of how the perceived world can be changed in collapsing time or reversing it.

Pixillation can also create life-size cut-out animation in the studio, using the 'Black Theatre of Prague' technique. This involves shooting single-frame, against a black background, actors dressed in black, either carrying cut-outs or wearing them. The closer to white the 'artwork' is, the more it will stand out, though any light-coloured material can be used. The cut-outs themselves can be worked on and animation can be applied to the surface. The technique is identical to pixillation, but the added dimension makes it possible to create a completely artificial perspective and movement. This technique is very appropriate for group work – Caroline Leaf has used it extensively in workshop projects. It can involve as many people as are available and, since the actors are hidden, they can change roles and be replaced by others as necessary.

Handmade animation provides a useful set of techniques for a workshop situation. As well as catering for many different levels of expertise, from the beginner to the most experienced film-maker, these methods can be adapted to the materials and the funds available.

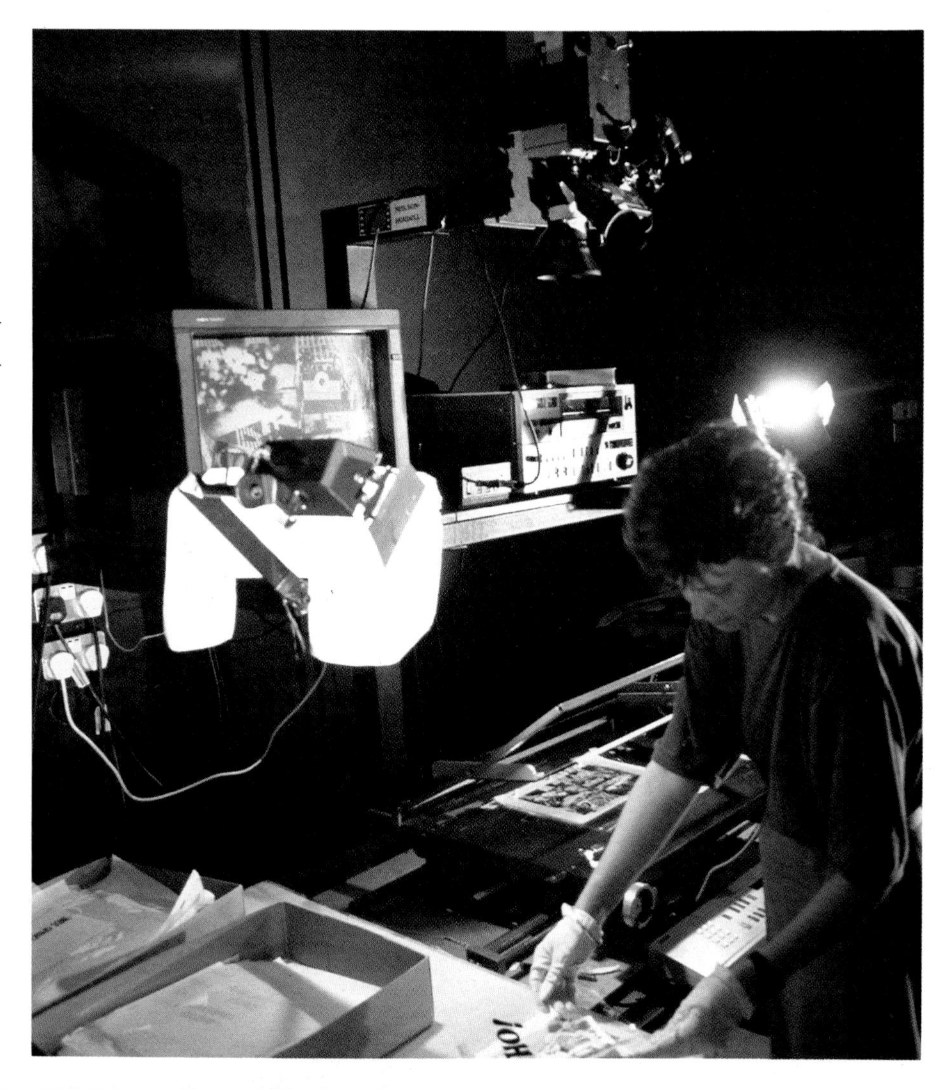

SINGLE-FRAME VIDEO

The single-frame video rostrum has had a great impact on animation production. Though in the commercial studios it is mainly used to test animation, in education and workshops it has come to play a major role as an inexpensive production tool. Even though the video rostrum is cheap to use, it still requires the same care in shooting.

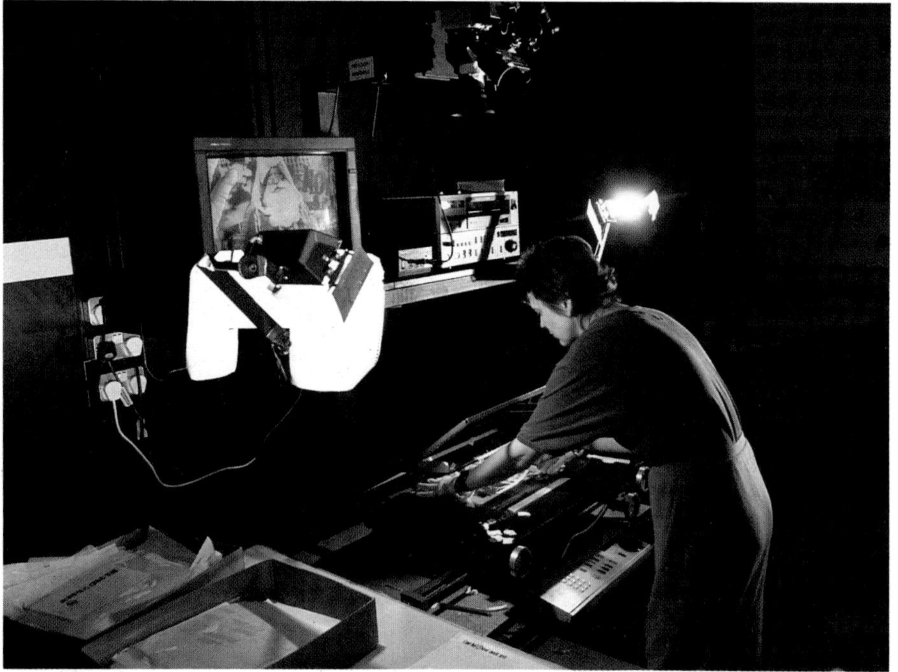

Above: When using cel it is important to avoid getting any smears or scratches on the surface by wearing cotton gloves. Scratches are picked up by the lights and can cause reflections. When cel is prepared for an aerial image or optical work, the scratches show up as black marks on the film, so avoiding them is vital.

Left: Joanne Gooding placing the artwork to be shot on the pegs.

Left: When the artwork or the cel is placed on the pegs, a platen – which consists of an optically correct pressure glass plate – is brought down to hold the artwork flat. Downward pressure may have to be applied to the platen if there are few cel levels. Tissue placed under the background will also help ensure that the artwork is kept completely flat.

Below: The single frame is exposed using video. The number of frames to be exposed can be pre-set from 1 to 99. It takes a little more time exposing video, as the tape winds back before each frame to build up speed. This can take up to 15 seconds.

6
STUDIO PRODUCTION

Most of the animation that the public sees on screen today is the product of small commercial studios, where skilled teams work either on high-budget 'full' animation or low-budget films, or else explore the rapidly expanding area of model animation.

Above: Rupert the Bear, Grand Slamm Partnership Ltd, © MPL Communications Ltd

The application of studio animation techniques to the character of Rupert the Bear in a new production from Geoff Dunbar. Even in this simple scene from the film, the range of colours and the detailed background give an indication of the reason for the high production costs.

The structure of the animation industry has constantly altered over time to keep up with changing conditions. Since the rise of television and the growth of new technology, the large Disney-style studios have lost their dominance and smaller units are now responsible for most animated film production. But the disciplines that Disney recognized – the need to organize the flow of production efficiently, to break down the process into separate activities, to deliver a product of consistent quality, and to work within a set budget – still apply to any commercial studio animation.

Budgets and production values

A studio product is normally categorized as either full animation or limited animation, depending on its budget and production values. Full studio animation pursues very high production values and usually has a suitably high budget. Conversely, limited ani-

Left: The studio producing *Count Duckula* at Cosgrove Hall, Manchester, the largest single permanent animation studio in Britain. The amount of paper generated can be seen, with each of the sequence boxes containing several hundred drawings. In the background is the Quick Action Recorder, used to obtain an immediate line test of the animation action.

Below: As well as two-dimensional animation, Cosgrove Hall produce three-dimensional animation, often in the form of TV specials. This kind of studio production is normally divided into three sections: model-making, set and prop construction, and animation and film. (Cosgrove Hall Productions 1988)

mation is produced on lower budgets and tends to stress the quality of script or characterization rather than production values.

Production value essentially means seeing the budget on screen. At the time of the Disney classics, production values were found through a return to what an audience would recognize as traditional quality – academic figurative art. But times change, and nowadays it is the demonstrable use of expensive computer technology that represents the height of production value. It can also relate to the 'fullness' of the animation, the range of colours used, and so on.

Budgets for animation, calculated in terms of pounds or dollars per foot of film, vary considerably. Television films for children have some of the lowest budgets, though this is offset by merchandizing – the sale of products exploiting the popularity of cartoon characters. Indeed, merchandizing often becomes a more significant source of profit than the animation itself.

At the other extreme are television and cinema commercials. Although most animation commercials have lower budgets than the equivalent live-action product, they are still well funded to provide very high production values. Inevitably, commercials attract animators who want to develop their technical skills. There is more time to polish the work – a low budget series will be churning out more than 100 feet of film a week, compared with only a few feet for a commercial.

Preparing budgets is an important skill. Budgets are broken down into three major areas: pre-production, production and post-production. Pre-production budgets cover the preparation of the script and the storyboard, the initial soundtracks, breaking down the sound, and bar charts. Production budgeting covers the animation costs, artwork and materials, film-stock and processing, as well as camera hire and special effects. Post-production will have all the costs of editing, dubbing and additional sound, negative cutting, and production of the first married print. Budgeting must also allow for video effects, video editing and computer inserts, and for overheads such as studio rental and legal fees. It is normal practice to finance the work on the same three-part basis. So funds are received in thirds, at the start of each of the three stages.

Kellogg's 'Sunpin', Richard Purdum Productions (agency: J. Walter Thompson; client: Kellogg's Sunpin)

The levels of cel (above) build up a single frame (left) – in this case frosted cel rather than clear cel. Frosted cel, a new material, allows the application of pencil and crayon, which clear cel does not accept. The areas which need to be transparent are then sprayed with a solution to clear them. Alternatively, frosting solution can be sprayed onto the small areas of clear cel. This sort of pencil and crayon rendering is even more time-consuming than traditional cel painting, though the results are sometimes exceptionally subtle.

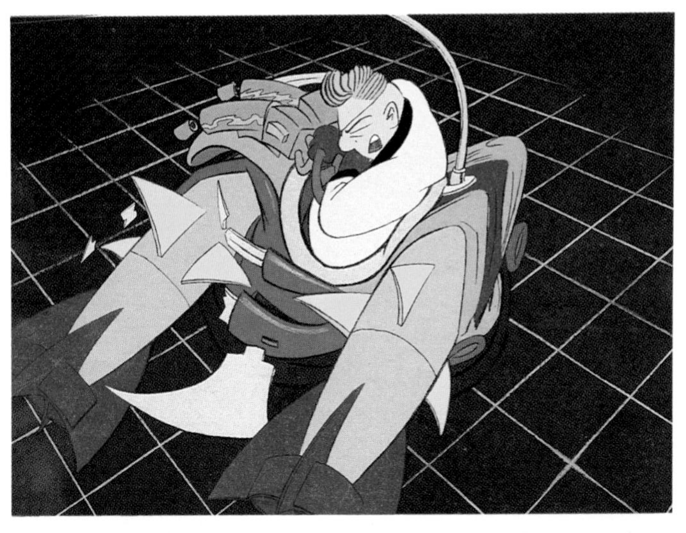

Above left, above and left: The Victor, Animation City
In Animation City's film, a bold contemporary comic-book approach is combined with traditional cel animation to retain fluidity of movement. Here a soldier, victim of military drug experiments, finds himself hallucinating in a fairground. In some cases a stylist is specially employed to design the 'look' of a film.

Below: Superted, Siriol Animation Ltd, © Petalcraft Demonstrations Ltd
Relatively low-budget production can on occasions also achieve a surprisingly high quality of animation. *Superted*, made for the Welsh-language TV station S4C, gained a wide popular following outside Wales.

Full animation
The term 'full animation' generally refers to drawn animation that uses the maximum possible number of drawings – a drawing for every one or two frames of a sequence. There are good reasons given for using this costly process. The first is that audiences find it easier to watch long films made in full animation. It is said to be easier on the eye and less of a strain. It may well be that audiences have become used to this technique being associated with strong narrative over the years, because of their familiarity with the Disney output. Another reason advanced for using full animation is that it achieves maximum impact in a highly concentrated form. There is some truth in this. Certainly, in the short time which a commercial has to communicate its message, full animation can make a strong impression.

But there is a danger in confusing full animation with good animation. At its best it can be excellent. But if full animation is used as the norm by which all other animation is

Above: Trebor Dandies, Ian Moo-Young, Moo Movies (agency: Collett Dickenson Pearce & Partners Ltd; client: Trebor Ltd)
When the finished painted cels are combined in the final phase of production, the result can be very complex. Even in a short commercial like this, no expense is spared to obtain such an image.

judged, this can promote a crude and narrow attitude. It is best to judge the different categories of animation on their own terms, rather than imposing a single set of criteria onto a very wide spectrum of work.

There remains a great deal of potential in classic full animation and in the narrative tradition itself, as long as it does not stand still. Much recent work has attempted a renewal of a form which it once seemed would die with the great masters of the past.

Drawing

The ability to draw quickly and accurately is essential in the full-animation technique. But it can be a difficult step from the production of competent still images to drawing for animation. One common problem lies in the tightness of the drawing style. If this seems to be a difficulty, the only solution is to abandon any idea of style, particularly what might be seen as a cartoon stylization, and draw from movement. Often established draughtsmen find they just cannot make the leap into animation, while others who have previously lacked the confidence to use their drawing ability find that the new challenge produces a great improvement in drawing.

Many individual animators and studios use life drawing as a way to develop drawing skills. But the traditional methods of life drawing do need to be adapted to meet the particular problems of animation. Style and technique can detract from the development of the skills of visualization and the conceptual grasp of movement. The main emphasis should be on short poses and on the figure in movement. If this can also be related to a real situation developed through a series of poses, it will improve the dramatic use of the figure.

Drawing is an essential part of classic animation, but it is not always the kind of drawing which would be considered 'good' in other fields, where static images alone are used. These are generally too overworked to be of use in animation. Animation drawing can, however, be an excellent discipline for an artist working in the still medium. The principles of economy which it teaches can be a liberating experience for the artist.

Key drawings, breakdowns and in-betweens

The first images the animator produces for a drawn animation are the key drawings. These show the first and last positions of each movement. Put together they indicate the development of the action through a sequence. The number of key drawings or 'extremes' that the animator produces for a given sequence varies according to the complexity of the movement. Every change of

Right: An American Tail, Sullivan Bluth, © 1986 Universal City Studios Inc and U-Drive Productions Inc, courtesy of MCA Publishing Rights
A cleaned-up animation drawing from *An American Tail* which is now ready for the paint-and-trace department. The drawing will be traced on to cel and then carefully painted on the back with special animation paint according to the character colour chart.

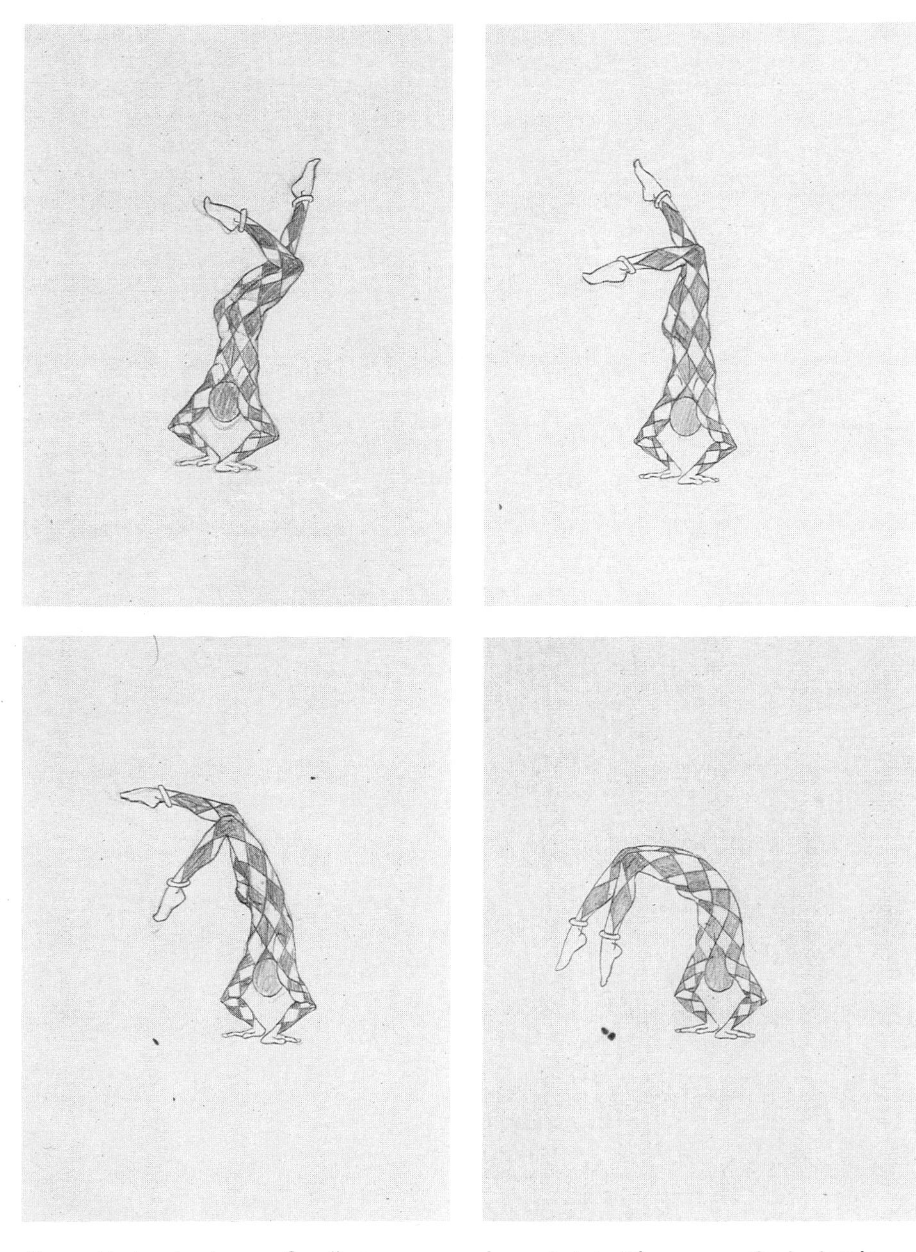

Above: Harlequin, Joanne Gooding
Here the key positions of a movement are shown. The animator will indicate, using a scale entered on the key drawing, what kind of in-between is required–whether it is to be one with even movements or if a buffer is needed. In this case, as the harlequin figure reaches the highest point the animator will ease into the position and the movement will speed up as the character's flip reaches completion.

action or change of expression is marked by a key drawing. These are then 'in-betweened' by an assistant animator – that is, the additional drawings between the two keys are added. It is unusual for an assistant to be asked to draw more than three in-betweens between any two keys. The animator sometimes also does a breakdown position drawing to aid the assistant.

Keys are important for the timing of a sequence. They give the movement its coherence, establishing the lines of the action. If the key drawings are shot alone, as they often are for a test, it should be possible to read the film easily, without any ambiguity.

The breakdown drawing is the main in-between drawing. It is essential that this is accurately positioned and drawn. It can be deceptive to use the light table, as there is a temptation to trace it off mechanically from the keys, producing stiff, inaccurate movement. The movement is the important thing at this stage – mistakes in drawings can be corrected or cleaned up later. Mistakes in the movement of the animation are more difficult to detect at an early stage and may not be found until a line test is completed.

The in-between drawings introduce a flow into the action – they in fact perform a function that the eye can do for itself. Faced with a sequence of key drawings, the viewer connects the actions and makes allowances for any inconsistencies; the in-betweens now intervene in this process. The viewer is no longer doing the work of bringing the keys to life. The in-betweens assume this role. In-betweening is a skill in its own right, calling for a very precise understanding of movement, and of different animators' approaches to movement.

Animators value the work of good assistants highly. It involves much more than filling in the drawings. The in-betweener works to a guide placed on the key animation by the animator. This marks the two key drawings, the breakdown drawing and the two or three in-betweens required. The position of the in-betweens and the breakdown is given by marks on a horizontal scale drawn between the keys. The positions may be evenly spaced if the movement is even, or they may be staggered if the movement eases out or in. In some cases there are only two in-betweens, which presents problems for the assistant, since it is much more difficult to assess the movement with no central breakdown position. Even when the movement eases in or eases out, the breakdown indicates the mid-point of the movement and the ease-in is placed between the breakdown and the first key.

Even if the animator is working alone and is

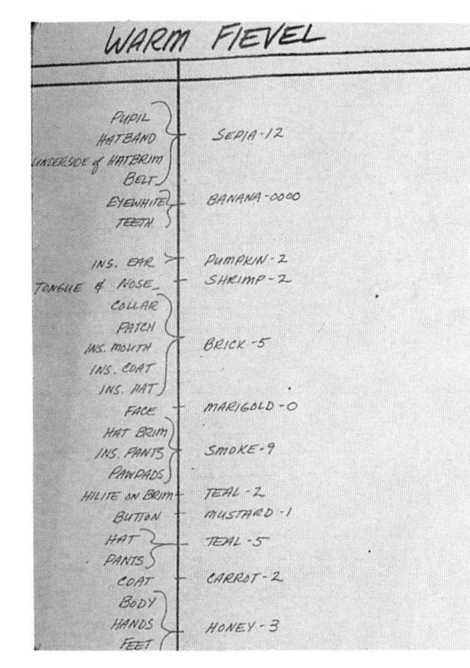

Left: An American Tail, Sullivan Bluth, © 1986 Universal City Studios Inc and U-Drive Productions Inc, courtesy of MCA Publishing Rights
The colour chart for a character in *An American Tail*, showing details of the colour to be used on each area of the character, with the colour changes required for changes in the cel level. Several levels of cel can alter colours to a noticeable extent.

Below: These charts indicate the kind of movement required for the assistant to make the in-betweens. The first shows an even movement. The second shows easing in and easing out of a movement so that the distance between the keys and the following drawings will be smaller than that between the in-betweens and the breakdown drawings. The third shows the unusual situation of 'thirds', where only two in-betweens can be used in the movement.

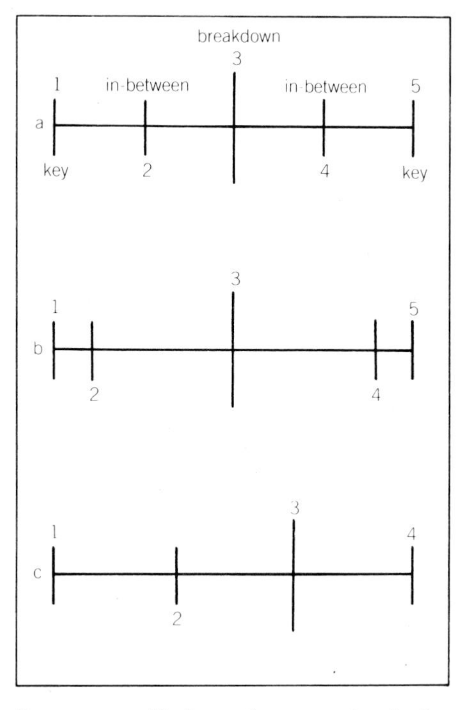

personally providing the in-betweens, it is essential to move from key drawing to in-between in order to make the animation flow. The most common mistake of the beginner is to attempt to animate 'straight through', from the first drawing of a sequence to the last. It is impossible to control the movement or animation in this way and the animator quickly gets lost.

On the animation paper

Apart from the animation drawing, a number of other marks appear on the animation paper to aid the assistant, the animator and the trace-and-paint. This may seem a mundane part of animation, but if it is ignored it can cause the animator and the assistant a good deal of anguish. The start and end positions of the movement are marked on the second key drawing, together with the mid-point of the action for the assistant (marking the scale on the second key means the assistant does not have constantly to refer back to key one). If necessary the in-between positions are then also marked. The number of the key drawing is placed next to the peg holes (on the right) with the scene and sequence number on the left. Any changes in numbering must be entered on both the dope sheet and the animation. It is important to be systematic about this – other people will depend on the information at a later stage in the production. A large amount of artwork is involved in any animation film and a lost sheet of animation can cause considerable problems.

The in-between is sketched out roughly using a blue or orange pencil and is constantly checked by flicking back and forward to the key drawings, before it is finalized. The tradition of the blue pencil dates back to the days before the introduction of panchromatic film. The orthochromatic film then in use did not register blue pencil marks. In most cases, it does not matter nowadays whether a blue or an orange pencil is used.

Traceback, flipping and testing

It is common practice to 'trace back' the line on any part of the animation which is not moving, rather than holding that part of the image in the filming, which can look crude. So if the arm and head of a character are animated but the body remains static, the body is traced back. Tracebacks need to be very accurate, as they are in effect an animated hold. They are traced from the key drawing and never from in-betweens or other artwork.

Flipping is a way of judging the animation movement. The sheets of animation paper are flipped, just like a large flip book, so the images appear to move. Flipping is used in conjunction with the light box to position the animation accurately. Using a light box alone, the in-between drawings can become mechanical tracings rather than drawings. There is some debate over whether flipping is enough in itself or if other methods should be used in addition. In cycles, line tests are essential. As always in animation, it is the movement which is the important factor and not the single drawing.

There are now many sophisticated ways of testing animation using computer frame stores and single-frame video. These avoid the cost of shooting line tests on film and the inevitable delays with processing. There are, however, drawbacks. Video tests can soften the movement between frames and make the animation appear smoother than it in fact is. There is a temptation to use the test facility too extensively, until it becomes a substitute for judgement. But this equipment can also liberate the creative animator and permit a much more open and experimental approach to animation work.

Loops are a useful technique for testing a movement or sequence. Rather than shoot it a number of times so that it can be studied, a loop of the test is made by joining the head of the film to the tail. On some equipment, such as the Quick Action Recorder, you can make loops electronically, as well as changing the doping and adjusting the projection speed. There is as yet no facility on single-frame video which allows for this, so there is no alternative to shooting the sequence a number of times or using rewind and replay.

Cycles

A cycle is an economical method by which an action repeated a number of times can be integrated into an animated film. It differs from a loop in that the last frame of the action is also the first frame, so that a movement can be repeated endlessly.

The most common example is the walk cycle. If we break down the action of walking, we can examine it in detail. First of all there is the step: if the left leg is in the back position, it will move forward, leaving the ground, and pass the right leg which takes the weight of the body. The left leg will then be in the lead position. This completes one step. A common mistake is to believe that this completes the action, whereas in fact it is only half of the walk. The step must be repeated, so that the left leg returns to the back position.

The crucial movement in the walk cycle is the crossover position. This is the position of balance when the figure is at its highest point, with the supporting leg straight. This position seems to cause the most trouble for the beginner – legs detach themselves and move to other parts of the body without reason. It is important to understand how the walk works by trying it out, looking hard at the crossover and how it relates to the rest of the movement, and at how the cycle relates to the movement as a whole. Crossovers determine the character of a walk cycle.

The number of drawings in a cycle is designated as, for instance, 1×17, in which case there are 16 actual drawings, and drawing 1 is the same as drawing 17 (it actually is drawing 17). The principle is simple and can be applied to all kinds of animation. Any identical drawings or scenes offer a potential takeover point and, accurately registered, allow whatever movement is between to be repeated.

The technique of cycling is particularly useful for panning backgrounds. If the start field and the end field on the panning background are exactly the same, the background can be kept moving as long as needed. If you do intend to repeat the background a number of times, however, it is important not to put in too much detail – when the same very recognizable house goes past four or five times, the illusion is broken. The fields at the beginning and the end must be exactly the same, and they must be full fields. The takeover point is at the centre of the two fields.

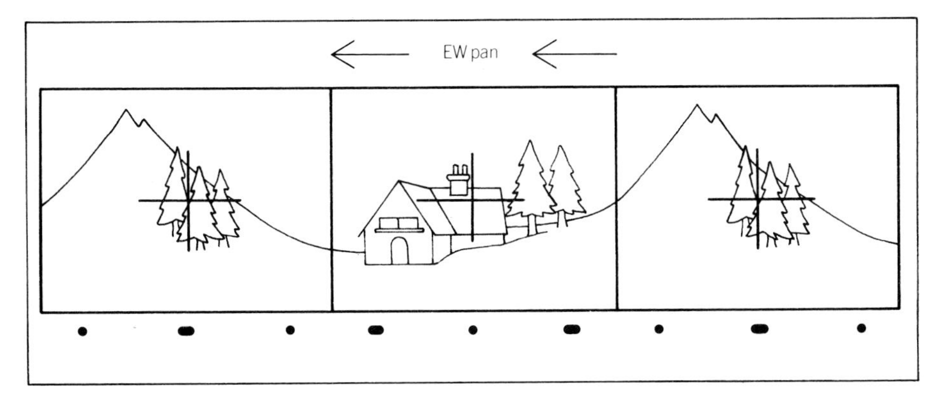

Above: In a panning background the centre of each of the takeover fields must match; the detail of the field will be identical. If the field moves when the takeover is being performed, there will be a jump and the illusion will be lost.

Whenever a takeover is being performed, the peg on the rostrum is wound back to the start position. It is vital that the background does not move, so it must be securely taped to the table top during this operation. As always, use a number of short strips of tape rather than one long tape which is more likely to buckle or distort. A panning background combined with a walk cycle provides a very economical means of getting from point to point in animation.

Cycles can also be used in perspective to create the illusion that an object or character is moving continuously towards the camera, or that the camera is travelling down a road or a corridor. To create a perspective cycle, you need to choose strong verticals that are known normally to have equal spacing – for example, lampposts, telegraph poles, an avenue of trees or a row of buildings. The perspective background moves in the same way as perspective animation, that is, the increments in the distance are much closer together than those in the foreground. This applies to the in-betweens as well as the key positions.

Below: Pretend You'll Survive, Leeds Animation Workshop
Cel animation can be combined with other techniques such as cut-out. This is especially useful in low-budget productions, like this film made in a women's workshop. Even though the production process was non-hierarchical, cel animation was used.

Extra dimensions

There are a number of animation techniques, associated with action and reaction, which give an extra dimension to the timing and movement of the animation. The classic exercise of squash and bounce in the bouncing ball is a good illustration. It shows how the stiff and ridged movement of a circle can be changed into a ball with weight and mass, which can create the illusion of the third dimension by the way it moves. When the ball strikes the ground, it flattens; immediately it leaves the ground, it elongates; as it reaches the highest point, its own weight slows it to stalling point; as it goes over the top, it begins to speed up again; and as it approaches the ground, it elongates in anticipation. This anticipation need not have a parallel in the physical world. It is rather the way in which an animation movement is signalled to the viewer. An imminent impact or movement is communicated before the event, making it easier for the viewer to follow the line of the action. For instance, a figure may move slightly backwards and then forwards before the movement actually begins.

The 'take' is a very exaggerated form of anticipation normally used in character animation. It is a hallmark of the classic cartoon, such as the work of Tex Avery, and needs to be understood in relation to this tradition. The take is sometimes very extreme – fitting in well with daring distortions. Chuck Jones, for instance, imposes on his stock of characters the full repertoire of different ways in which the body can be distorted as it goes about its legitimate task of hunting road runners or aggravating ducks. But the exaggerated take is not suitable for many kinds of animation where expression can be achieved in more subtle ways. It is a device to be handled with care.

Many of the techniques of full animation can be applied to other kinds of animation as well. Their importance lies in the principles of timing and movement that they embody. These do not always correspond to simple observation. Animated film deals with illusion – the illusion of projection and the phenomenon of the persistence of vision. It deals with the way in which an audience responds to this illusion and accepts or conspires with it. This gives animation the freedom to attempt to stretch 'natural' laws. But there is also a responsibility to understand the relationship between the animator producing the animation and the audience's perception of the animated film. Clichés are the result of ignoring this interaction.

Limited animation

Those who have the opportunity and the skill to work in full studio animation take a quite understandable pride in their craft. But limited animation has its own qualities – it is not just animated film with the animation left out. The budgets for limited animation are usually tiny, as the productions are in the main for children, who have no power over the broadcasting institutions which commission or buy the films. Yet even so, excellent work is produced, often depending for its success on strong communication and characterization.

There are many ways of shifting the emphasis from the production values embodied in classic animation to those values more effective in the limited form. The rostrum camera can be used very productively to achieve effects that in full animation may take many layouts and drawings. Once strong character-

Beaks to the Grindstone, Bob Godfrey Films/Steve Bell

Cel can also be used behind the background, as in this animation by cartoonist Steve Bell. The penguins are on a cel overlay, but the picture of Mrs Thatcher is behind the background, which has a hole cut in it representing the video screen.

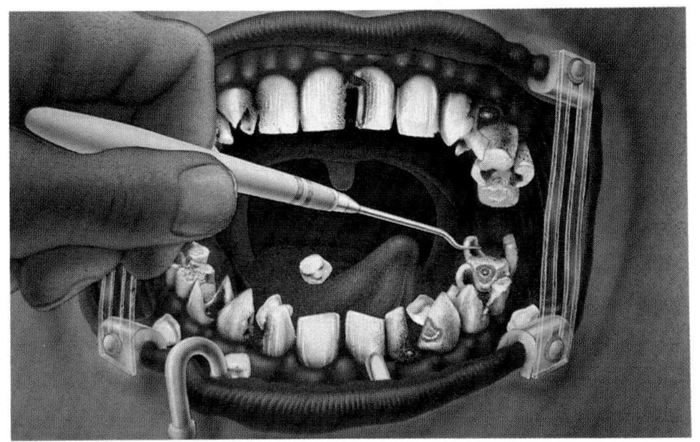

Above left: The Cold War Game, John Challis for Triple Vision Ltd
Above: An Inside Job, Aidan Hickey
Cel overlays are sometimes used to 'jump on' effects which remain on the screen for a very short time, such as the 'Biff' in *The Cold War Game*. They can also combine with a very complex background, as in *Inside Job*, where the small amount of animation is used very economically and effectively to complement a witty script.

Above: John Lennon Sketchbook, John Canemaker Productions Inc, © Ono Video Inc 1986
Even a single cel can be effective. In this case a run cycle, inked and painted on to cel, is combined with a panning background to produce a sequence from limited means. The use of flat, even colour is also important – any blemishes in the colour would destroy the overall effect.

ization is established, point-of-view shots will often serve as an alternative to an animation sequence. A character's reaction to dialogue can be shown instead of the speakers' faces, avoiding the need for lip-sync. The framing can mask out areas which would require elaborate animation. Where this is not possible, simple cycles provide an economical alternative. Pans and zip pans can be used to show movement. There is also a place for camera effects – short mixes between drawings create an illusion of movement, and dramatic effects are often achieved by using superimpositions and multiple exposures.

The judicious use of effects is a great help in limited animation. Effects have always been used by film-makers in both live-action and animated film to get around difficulties of logistics or to provide cutting points. To see a master at work, just look at Orson Welles's *Citizen Kane*. During the famous supposedly continuous shot in which the camera descends through the skylight of the Zanzibar, a flash of lightning occurs just as the camera reaches the skylight, and the track continues down into the room. The lightning cleverly covers the join between two shots, giving an impression of continuity.

Atmosphere is another economical aid to animation. Night effects – a black screen with voice-over is about the limit of what can be got away with so far – mist and fog can all be quite useful for the animator short on time and money. They can be put on cycles and continued as required. So can smoke which, especially if preceded by an explosion, can save a good deal of animation work.

Explosions are a very economical kind of screen business that can be used creatively. There are many ways of producing explosions or similar effects, but the simplest is a five-frame cycle. Like Orson Welles's flash of lightning, explosions are useful as a cutting-point within a scene, as well as saving on animation. This is particularly helpful in a long scene without cut-aways.

All of these time-saving devices are in a sense clichés and are obviously only suitable for certain kinds of film. However, the principle applies more widely. There is really no limit to the use that can be made of very simple sequences such as these.

Finally, it is worth mentioning simple animation on paper. This is often very effective, producing lively animation in a low-budget way. Felt-tip pens now provide a means of applying colour and line efficiently, cutting out a number of steps in the production process – the animation and colouring can be executed directly by animators producing sequences, without in-betweens carried out separately. The felt pens tend to get used up quickly, so it is important to decide before the production begins what area they will need to cover.

Paper animation calls for a strong style and a good knowledge of editing techniques. One of the first and most successful of such productions was Bob Godfrey's *Roobarb* series. It had all the necessary elements – strong identifiable characters, both in terms of the design and the voices used, good stories, strong editing and a simple but robust graphic style. Godfrey has continued this approach in the *Henry's Cat* series.

Model animation

Model animation is a rapidly growing area. It has often been treated as quite separate from other animation and yet it has a history stretching back to the earliest work in animation and trickfilm. It also has a future which is already encompassing new technology and the developments in model work that this technology makes possible. Many of the great works of animation art and culture have been produced in three dimensions, and increasingly this area is contending with two-

Left: Sundae in New York, Jimmy Picker
Claymation and the use of Plasticine for modelling have become a significant form of animation. In the hands of experts such as Will Vinton and Jimmy Picker, the vitality obtained by working quickly has been harnessed to both comedy and, increasingly, more serious themes.

Top and above: The Pied Piper, Jiří Barta, Krátký Film Praha
Carving has often suffered at the expense of other speedier techniques. Yet here the carving of the wooden walnut characters produces a medieval atmosphere full of gloom and horror. In these scenes, the burghers of Hamelin plan to cheat the Pied Piper of the price they have agreed for him to rid the city of rats, and the tailor finds that the rats have eaten his prized cloth.

Above and top: A Crushed World, Boyko Kanev, Sofia

Almost any material is suitable for model and three-dimensional animation. In this case paper is used. The first still (top) shows how the chosen material can build a completely plausible world. The second still demonstrates how the lighting can play an important part in model work, establishing mood and disguising the inevitable mechanisms for support and movement.

dimensional animation as a viable production method for commercials and specials.

Conventionally, the discipline of studio model animation has distinguished sharply between those who make the models and those who animate. But the distinction can never be that clear. The animator is also the designer, who needs to have a knowledge of what is possible using a given material. The engineering or specialized construction may be sub-contracted, but the specifications of the model have to be given and this calls for an understanding of the materials.

Glass, metals, wood, card and the ubiquitous Plasticine have all been used either as the primary material or in combinations. The essential characteristic is that they must be light and flexible. If metal is used it may even be necessary to hollow out the larger sections. The choice of materials sometimes carries a specific cultural meaning. In the great work of the Czech animator Jíří Trnka, the use of wood corresponds to the folk traditions of his country. Where very many materials are brought together, such as in the work of the Brothers Quay, it relates to the art of the *bricoleur*. There is no limit to the kinds of material used. In Alexeieff's film *La Sève de la Terre* (1955), dripping oil is represented by glass droplets animated into a fully controllable oil cycle sequence. Each droplet in the sequence was made separately.

Each country has traditions and materials rich in cultural connotations. The Japanese film-maker Kawamoto makes use of Japanese theatrical traditions, such as that of the Noh theatre, in which masks are used and there is no expression – each mask has its own meaning. He also uses traditional Japanese stories and folk tales, elaborating them. The effect of this style is astonishing in its power of expression. Everything is concentrated in the movement of the puppets and in the staging itself.

As well as the art of puppet-making, the art of carving has been widely used. The remarkable feature film *The Pied Piper* (1985) by Jíří Barta adopts an ornate Gothic wood-carving style to re-tell the traditional tale. The way that the technique is handled makes the medieval town and the style of the puppets a coherent whole. Barta used 16 carved walnut puppets and over 170 sets for the film.

In the film *A Crushed World* (1986) by Bulgarian Boyko Kanev, paper is used for both the sets and the characters. The nature of the material is clearly shown, so that the images and the texts on the paper form a part of the meaning of the film, as the paper character is crushed and torn in the search for enlightenment. In this case the text becomes the texture.

The Wind in the Willows, Cosgrove Hall Productions 1988
Characterization is especially important in narrative work. In *The Wind in the Willows*, the characters of Toad, Badger, Rat and Mole are known to generations of children. Not only must they be recognizable, but the designer and model-maker must ensure during the planning and construction of the model's skeletons that they will move in the correct way. If this is achieved, as it is here, model animation can be an excellent medium for children's film.

Model animation in action
Staging the action is of the utmost importance in model animation. It goes far beyond the simple placing of camera and models. The staging should reflect the meaning of the film, the scenic truth. It is the orchestration of all the elements into one highly focused direction. In some cases the vocabulary of live-action film-making is the one employed. Model and three-dimensional animation can approximate to the live-action film more closely than any other form of animation. Films such as the Cosgrove Hall *The Wind in the Willows*, based on the story by Kenneth Grahame, use live-action devices to portray the characters of the animals that make up this miniaturized world by the river bank. In contrast, the films of the Brothers Quay eschew this approach in favour of a style in which there is a play of recognition and identification between the real and imagined worlds of the objects and material.

There are many techniques which are common to both model and two-dimensional animation – the timing of movements and of action, lip-sync techniques, framing and storyboards all have a place in both forms. Some techniques have no parallels, however. It is not possible, for instance, to use cycle and loop techniques in three-dimensional animation. Key drawings and the technique of in-betweening, which are so important in giving a controlled timing and consistency of movement to two-dimensional animation, have no equivalent in model animation, and other means of timing and registration have been developed.

Commercial model animation makes a clear distinction between animator and model/set-maker, as well as reserving the technical areas of camera and editing for specialists. But it is important that in designing and making sets and models, the final result of the whole endeavour, the film itself, is not lost to view. Many film-makers producing model animation operate outside the commercial system and develop their own particular ways of working, but although the methods, procedures and philosophies differ, some essentials are shared.

Sets and lighting
When constructing the set, it is important to consider the way the film will be shot. There may be shots indicated on the storyboard which will require the removal of sections of the set to enable camera movement or the animation of models to be carried out effectively. And lighting has to be considered – there is little point in building an elaborate set which then cannot be lit adequately. You may not need to build sets with removable sections if the normal openings of doors and windows are placed with sufficient care. Where the set is large and it is impossible for the animator to work entirely from the front of the set to the back, such foresight is particularly important. In the Aardman film *Babylon* (1985), double doors which were a part of the set and integral to the action also gave access to the rear of the set, enabling the animator to carry out the movement and manipulation of the characters.

It is vital that the set is firmly secured. If there is any movement of the set itself, this has to be related to a cutting-point in the action. Animation is an illusion and the art of the three-dimensional model-maker is to create from bits and pieces of materials a world with its own authentic miniaturized scale, while at the same time maintaining the freedom of movement of camera and model.

Lighting plays a significant role in model animation. Most lighting units designed for live-action filming produce too much light over too broad an area to be of great use. Much smaller specialized lighting units have been developed, which are ideal for the kind of lighting control required in three-dimensional animation. This calls basically for accurate lighting over a small area.

Peppers are miniature lighting units which produce 150 or 300 Watts. Slightly larger units produce 500 Watts and the workhorse Red Heads give an output of 800 Watts. This is normally too much except for large sets, and it is uncommon to employ units which are any stronger.

As usual, the lighting plays a role in orchestrating the way that meaning is produced in the film. But it has another more prosaic function of masking all those devices – the pieces of tape, screws and wires – which make it possible to create the illusion of

Above and left: The Web, Joan Ashworth, © NFTS 1987
This is an adaptation of Mervyn Peake's novel *Gormenghast*. The style of the Gothic melodrama is captured through strong characterization and dramatic lighting – even the smaller sets used have minutely detailed lighting. The sparks which accompany the sharpening of the chopper (left) were shot separately and added optically using a bi-pack superimposition.

Left: Dreamless Sleep, David Anderson
The final scenes from *Dreamless Sleep*, depicting the end of the world, make use of stylized figures and mesmeric movement to establish a dreamlike, strangely clinical atmosphere. The film integrates two- and three-dimensional techniques to show the whirling vortex created by the final holocaust.

movement. It is sometimes necessary to suspend objects or characters with wires while at the same time directing light onto them. Though the specialized lighting gives great accuracy, you can further check whether the wires or fishing line are visible by using a 'pan glass'. The pan glass gives a panchromatic range for the spectrum, the range which would relate to a black-and-white image. It also shows the contrast ratios, so that if a wire is visible through this glass, it will almost certainly show up on the final film. As single-frame video becomes standard the lighting can also be checked through a video system, even though the final production may be on film.

The model

Any moving model will need support and, at the same time, some flexibility of movement. There are two alternative ways of achieving this. The first is to start by making elaborate armatures which are placed at the main joints. The support structure of the model is then built around this framework using a variety of materials. The second method is to make a support from wire, without armatures at the joints. This is easier for those without a technical background or the funds to commission the skeleton of the model. But it does not achieve such a realistic performance as armature models and is prone to wear and tear, especially at the joints. The advantage of the wire frame, on the other hand, is that it takes on an organic movement which may sometimes be appropriate to the subject dealt with in the film.

A basic armature consists of a ball-and-socket or a double ball-and-socket joint, which is pinned to the appendage forming the arm, leg or other necessary extremity. The joint is the most vulnerable part of the model. Unfortunately, it is rarely possible to purchase a suitable ready-made joint of the right size and scale. But most of the parts can be bought off-the-shelf and assembled to make a strong working joint without resort to engineering.

This tradition of model animation which relates to puppetry and theatre is matched by an equally strong, if more elusive, tradition which draws on trickfilm and the idea of 'making strange' – of placing ordinary objects in situations which make them odd and threatening. This relates to the uneasy artistic traditions of mannerism and *bricolage*. Jan Svankmajer has pursued this path for more than a decade, often taking his themes from the world of children. Trnka and his generation in Czechoslovakia set the innocence of children against the Fascism of the Nazi master race, but Svankmajer rather places the child-viewer in the position of coming to terms with, understanding and opposing these real fears. Innocence is no defence for Svankmajer. Thus all of those tempting objects, like the glass jars in *Alice* (1987), may contain a mass of seething worms. He celebrates the courage of children in overcoming the fear of the world, rather than indulging that fear. Given these preoccupations, the objects used in the animation take on a great significance. Sometimes this is achieved through changes in scale, as in *Punch and Judy* (1966), where the doll-like figures are shadowed by giant puppets. At other times the selection and juxtaposition of objects plays the most important role.

In the work of the Brothers Quay, too, selection and juxtaposition are central to the meaning of the film. Organic figures haunt decaying mechanical landscapes of fraying veneer, from which a sudden flash of metallic surface can transform the object or character in a moment. Found objects carefully collected or artfully improvised form the basis of set and characters in their recent film *Rehearsal for Extinct Anatomies* (1988). The main character is constructed from dessicated vine, garlic husk and old potato skins.

Left and below: Alice, a film by Jan Svankmajer/Condor Features/Film 4 International/Hessischer Rundfunk
Svankmajer is able to combine models, puppets and live-action to pursue increasingly a concern with the 'mistaken idealization of childhood which we adopt as we get older'. These artefacts from childhood are ripped out of the cosier and more comforting traditions of stories for children and their real cruelty is exposed. Svankmajer's film based on *Alice in Wonderland* by Lewis Carroll transcends the normal sanitized view of the tale, though not the original darker disturbing story.

Above: This Unnameable Little Broom, Channel 4/Brothers Quay
Decor is a central element in these films by the Brothers Quay. Rather than construct a homogeneous world for similar materials, they made the sets from many different found materials and objects.

Above: Street of Crocodiles, Brothers Quay, a British Film Institute Production in association with Channel 4
The characters are also sometimes made from found materials, which are blended to create new meanings. The Brothers Quay are always at pains to reveal the creaking machinery behind the illusion, as materials appear and vanish.

Plasticine and claymation

Most model animation techniques are related to moulding, casting and carving rather than to constructing models from manufactured or found materials. But the modelling techniques used in clay and Plasticine animation make use of both.

For many young people, clay and Plasticine animation has been their first introduction to the potential of the moving image. Some have gone on to live-action film or to different areas of animation, but others, such as Will Vinton, have persisted with the medium and achieved remarkable results. As a production method, clay and Plasticine has a history stretching back to the inventive Fleischer studio. The earliest clay films in America were those of Helen Smith Dayton in 1916. Clay appeared again in a Koko the Clown film of 1921, but then as the Disney production methods and narrative ability came to dominate production, it disappeared. Three-dimensional work became associated with special effects.

Left: Lurpak, Aardman Animations Ltd (agency: Gold Greenlees Trott; client: Danish Dairy Board)
Any material can appear to come to life. Here a sailor is created from the butter on a toasted muffin. The 'butter man' is in fact made of wax coated with vegetable oil. The model is built around a wire structure.

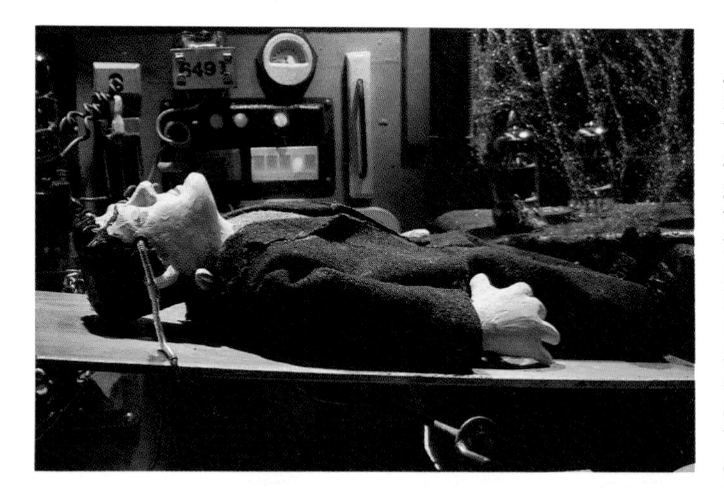

In the 1950s the character of Gumby appeared on NBC television in the United States in a short-lived series made by Clocky. Then Vinton gave a great impetus to the form, as well as to three-dimensional animation in general, when he won an Academy Award with *Closed Mondays* (1975). He continued to explore the medium with *The Great Cognito* (1982) and his feature *The Adventures of Mark Twain* (1985). Vinton eschews placing his Plasticine figures in a model background and insists that the whole set be constructed of the same material. The Plasticine is used to cover the surface of the constructed sets. This creates the impression of a 'real' Plasticine world in which the action takes place. Perhaps Vinton is at his most inventive when the traditional animation technique of metamorphosis is incorporated into the claymation, as in *The Great Cognito*, when the figurehead changes rapidly from John Wayne through General McArthur to a mass of battleship guns and a submarine conning-tower while maintaining a quickfire monologue with immaculate lip-sync. Plasticine has also been used to make documentary film, as in the BBC television series *Animated Conversations*, a number of which were carried out by the model animators Aardman (alias Peter Lord and David Sproxton). In these films the sound was prerecorded in documentary manner and then edited to provide the soundtrack for the films. The Plasticine animation was created afterwards. The effect in the film *Down and Out* is harrowing, as an incoherent tramp tries to deal with a patient but unbending official at a hostel who wants to see his identification before allowing him a free meal. There are few

Frankenstein Punk, Cao Hamburger and Eliana Fonseca, Embrafilme
There are obvious links between the alchemy of giving life to an inanimate object and animation. In this case, the recreation of a Plasticine Frankenstein's monster serves as a parody both of itself as a genre and of other films to which it refers. The middle still shows the monster in his heavy boots tap dancing through 'Singing in the Rain', in imitation of Gene Kelly.

animation films which have attempted to deal with this kind of difficult 'non-animation' subject-matter, and even fewer that have succeeded in lifting animation above the documentary fly-on-the-wall style and into a genuine comment on contemporary reality.

Movement
Sometimes the models achieve their movement through a process of substitution of parts, while in other cases the whole model is moved and manipulated. In the substitution method, a series of different heads may provide changing expressions for a character, or the entire movement may be created through substitution, as in Alexeieff's oil droplets. The great Georg Pal, who made the classic *Sky Pirates* (1938), used this method to add life to his puppets. After World War II, Jiří Trnka made extensive use of the technique of substitution in model films like *The Emperor's Nightingale* (1948) and the epic *A Midsummer Night's Dream* (1958).

Otherwise, the model is manipulated as a puppet or through the moulding and modelling technique of claymation. In this case, the animator plays a more traditional role in judging the nuances of movement and of timing. Key points on the model are established – fingertips, point of nose, toes and so on – and these are positioned using a template of bent wire. It is then possible to reset the position of the model and proceed to the next points of the path of the action with some certainty. As with all animation which calls for direct manipulation, working quickly helps maintain a continuity of movement. This is not always possible, given the complexities of model animation, so any aids to correct timing and positioning are useful.

Many of the magical elements of model animation are the result of careful planning and setting up of the shot, so that the 'wires don't show'. Even a character walking has to be created by firmly fixing one of the model's feet to the ground and supporting the rest of the body from positions hidden from the camera. Again, a judicious cut-away may give the illusion of smooth and unhindered movement when this has not strictly been achieved. Fishing line can also be used to support models. If the line is attached to movable brackets, it can very effectively transport characters or objects through space. Another technique is to use panes of glass to support the models. They can be panned and tilted to produce great accuracy of movement.

Three-dimensional work, whatever form it takes, has won a position at the centre of animation over the last decade through the dedication of a few individuals and the production of a number of key animated films. It has long deserved its place alongside the dominant tradition of two-dimensional animation and seems unlikely ever again to be dismissed as belonging to a mere secondary tradition.

Whereas the production methods of the classic school of Disney dominated animation through to the 1950s, new approaches are now making headway. The feature film industry continues to be mainly under the influence of full classic drawn animation, for reasons of efficiency of production methods, consistency and audience expectations. But there are signs that this may change and that there is room even in feature animation for a wider range of style. Narrative continues to dominate, as it does in live-action, but three-dimensional as well as two-dimensional images are now accepted and even sought after. The development of three-dimensional animation is proving to be much more than a passing fashion.

Business Animal, Redwing Productions Ltd (agency: Boase Massimi Pollit; client: Royal Bank of Scotland)

Taking great care in positioning the model for the *Business Animal* commercial – the model is being lined up to an adjustable and weighted pointer with a scalpel attached. As well as walking, the Business Animal (left) has numerous other moving parts which must be calibrated separately.

CASE HISTORY

MODEL ANIMATION

Model animation has become an important commercial production method in combination with the new technologies. It can take up a good deal of space and some of the most important studios are located outside what are considered the central areas of film production. In this case, a converted church in Bristol serves as a studio for the production of the award-winning Royal Bank of Scotland commercials 'Portcullis' and 'Business Animal'.

All illustrations in this case history from Portcullis and Business Animal, David Anderson, The Redwing Film Company (agency: Boase Massimi Pollitt; client: Royal Bank of Scotland)

The scale of the set can be judged from these three shots. The commercial is shot on 35mm film, using the reliable Mitchell camera noted for the steadiness of its film registration and gate.

Left: The video camera attached to the side of the Mitchell is often used to check the position of the model. When the model is shot in close-up great care has to be taken in the animation as the movement increments are much smaller.

Below: The effective close-up shot achieved. The detail which shows when 35mm film is used means that great care is called for in animating the models and matching them to the background.

Below: The effect of skilful lighting can be dramatic. Here backlight and modelling light combine to create an atmosphere of sunny expectation. It is important when designing the set to consider the placing of the lights. Backlighting can only be used if there is space allowed to place the lights. Alternatively, it is possible to hang lights from overhead gantries or attach them to the wall.

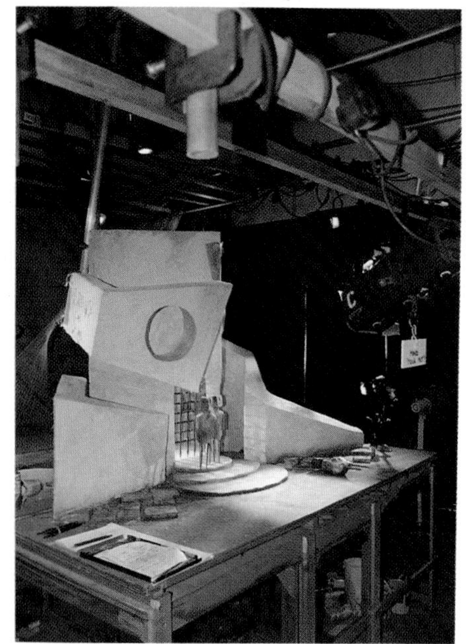

Above and left: The models can be positioned either, as here, by making the feet of material which can be stuck into the base, or by pinning the feet from a position hidden from the camera. The importance of lighting is evident—here a mixture of lights is used, with the smallest, a pepper set on the table top itself, serving to add modelling to the figures.

CASE HISTORY

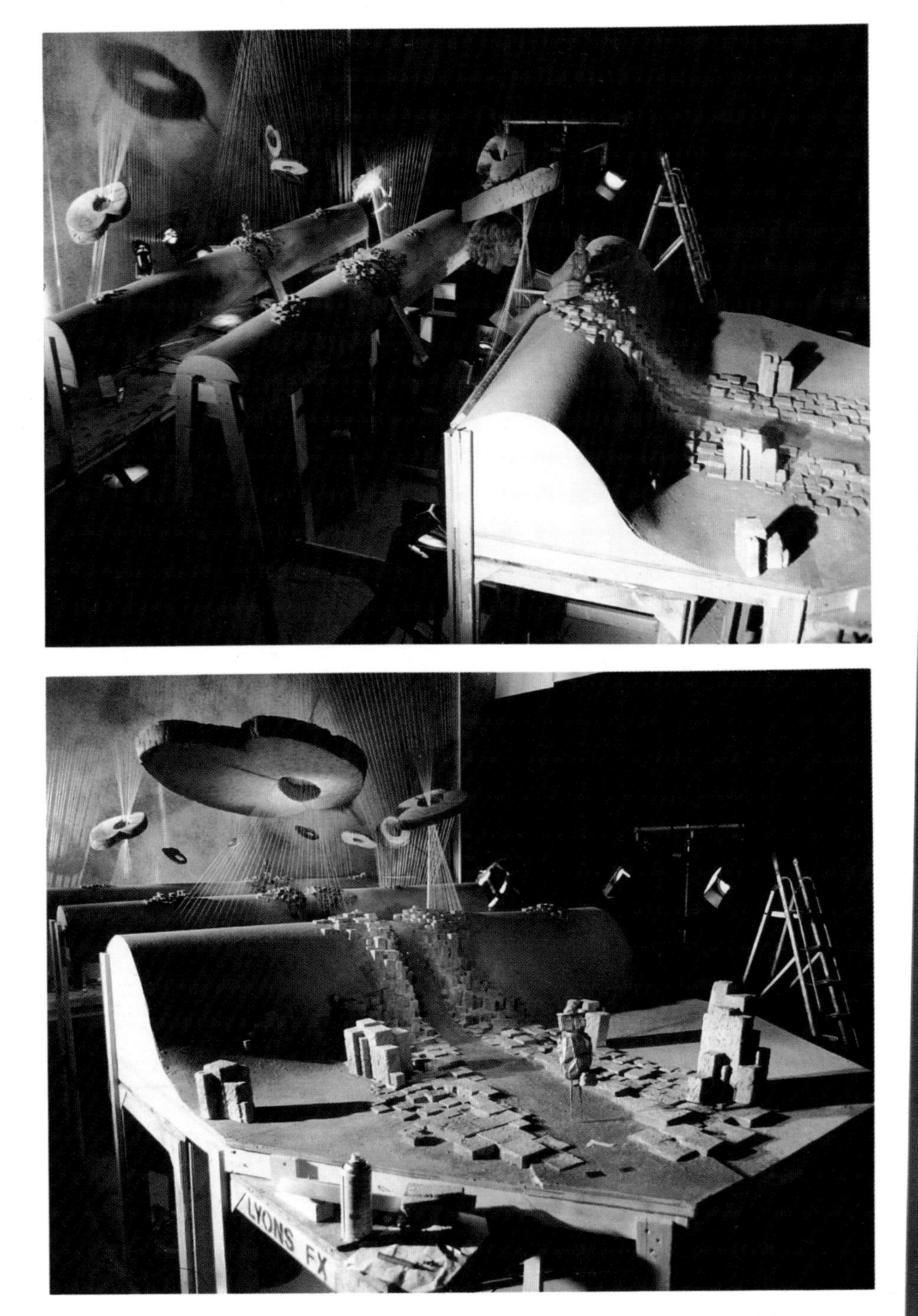

Top and above: Additional depth is often created by using false perspective in the construction of the set. This may take the form of a dramatic exaggeration of the depth, as in these stills, but even slight distortions of space in room sets or in backgrounds can be effective. The importance of pre-planning is also demonstrated here—the animator needs to be able to reach the model wherever it is on the set.

Right: The character of the model has an effect on the movement. In this case the model is not naturalistic, so the movement of the walk can be quite simple. The legs make only one movement – the leg is either raised or it is in contact with the base. If one leg was not strong enough to support the model, it would need wires.

7

THE NEW TECHNOLOGY

To a large degree, computer technology has transformed the practice of animation in recent years, and it seems certain to set the pace of change for the foreseeable future. But technological wizardry is no substitute for the old sophisticated disciplines of the animation tradition.

Above: The Adventures of André and Wally B, © 1984 Pixar
Seen as a breakthrough in three-dimensional computer-generated animation, this film was made by Pixar, an offshoot of Lucas film renowned for its innovative work in this field. Such realism of animated three-dimensional simulation was regarded as an important goal for computer animation.

The impact of new technology on animation has been very exciting but, at the same time, traumatic. Some animators have been inclined to bury their heads in the sand, while others lift their eyes to a bright new future. Developments have not always been predictable, nor has the trajectory been even. After the early work of the Whitney brothers and the excitement of the cybernetic revolution in the 1960s, it was some time before the new technology could supply a truly practical production method for animation studios.

A number of problems faced those who saw the computer as the key to the regeneration of animation. The first was the high cost of the mainframe computer systems required if animators were to achieve anything that could compete with the well-established production processes already in operation. The second lay in the divide between the disciplines of art and science. To achieve results that went beyond computer animation

clichés, new programs were needed. But the artists who had the desire and the imagination to stretch the medium did not have the scientific knowledge required to write the programs. It would be some time before a group emerged who could combine programming and animation skills. Finally, the computer systems themselves were slow and it took massive computing power to generate images which could match those produced by conventional means.

There still remain major questions to be resolved about the use of the new technology, but it is clear that some of the main lines have now been drawn. Applications of the new technology include the generation of two- and three-dimensional animation and the control of optical and mechanical equipment by computer. Other areas, such as the use of holography and robotics for animation, remain in the early stages of development, though the potential is enormous.

The most visible application of new technology has been in two-dimensional animation – the generation of graphic images using various forms of 'paintbox' system, which allow images to be manipulated on a screen. This kind of animation has been applied in areas as various as entertainment film, graphic titles, television weather maps, and graphs and charts for business or education.

Computer-generated images which are three-dimensional, or rather which create the illusion of three dimensions, were developed more for the solving of complex programming problems than for art, entertainment or communication. With films such as *Luxo Jr* (1986) and *Reds Dream* (1987) by John Lasseter, however, a new technical standard

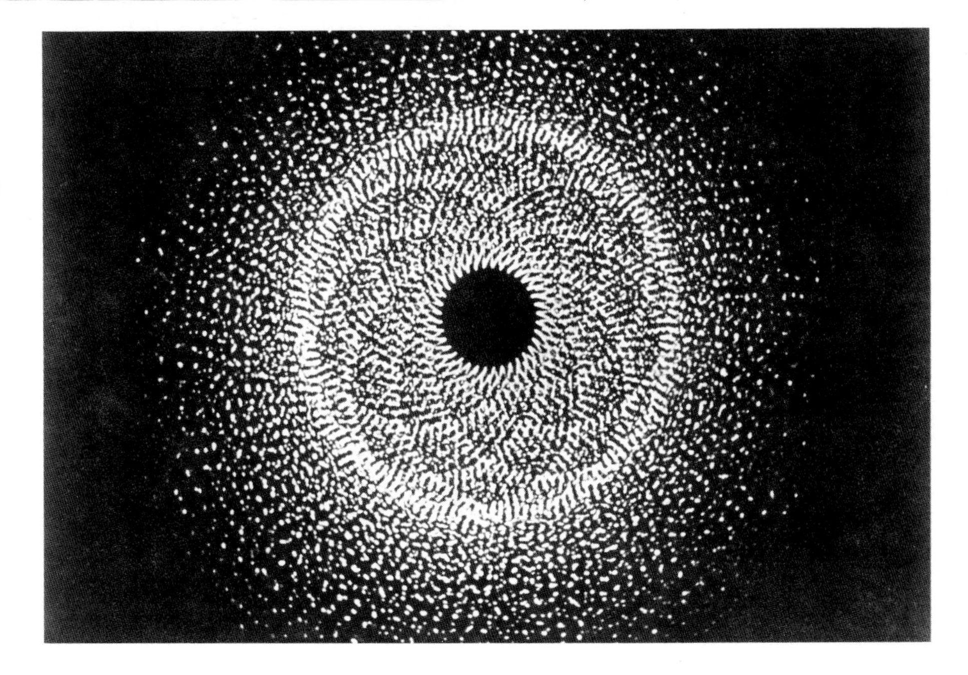

Lapis, James Whitney

***Lapis* was one of the first films using computers to make a general impact. Working with the equipment developed by his brother John, James Whitney made the film by computerizing tiny particles of light, using a development of the 1957 analogue computer. He had worked on similar films before, without a computer. These films required thousands of pin-pricked cards to give the light source.**

Above: Luxo Jr, © 1986 Pixar
Experienced animators skilled in traditional techniques are now working directly with computers. John Lasseter, an ex-Disney animator, made this film about the child-parent relationship of an anglepoise lamp. The quality of animation and the characterization are comparable even to the classic tradition.

has been set and three-dimensional computer animation is well placed for major progress. At present the cost of such productions is still prohibitive, except for animators like Lasseter working on such high-profile flagships of the new technology. So to some extent the future will be determined by whether or not the cost can be reduced.

The era of crude computer-generated effects is thankfully receding. Clients' constant demands for the most fashionable and up-to-date hardware has bankrupted many of the production houses specializing in this sort of predictable computer work. There is now a greater awareness of the potential for integrating traditional practices with new technology and broadening the application of computer-generated and computer-aided animation to fields other than entertainment. The present state of computer animation in some ways resembles the early days of the film industry – a restless and constantly shifting field, where companies continually emerge and vanish – and there are still few individuals with expertise to match the potential of the medium. Exaggerated claims for the new technology are countered by equally exaggerated rejection of everything it produces. The 1990s may well see the various sections of animation production finding common ground and working much more closely together.

Two-dimensional computer animation

The initial impetus for the development of computer animation came from experiments with simple analogue computer systems originally used in anti-aircraft viewfinders. It was John Whitney Sr. who reversed this military application of computers, enabling him to develop computer controls and imaging in the early 1950s.

Early computer animation took the form of complex abstract pattern, making the influential figure of Oskar Fischinger once more emerge as a mentor. He had inspired the Whitneys, who completed their first abstract film, *Five Film Exercises*, in 1944. This was not computer-generated, but its complex use of light beams, colour filters and optical printers clearly indicated interests which were technological as well as aesthetic. By 1961 James Whitney was using an analogue computer for his film *Catalogue*, in which abstract imagery attempted to combine modernist aesthetics with what was perceived as the liberating and non-elitist new electronic technology. Whitney's fellow experimenters Stan Vanderbeek, Lillian Schwartz, Charles Csuri and John Stehura, who were also pioneering computer

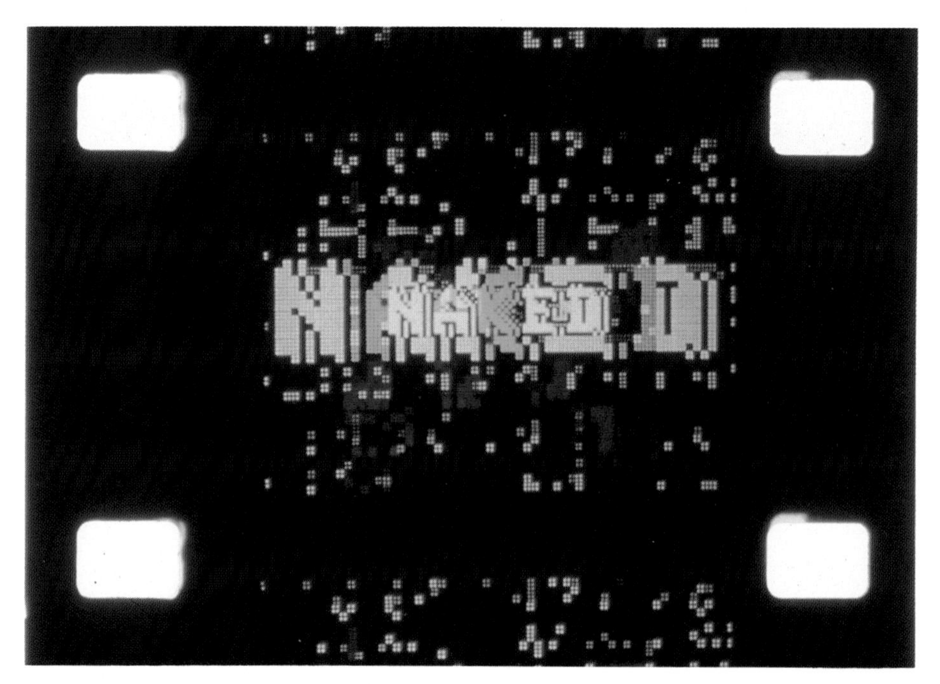

Below: Poemsongs, Stan Vanderbeek
The experimental film-maker Stan Vanderbeek teamed up with Bell Lab's technical computer expert Ken Knowlton in the late 1960s and 1970s to produce computer-generated films. This still is from one of eight films they produced, using the computer language BEFLIX on an IBM 7094.

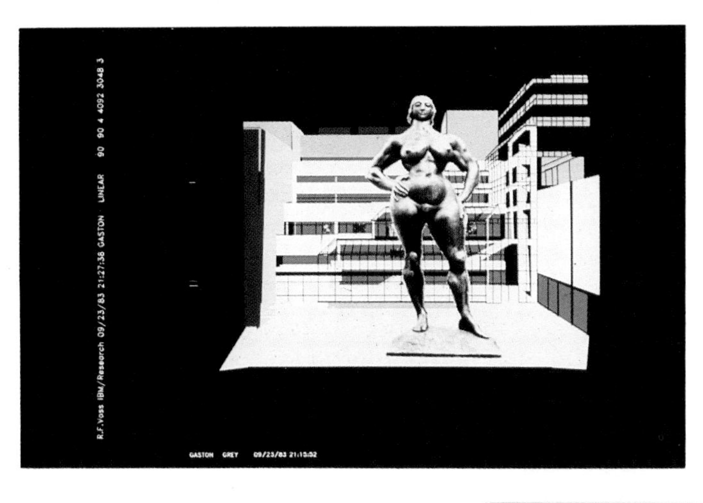

Above: Sculpture Garden; Right: Gallery; Below: Poster; all films Lillian Schwartz, Museum of Modern Art

The artist Lillian Schwartz began her influential computer work with Ken Knowlton at Bell. By the time she made *Gallery* (right), she had been working with computers for six years. This film extended her pointillist approach in which images are broken down and reconstructed using quantizing techniques. More recently, she has moved from a concern with abstract imagery to what she terms 'appropriations', bringing together her animation with the work she has carried out using computers for the analysis of paintings.

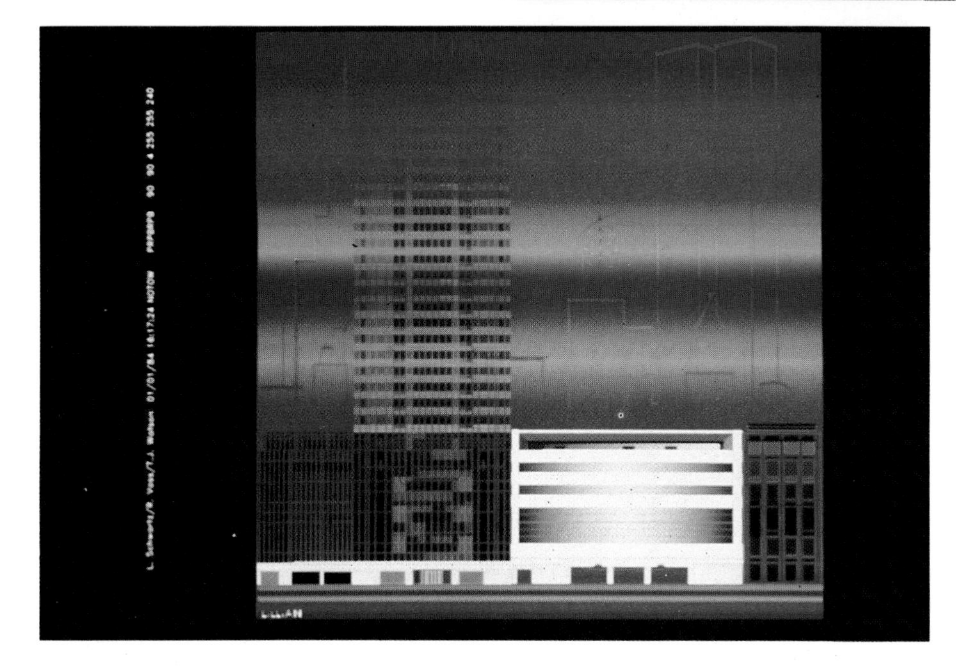

animation in the United States, shared these ambitions.

The large educational and industrial institutions quickly became involved with the development of computer-imaging. Whitney was employed by IBM, while Bell Laboratories worked with Vanderbeek and Schwartz through Kenneth Knowlton, a systems developer. Between 1967 and 1969 Vanderbeek produced a series of films, *Poemfields*, which extended further the abstract animation film. Schwartz combined her aesthetic preoccupations with a growing facility in the use of advanced technology to produce a number of seminal works, including *Pictures from a Gallery* (1976), a decisive move away from the abstraction of earlier artists and towards a more figurative imagery, in this case a kind of cubist interpretation of processed family photographs. The scientific use of computer-imaging was following a parallel course, sometimes, as in the case of Knowl-

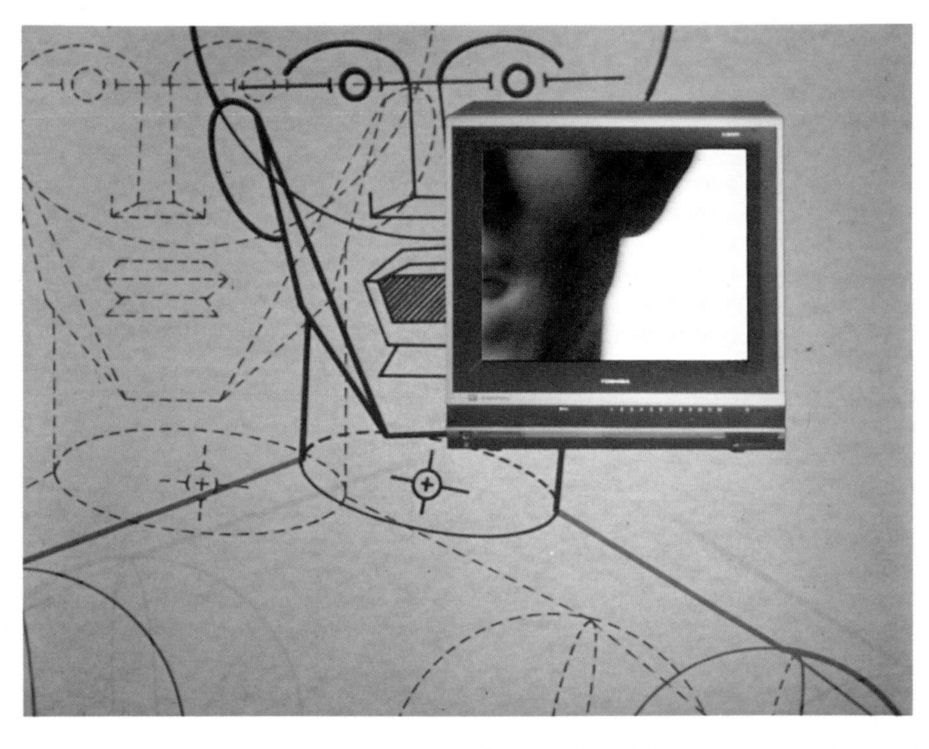

Toshiba 'FST' and Toshiba 'Hi-Fi', Speedy Films Ltd (agency: Gold Greenlees Trott; client: Toshiba UK)
The mythical aspects of high technology quickly entered the world of advertising. In this, one of the most exciting examples, wireframe computer images, which have become synonymous with new technology, are used to emphasize the technically advanced nature of Toshiba's hi-fi systems. These images are combined with film and conventional animation. Even though computer technology has advanced far beyond wireframe, it still remains the popular symbol for computer animation.

ton, crossing the path of the artists of 'the new age'. E. E. Zajec produced *Simulation of a Two-Gyro Gravity Gradient Attitude Control System* at Bell Laboratories in 1963.

However remarkable these early computer-animation works were, they depended to a great extent on a collaboration between the artist or designer and the computer scientist, with the scientist serving as translator between creator and machine. The key to the next step forward lay in making it possible for the non-scientific artist and animator to have direct access to the new technology. Ivan Sutherland developed the first Sketchpad, 'a man-machine graphical communication system', at the Massachusetts Institute of Technology in 1962. It allowed the user to draw with a light pen onto a digitizing pad. The image then appeared on a screen. At the same time, the system stored information as a model which could be recalled and manipulated as required. Of course, the scientist was still there as the invisible maker of the model, through having designed the system itself.

Nowadays, sophisticated systems such as the Quantel Paintbox provide a vast range of potential visual permutations for the graphic artist. But the artist still cannot go beyond the model of the visual world provided by the system in the first place. The relationship of system to user remains a central issue in the future direction of the art.

The development of two-dimensional animation followed the course marked out by the paintbox approach to producing images.

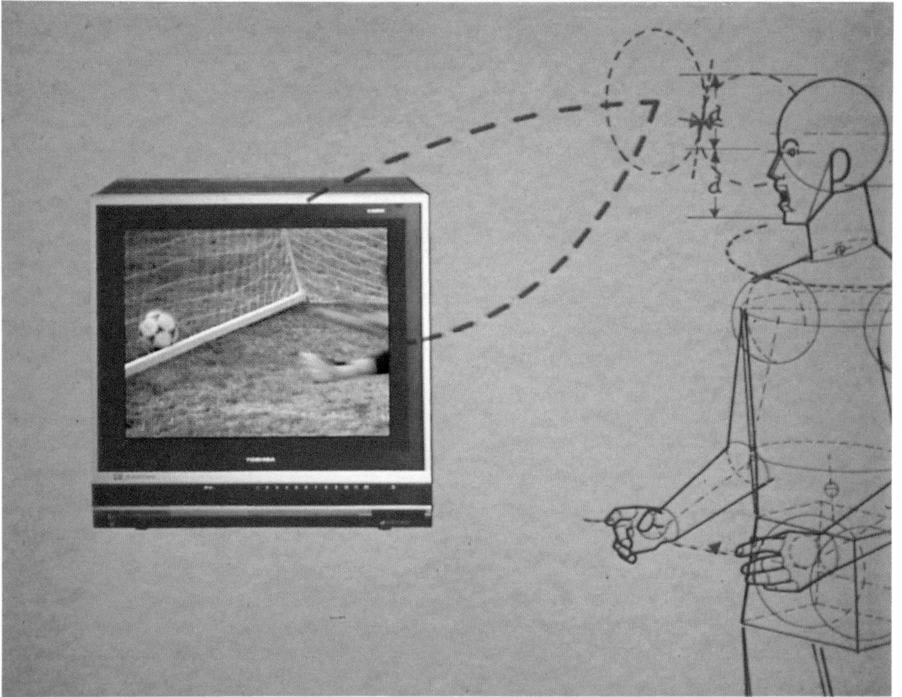

Images generated by these methods have become so commonplace they are for many people almost synonymous with computer animation itself. The early examples of this kind of animation which received a large audience, such as the *Think Electric* commercial made for British television by Ken Brown, used a system of wireframe graphics which was plotted onto paper and subsequently transferred to film and rephotographed, so that the lines in the film would have the luminosity of an electronically generated image. This film depended, as did many of this period, on the wireframe image that was produced by vector systems.

The use of computers to create scientific and technical simulations made great headway in the 1960s and 1970s. The programming for films such as Frank Sindon's *Force, Mass and Motion* was complex and was

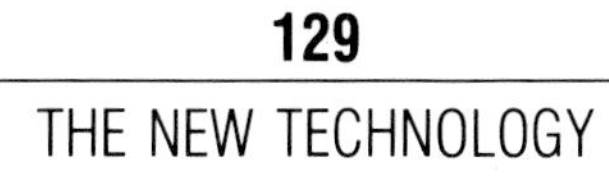

supported by companies such as Boeing and Bell Telephones. Bell gathered a group of programmers – E. E. Zajec, Kenneth Knowlton and Frank Sindon – who continued to explore the possibilities of simulation. Some of this work filtered through to the artistic community through scientific publications read by artists interested in the application of new technology. However, vector graphics, though suitable for scientific modelling and simulation, had drawbacks. The system required a very large amount of computing power and, while it was possible to produce complex modelled images, the process was extremely laborious until raster scanning was adopted in the mid-1970s.

The relative slowness of the vector system meant it had difficulty distinguishing what was in front of and what was behind the field. This problem is referred to as the 'hidden line'. The computer is seeing the model as a series of incredibly short straight lines and is calculating the movement between related points. There is no indication of surface – the lines have the same thickness whatever their

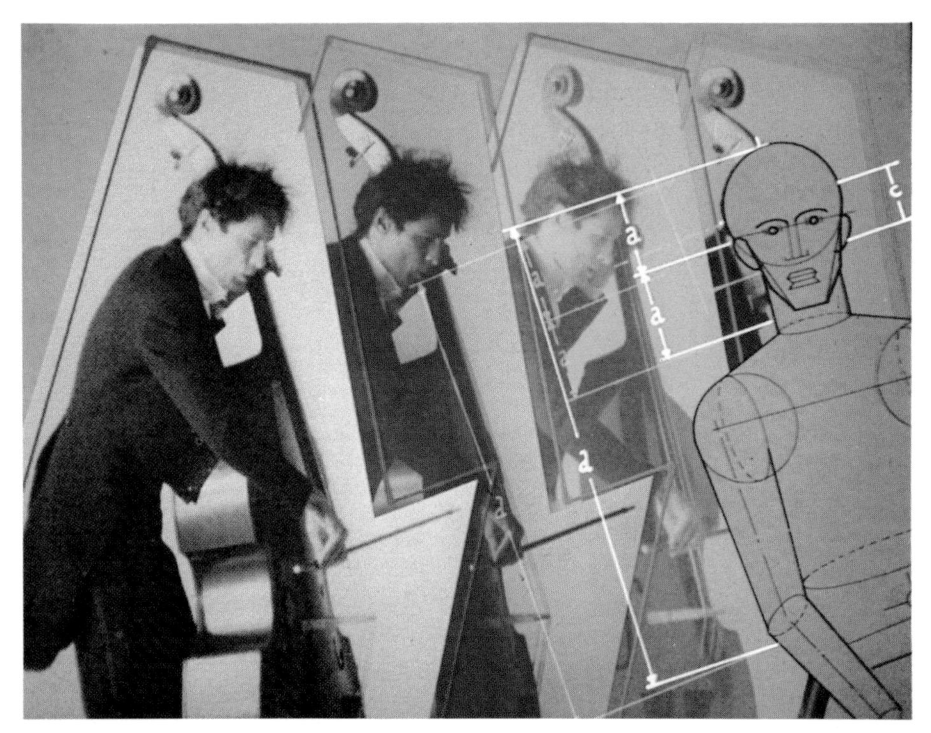

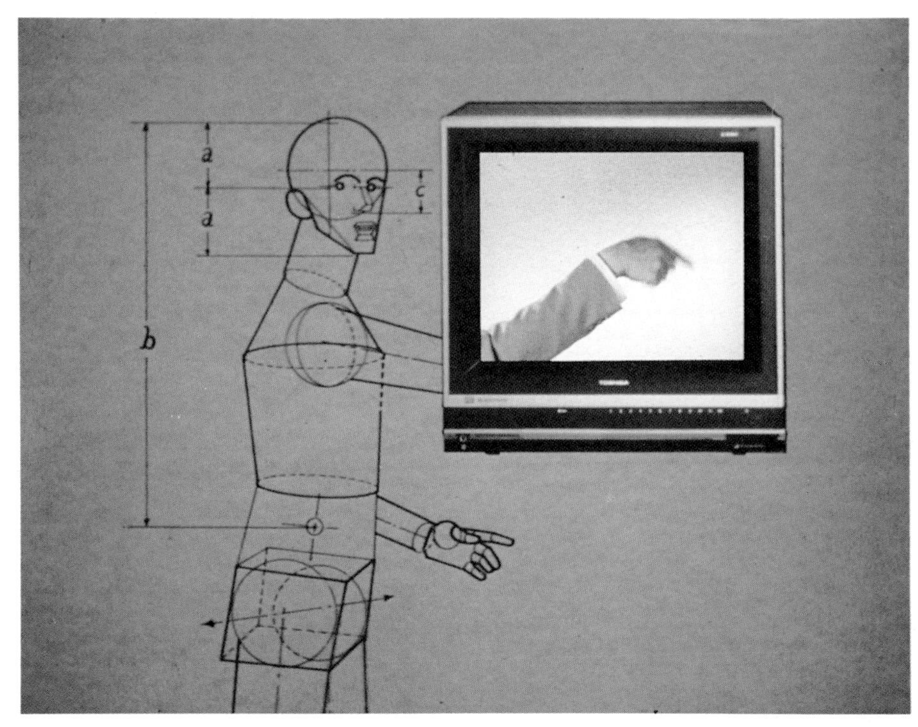

position. So the model is, in effect, transparent. The human eye and mind can interpret spatial clues and recognize objects instantaneously, basing their judgement on experience. So we can 'read' wireframe models easily. But the computer will have no reason to doubt that a nose might grow out of the back of a head, instead of the front.

Other problems arise from the need to make curved images out of a large number of straight lines. In general, for the computer using vector modelling to create a recognizable non-diagrammatic three-dimensional image is extremely difficult. One answer has been to generate wireframe models and transfer them into more conventional materials, especially by tracing off the screen, so that the lines can be removed. The images can then either be re-photographed and colourized, or simply transferred to cel and photographed conventionally.

The contribution of wireframe has been enormous, but the evolution of computer animation and graphics through vector systems may have served to distort the potential for innovative imaging. Certainly, the wireframe has come to represent a public relations image of high-tech fashion which has been difficult to escape. Computer images, as much as any others, are caught up in myths and ideology, in our perceptions of technology and change and our view of the world around us.

The computer and the in-between

A number of systems have been developed to use computers to deal with the animation in-between. These are seen as a labour-saving aid to the production process, as well as bringing the potential for imaginative metamorphosis through the computer generation of images. The idea is to take the key drawing, or in this case the key image, and use the computer to create the images between the keys. In the hands of an artist like Peter Foldes, this system is capable of creating powerful and original works. As an extension of his work in conventional animation, Foldes produced a series of films using the new technologies, working with the National Research Council of Canada and the Research Center of ORTH. *Hunger* (1973), one of the earliest films to use representational images in computer animation, shows the figure of a gluttonous civilized North so intent on satiation that after devouring the

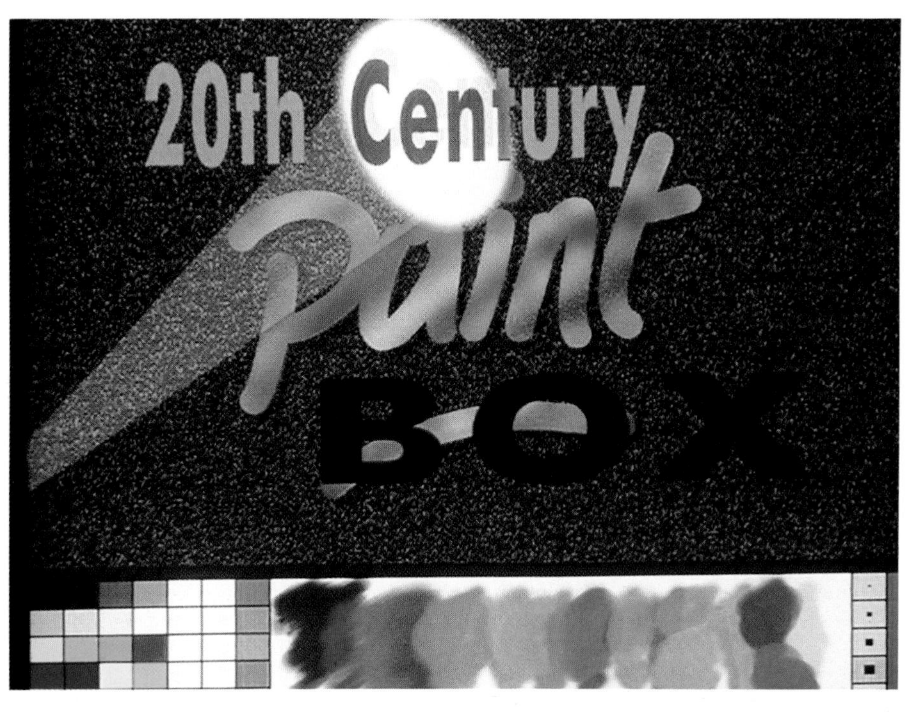

Left: The MEDIT materials editing system. All the surface characteristics can be defined using a set of on-screen parameters, from colour and texture to transparency and reflectiveness. Paintbox and edit systems such as these have had a tremendous impact on film and video in general, as well as on computer graphics.

Below: Using the digitizing tablet and pen. As on low-priced systems, with these you can draw in different styles and select items from the menu of options.

material commodities of the consumer society he turns his attention to the Third World. But the Third World resists and finally devours the now gross figure. Foldes fine line drawings are appropriate for this kind of animation – the lines disintegrate and re-form to provide a constant and shifting image of power and corruption.

A more recent film, John Halas's *Dilemma* (1981), also uses this technique, though advances in computing power now allow for the introduction of colour and limited modelling. The film, which shows the advance of the technology of killing, is based on a number of individual key images which metamorphose into each other. As with *Hunger*, there is a poignant irony in the application of high technology to a theme which is itself critical of simplistic ideas of progress.

It remains true, however, that this kind of in-between animation, which is now becoming more available to the microprocessor user, can give a far too mechanical movement. When this is apt, as it is in *Hunger* or *Dilemma*, it can be defended. But the subtlety which the traditional in-betweener brings to film is inevitably lost. This skill, perhaps not understood by the programmers developing this kind of computer animation, is one of the many which contribute to make traditional animation such a rich medium. Against this fact must be balanced the new opportunities given to many enthusiasts, who can experiment with animation programs and experience some of the pleasure of creating animated 'films' without the laborious processes required for conventional cel animation.

Paintbox

Computer-generated or manipulated images flourish on television – in commercials, of course, but also increasingly in the form of titles, diagrams, maps and other graphic inputs to programmes. Given the very tight schedules of television production, as well as the limited budgets, speed takes precedence over innovation and quality. There would be little point spending the four years it took to produce *Luxo Jr* on a television title which, in any case, may be viewed in less than ideal conditions. So a number of 'turnkey systems' have been developed, which are user-friendly so that designers can operate them with the minimum of computer literacy. The drawback is that the range of possibilities they offer is, of necessity, limited. The computer provides a menu of effects and graphic styles that are combined in different ways and used to manipulate frame-grabbed images. These systems have been greatly reduced in price and the slower ones, such as Image Artist, cost a fraction of the price of a sophisticated system such as the Quantel Paintbox.

The Quantel Paintbox itself is the system

which established the current standards for graphic-image generation and the manipulation of images. It makes available a vast number of combinations of colour and effects. In conjunction with Harry, a video editor and effects generator, the Quantel Paintbox is one of the most widely used systems in the world. Its flexibility and its very high quality may only be stretched to the full when high-definition television becomes the accepted standard for receivers. It would be a pity if the deservedly poor reputation of the flip, spin and twist of the early paintbox systems, which once saturated television graphics, prejudiced the use of the much more sophisticated systems now rapidly developing. The paintbox has also changed the role of the designer/animator in television from the simple production of artwork to a more central position. The work can be designed as it will appear in its final form on screen.

Most importantly, the linking of the Quantel and Harry systems has opened up an almost unlimited capacity to combine and manipulate images. Using Harry, single frames can be isolated and then transformed with the paintbox. They can be coloured, very small sections can be focused on and altered or enhanced, and special effects which were costly and time-consuming on film can now be carried out at the press of a button. Increasingly, the images we are looking at have been constructed from many different elements brought together electronically. Using digital video recording, these combined images do not lose quality as they would if film alone was employed.

There are a number of paintbox systems which are of relatively low cost and still provide an acceptable range of graphic elements. They can be used to make non-realtime animated sequences in conjunction with video and frame stores.

Three-dimensional computer animation

It is the field of three-dimensional computer animation which offers the most promise and at the same time presents the most difficult challenge. It calls for a massive amount of computer power, requiring the use of large mainframe computers such as the Kray or VAX series. The reason for the amount of computing power needed lies in the complexity of building a three-dimensional model for animation. The familiar wireframe image created by vector graphics represents a transparent two-dimensional figure. To make the wireframe become solid, the surface of the figure has to be defined as well. This can be achieved for flat surfaces by using polygons, which build up to create three-dimensional images, just as short straight lines can be used to create curved figures.

First, however, the model has to be input into the computer. Unlike the two-dimensional model, which can be input using

Esso, Amazing Array Productions for Esso UK plc

These stills are completely computer generated, using the latest technology which allows for reflections and transparency as well as the normal hard edge associated with computer images. In this case the nozzle of the petrol pump was given a slightly worn surface to further enhance the realism.

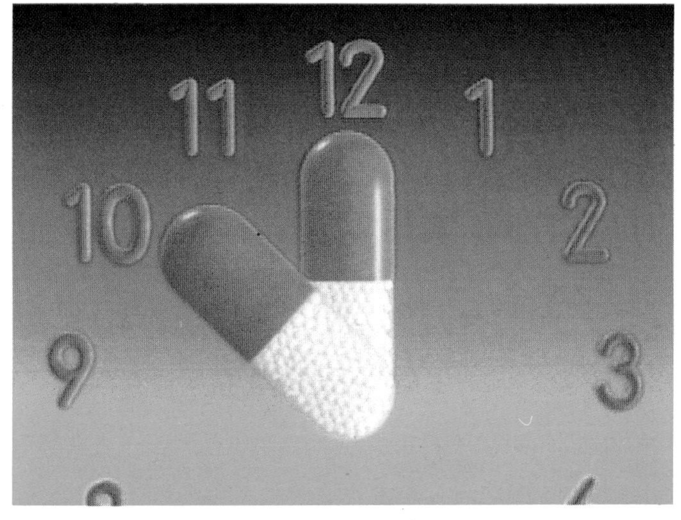

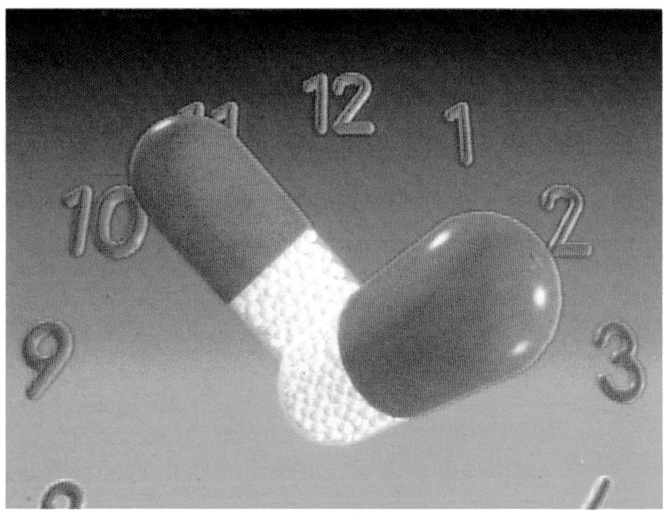

a cursor and light pen, the three-dimensional object has to be described in space, with only two-dimensional means. One way of achieving this is to construct an actual model and enter all of its coordinates into the computer, so that it can reconstruct the model in any configuration. This method was used in early modelling, but it is a time-consuming procedure.

In 'procedural' modelling, a number of three-dimensional figures, such as cones and cubes, are defined, and then these are brought together to form the precise object required. It is a comment on the speed at which computer technology is developing that some simple forms of procedural modelling are now becoming available to the micro-user. Even so, this kind of modelling has its limitations, especially the complexity of the construction and the time-consuming nature of the task.

A method of producing complex models that is more economical of time and computer power is that based on a mathematical principle called fractel geometry. The object is grown – it is developed organically rather than constructed. The method works by recognizing that any object may be made up from a number of larger or smaller objects with similar characteristics.

Finally, surfaces can be modelled by particle systems. This method creates many different effects by generating minute dots. The dots are recorded as blurs on film, opening up the possibilities of three-dimensional models for objects such as smoke and fire, where the hard surfaces of other modelling methods are not appropriate.

The display

The way in which the images are displayed and stored depends on how the screen is activated. Before the 1970s, the images were produced by continuous vector scanning. This was a slow process and was replaced by the introduction of the more efficient rasters. In the raster system the screen is made up of many small coloured squares called pixels,

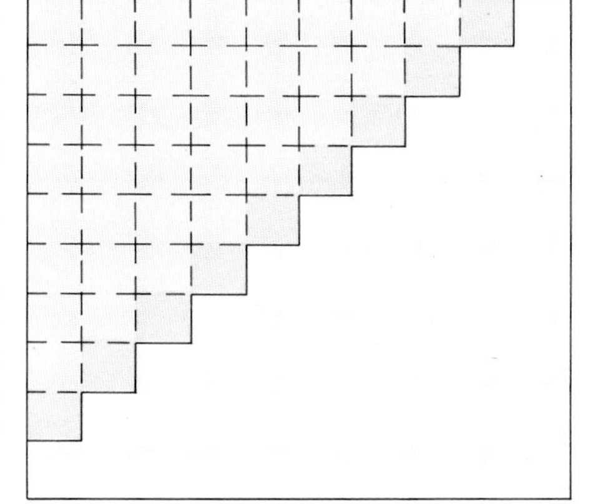

Anti-aliasing. The computer-generated image is built up of pixels, which are small rectangles. On diagonal lines this results in a staircase effect, which can be acceptable in still images but becomes obtrusive when the image is moving. In order to overcome this, the pixels which lie along the diagonal are given an average shade and colour which lies between that of the two adjacent ones.

which are triggered to produce the computer image. Obviously, the edges of any image which does not lie directly on a vertical or horizontal will be jagged. This phenomenon is known as 'aliasing' and appears on the screen as a flickering pattern. On many user-friendly systems, it is possible to 'zoom in' to examine the pixel structure and manipulate individual pixels. To eradicate aliasing, the mean colour of the pixels lying on the edge is worked out and then used to give a smooth transition between the different colours. When this effect of anti-aliasing is called for in an animation sequence, the picture is sampled over a very short time, so that once again the mean can be determined and a smooth sequence produced.

Animation aids

As well as computer-generated images, new technology has brought other advantages to animation. It has provided aids to the production process itself, alleviating some of the more arduous tasks. It has also been applied to the control of animation equipment, opening up a highly creative area of new effects. And it has revitalized some older optical effects which had fallen into disuse due to the time and expense of production but have now become viable once more.

The Quick Action Recorder is basically a line-testing machine. It is based on a computerized frame store which holds black-and-white digitized images made by photographing the original artwork with a video camera. The stored images can be replayed at normal speed, speeded up or slowed down. Or they can be moved to different positions in the sequence. It is also possible to insert images, to change the number of frames of 'exposure', and to replay all of this on an endless loop. Although the machine is designed for line-testing, because of the high-contrast image produced it can also be used for more experimental purposes. Exciting effects have been produced by making high-contrast images from artwork or from life, colouring them and using them with a two-dimensional paintbox system. In the main, the system is simple to use and provides an excellent way of learning about animation movement.

This page and facing page: Proflex, The Moving Picture Company, director Bernard Lodge (agency: Colman RSCG & Partners; client: Ciba Geigy)
The pack and the titles are generated using a Bosch BTS 4500 computer graphics system. The remaining shots of the pills were generated with the popular Alias computer graphics system, the pills explosion being programmed in house by Moving Picture Company programmers.

Other systems have applied computer technology to the production of a video recorder accurate enough to 'shoot' a single frame and reproduce it in high quality. The single-frame video recorder is, in effect, making a single-frame edit for each shot taken. This equipment is now standard in most animation studios and widely used in education. Nevertheless, many professionals still in the final instance test complex animation on film, since film shows up all the errors of timing.

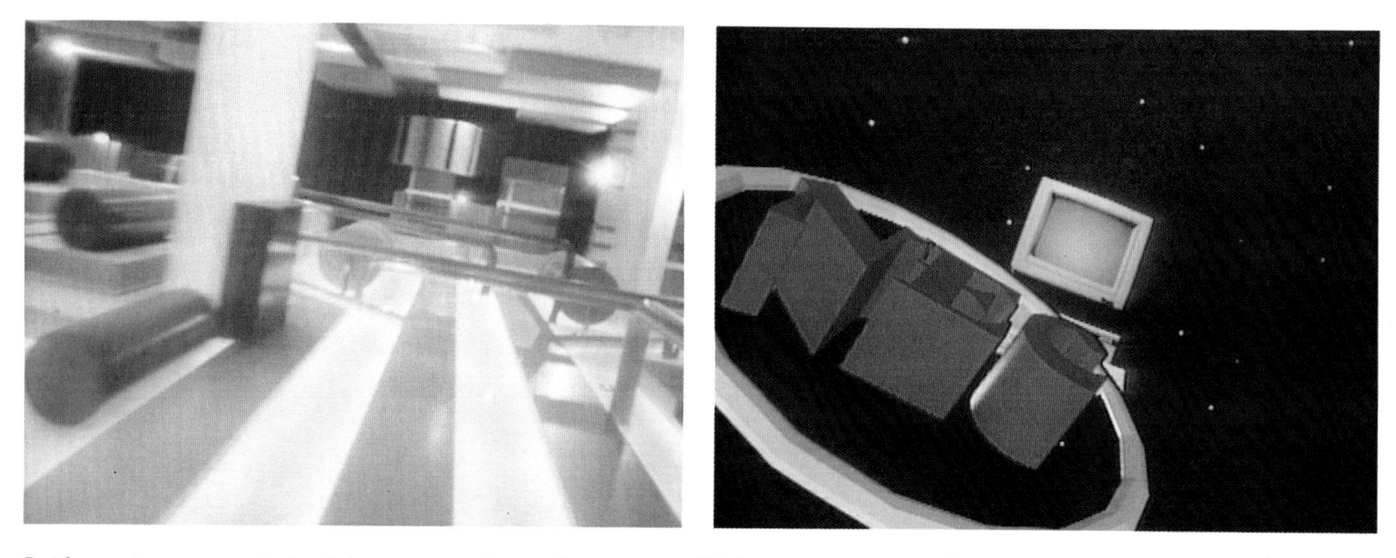

But for most purposes, electronic images are more than up to the task.

Motion control

Motion control involves the combination of stepping motors which operate with a great single-movement accuracy, and computer control and memory. The introduction of computer-controlled rostrum cameras was initially seen simply as an aid to productivity. It increased greatly the speed at which complex 'shoots' could be carried out and reduced the possibility of camera errors occurring through inaccurate calibrations of the movement or mistakes in the operation of manual controls.

However, it quickly became apparent that much more ambitious use could be made of the device. The very high degree of accuracy which could now be achieved meant that optical effects involving multiple exposure or minute movement could be carried out very effectively. Before the new technology was available, effects of this kind had to be judged by eye. It was now possible to repeat a camera or, increasingly, a rig movement almost infinitely. Previously, effects like travelling mattes, which combined camera or artwork movement with multiple exposures to create a composite image, were difficult to achieve and therefore largely avoided. Now the travelling matte and other optical effects which called for great precision were much easier to carry off.

The first spectacular public demonstration came in Stanley Kubrick's *2001: A Space Odyssey* (1968), which made extensive and innovative use of travelling mattes. The film's creative special-effects adviser, Zoran Presnic, devised the slit-scan technique. Though this has since become something of a visual cliché and is not widely used, it did demonstrate the extraordinary potential of motion control. A matte is a piece of artwork, in some cases a camera filter, which masks out part of the frame so that it remains unexposed. Subsequently another different image is exposed in the space, filling out the whole

Above left and above: NEC, The Moving Picture Company, director Peter Truckel (agency: DDB Needham Worldwide; client: NEC)

The first picture from the NEC commercial is made using a motion-control rig. The second shows the combination of a motion-control background and a computer-generated logo. This is achieved using the Bosch computer-graphics system.

Below left and below: DHL, The Moving Picture Company, director Peter Truckel (agency: Ted Bates Communications; client: DHL)

The jukebox shot from this commercial uses motion control. The live-action man-moon red streak was created using the Quantel Paintbox, and the final combination of images was made with the Harry computerized editing system.

Olivetti, The Moving Picture Company, director Peter Truckel (agency: CBC, Milan; client: Olivetti Italia)
Model television sets shot with motion control. The live-action sequence is matted in frame by frame, in an edit suite using ADO.

frame. It is often used in live-action films to combine separate foreground and background shots. The matte needs to be very accurate, as it will often be butted next to an image with a complex outline. Obviously, introducing movement into this, as in travelling matte, multiplies the difficulties, since in such a case the outline to be marked constantly changes.

In slit-scan, the matte consists of a narrow slit through which the image is exposed. This matte is moved across either an artwork or a projected image a number of times. Simultaneously, the camera tracks in. Again, this movement is repeated a number of times for each slit. The slit is exposed for the required length of the track as well as its movement across the field.

Motion control can also be used in conjunction with optical printer systems such as the Cinetron and Aces to create a whole range of optical effects – changes in exposure, skip framing and multiple exposures. When these systems are used in conjunction with rigs having multiple camera systems, even more specialized effects are possible.

Motion control has been applied not only to rostrum cameras and rostrums, but also to complex rigs. A rig is any system in which camera, objects or artwork can be moved in relation to each other. Some are relatively small, while the largest can cover the area of a small studio. The Aces system has a 68-foot track. Whereas a rostrum stand is positioned on the floor, a rig may be entirely mounted on an overhead track, permitting movement in any direction. It can, for instance, enable the camera to move very close to small objects and through sets. Combined with systems based on pencil-thin optical fibres, this creates the potential for minute movements which can be very accurately calibrated and controlled by the computer and which can then be repeated at will. At the forefront of developments in this area have been the Moving Picture Company, who have employed motion control in a number of their films, as well as pushing back the frontiers of the technology.

Robert Able Associates have gone further with the LORI system. This permits the manipulation of models and graphics, as well as camera controls which can be operated from a paddle on the computer. The models themselves can be read from blueprints before they are in fact built and all of the movement can be preset and analysed. Once the system has been set, the camera controller simply has to film the models or animations as planned.

Increasingly, the full resources of the new technology are being combined to produce animated films far removed from the stereotypic image of high-tech.

The future

In the last decade animation has undergone many changes. The effect of some of these can be clearly seen; others have yet to seep through to mainstream production. New technology has made possible many of these changes and seems likely to set the pace in the future. The possibility of combining and manipulating animation with other forms of image electronically has made it much more visible. It appears regularly on pop videos, in commercials and as spectacular sequences in live-action feature films. Yet animation studios face the unpleasant possibility of becoming little more than producers of interesting animated images to be used as elements in electronic collage.

It seems likely that the role of the animator will change in the 1990s, as the role of the designer has. The animator will take control of the electronic process and engage much more directly with the total production process. To some extent this has begun to happen. The use of sophisticated electronic equipment is increasingly a part of the animation world. Few studios or workshops are

Above: Mid-Air, Vera Neubauer
The place of the individual committed film-maker who works with limited funds and resources has always been assured in animation. Increasingly, film-makers like Vera Neubauer have used the medium to express what is seen as more difficult subject-matter.

Above: Radiocity, Amazing Array Productions
The sophistication of computer-generated moving images is now such that real-time three-dimensional computer animation which the animator 'directs' seems within sight.

Left: An American Tail, Sullivan Bluth, © 1986 Universal City Studios Inc and U-Drive Productions Inc, courtesy of MCA Publishing Rights
After a period of apparent decline, feature animation has how re-established itself as an equal partner of the live-action film. Storytelling skills, so much a strength of Disney's production, have emerged as the driving force behind this revival.

Right: Business Animal, Redwing Productions Ltd (agency: Boase Massimi Pollitt; client: Royal Bank of Scotland)
One recent development has been the increase in the production of three-dimensional animation, previously consigned to a place on the margins of the classic animation tradition.

Below and below right: Love is the Seventh Wave. The Moving Picture Company/ Kaleidoscope, designer Pat Gavin, © A & M Records
Pop promos have introduced new audiences to the exciting potential of animation. Though the productions themselves have not always been even in their quality, the best of them have brought together imaginative imagery and an experimental approach, revolutionizing the way animation is seen, and incidentally changing the look of mainstream commercial production.

without at least some electronic aid to the production process.

The earlier claims of the advocates of the electronic future that the electronically generated image – in particular the three-dimensional fully moulded computer animation – would see off the archaic, laboriously produced animated film now seem to have been exaggerated. The development of this area has been neither as spectacularly swift nor as problem-free as the first heady years led people to believe. However, there are significant research programmes taking place which make the future economical production of computer-generated three-dimensional entertainment animation a certainty. The time-scale for these developments remains less sure. Motion control also seems set to progress technologically.

Research is also being carried out into evolving further aids for conventional animation production. A computer is being developed which will accurately in-between animation, rather than provide a metamorphosis between key drawings. The use of fully computerized paint-and-trace is also imminent. The colourizing of images is already a part of current practice (sometimes applied disastrously to original black-and-white films), and the range of colour and graphics surpasses that of conventional production methods. The output of these electronic devices is, of course, to videotape or other electronic receiver. Although still dependent on very high levels of lighting, the high definition television, coupled with laser transfer between film and tape, seems likely to benefit the development of electronic animation. There has been a steady increase in the production of computer animation either in its pure form or operating with other systems, and this steady growth – rather than a sudden boom – seems set to continue.

Animation production in the conventional sense has also developed both in quality and quantity. That high-quality work is still compatible with economically viable feature-film production has been clearly demonstrated. There is a renewed confidence in the future of animated features.

As a result, there has been a rapid development of animation education, both formal and informal, within colleges and workshops. This has taken place on an

Left: Network 7, Matt Forrest, Snapper Films Ltd for Sunday Productions
This highly original youth current affairs programme for British Channel 4 TV made use of titles in pop-video style to announce its aim of bringing the visual imagery of new technology to studio-based television production. Snapper Films, specializing in music promos, produced the title sequence.

Above left and above: Okavango, The Moving Picture Company, designer Nick Wall, © BBC
The branch and the droplet are motion-controlled and the background is back-projected. Live action is matted into the droplet and the curve is achieved by using Mirage. The use of the traditional optical technologies with new technology has led to a revival of some of these crafts. The precision of movement that can be achieved using motion control also presents the potential for the creation of totally new effects.

international scale and the educational value of the medium as a discipline in its own right is now widely accepted.

Pop promos have carved out a niche and animation has played a considerable part in this. In addition to the impact that they have had in themselves, the better promos have also introduced audiences to images which a decade earlier would have seemed avant-garde. One effect has been to make film-makers themselves more aware of the history of experimental animation.

This demonstrates another feature of the changes that have taken place: there is now, among the makers of animated film, a broad and substantial knowledge of their own history. Sometimes this is drawn on through direct references; at other times it can be seen informing their practice. Yet the history of animation remains under-researched, considering the richness of the material.

One area for some concern is the production of animation for children. Animation has always been a popular form with children, but recently the films themselves have sometimes been seen as little more than commercials for the toys and characters associated with them. The economic pressure on production, coupled with low rates of return, is leading to lower quality in animation for

Esso, The Moving Picture Company, director Bernard Lodge (agency: McCann-Erickson; client: Esso Petroleum Co Ltd)
These computer images for an Esso commercial were generated using the Alias computer-graphics pack. Pack shots were frame-grabbed into the system and texture-mapped on to billboards within the computer-graphics system. Although many of the programs and systems used in computer animation are bought in, there is still a significant amount of development carried out in-house to create custom-made systems for specific purposes.

children. The kind of innovative work demonstrated by *Sesame Street*, which provided a variety of styles, approaches and access for animators, now seems threatened by the dominance of the cartoon series.

On the other hand, there has been a growing support for animation dealing with adult subject-matter, with Britain's Channel Four playing a leading role. Other television channels show every sign of following this lead and even surpassing it.

The imminent explosion of satellite broadcasting should provide many more opportunities for the production of animation. However, it will also place an added pressure on the already hard-pressed studios to economize on production costs and cut production values. Early indications, through the experience of music stations such as Sky and MTV, suggest that there will be an incentive to produce innovative animation which makes use of low-budget and experimental techniques. But this is also likely to become a highly competitive area.

A particularly interesting phenomenon has been the growth of genuine three-dimensional animation. It crosses from the most experimental and challenging work, through films of wit and social concern, to high-quality narrative productions. The models may be made of many different materials and created in a variety of styles and methods. Nor is production limited to the countries which traditionally specialized in puppetry. If the growth of this area is sustained at its present rate, the three-dimensional work, with its emphasis on the handmade approach to illusion and magic, may emerge as the antidote to the computer-simulated view of the world. Perhaps the late twentieth century's difficult relationship with new technology is reflected in the enthusiasm for this most physical form of animation.

NEW TECHNOLOGY

One of the most exciting recent developments in animation has been the application of new technology and its combination with traditional film crafts. The areas of computer-generated imagery, computer-controlled equipment, optical techniques and video editing have made a great contribution. This example from The Moving Picture Company shows many different techniques at work.

All illustrations in this case history from Monkey Business, The Moving Picture Company

Above right: A computer-generated image of a city street at night, in this case made from 1600 generations and produced using ADO and Abekas. This system is at the top end of the market and costs in the region of £95,000 (US $174,500).

Above: Motion control – the camera is controlled by computer as it tracks over the landscape. The movement of the rig which supports the camera is provided by single-frame stepping motors.

Left: Here the motion-controlled disc which is shot stop-frame is combined with the background using a film optical printer. The mattes essential for optical printing were once laboriously produced by hand, but can now be created electronically.

Above left: The live-action background has a Bosch computer-generated matchstickman superimposed over it. The flame which is coming from the head of the matchstick is added using Harry, the computer editor. Harry allows frames and sequences to be isolated and manipulated using a paintbox system.

Left: A computer-graphics sequence generated using Alias software. Alias is at the top end of the computer market, and when used with an Iris 4D workstation it costs in the region of £75,000 (US $138,000). In addition to this the costs of servicing such complex equipment can be as much as £11,000 ($20,000) per year.

Right: The arch is created using Alias. This is then matted over a Paintbox-generated background, and combined with lighting effects using the computer editor, Harry. Paintbox and Harry can be used interactively; the operator can move from one to the other on the same screen by switching menus. All of the controls can be operated using a light pen.

Above right: A live-action filmed background with stop-frame model animation of the gorilla matted into the television set. The matchstick figure is computer-generated using the Bosch computer-graphics system and is also matted over. The reflection of the flame in the bottom right of the television is another product of Harry.

Right: Harry is also used to make the combination shot of the candle and the counters.

Left: The bed is a live-action shot with the background wall created using a paintbox. The helicopter is shot single-frame with motion control. Finally, all the elements are combined using Harry. Harry allows elements to be edited out and added to individual frames, making it ideal for creating mattes.

Left: A live-action background has falling dice and counters matted on to it. The dice and counters are again generated by the Bosch computer-graphics system. Mattes allow one image to be superimposed over another without any of the background showing through.

Below: An animator using the Iris workstation for modelling and choreography. Both the keyboard and the mouse which controls the on-screen cursor can be used to create images and movement. This may be interactively controlled utilizing a real-time playback system.

ANIMATION KIT

Each phase of the production process – making the animation, shooting the artwork, producing the sound and editing the picture – calls for different kinds of materials and levels of equipment.

Light box and peg bar

The light box and the peg bar form the basis of cel and paper production techniques. They are also useful for many other kinds of production. A light box can be made from chipboard, a half an inch thick for the top, bottom, front and back, and five-eighths of an inch for the sides. Six-millimetre perspex is placed in a hole cut in the top. The board is usually angled at 30 degrees, but if the box is custom-made this angle can be adjusted to suit the individual. For professional work, an animation disc with sliding pegs is often set in the top rather than the sheet of perspex. A hole cut in the back of the box helps cool the light and serves as a handle for carrying. The light source is 60 watts – a 60 watt Linolight is most appropriate.

Light boxes can, of course, be bought from specialist animation suppliers. They vary a good deal in price depending on the level of sophistication. The light source should not be too strong – it is important not to buy the kind of light box made for viewing transparencies in photography.

The peg bar, used to position the artwork, can also be made using a cast and resin, but it is far easier to purchase one. Metal peg bars are strong and durable. They are, however, expensive, and plastic peg bars are now widely used by students. There are different standard and non-standard peg bars, Acme and Oxberry being most common. The kind of pegs required depends on the camera system used. If you are in doubt, the three-peg Acme system is perhaps the best bet.

Paper, punches and cel

If you do not have easy access to a punch or a guillotine, it is advisable to buy special animation paper. This is already cut to size and punched. A cel punch is an expensive piece of studio equipment and, because of the accuracy needed, second-hand punches can cause problems if they are excessively worn. A punch is certainly worth purchasing for a group or workshop.

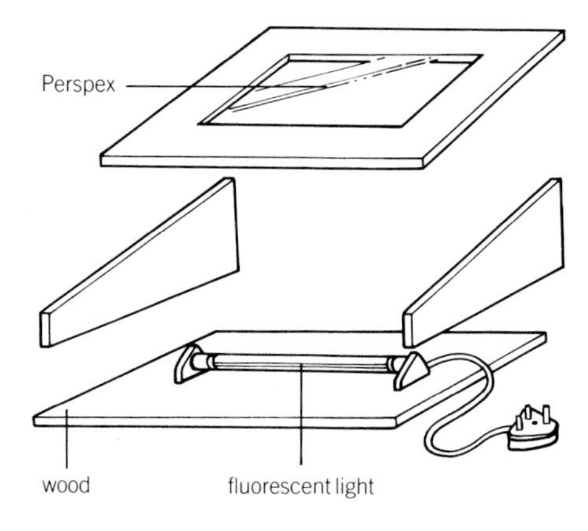

Above: The right kind of light box is essential. Although these can be bought from specialist stockists, they are relatively simple in structure and easy to make.

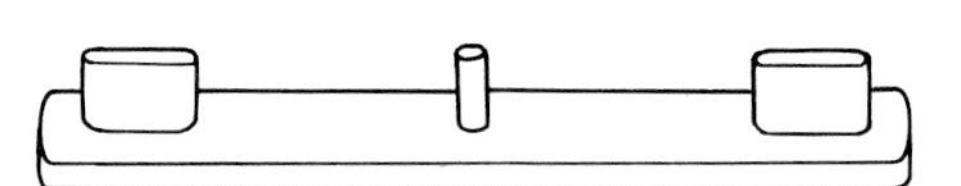

Above: A peg bar ensures that the various layers of cel, drawing and background are aligned exactly. Each layer has a row of holes at the end for placing over the pegs.

Cel is the transparent acetate on which the animation is traced and painted. Cel sheets come in various thicknesses, from 75 to 125 microns, and are sold punched or unpunched. The field sizes are standard 12 and 15 inches or larger specialized cel. Panning cels, used for animation which is to be laid over backgrounds, are usually two and a half or three fields in length.

Normally cel is transparent, but frosted cel is opaque. A special spray makes it transparent where required. Frosted cel can be drawn on with pencil or crayon. Frosting spray is also available, so that small areas of transparent cel can be frosted.

Paint and gloves

There are various paints made specially for animation. The main requirements of an animation paint are that it should flow easily, that it should not crack when exposed to heat and, of course, that the colours should remain true over a period of time. The paint's consistency should be such that it hangs from the brush without dripping.

Cel paint should never be brushed on. It is guided over the surface of the cel up to the traced line. The paint is always applied to the back of the cel. This is the side with edges which curve upward; the top of the cel will be curved down, so that when it is placed under the camera platen it lies flat.

Cotton editing gloves should always be worn when handling cel, be it tracing, painting or shooting. The thumb and forefinger of the gloves are cut off at the top so that pens and brushes can be easily manipulated.

Graticule

A graticule is an essential item for two-dimensional animation. Graticules are manufactured in two sizes, 12 inches and 15 inches. Although it is possible to make copies of an existing graticule, this is not recommended, as a degree of inaccuracy inevitably occurs when repeated copies are produced. It is essential that the graticule gives a very accurate picture of the positioning of animation, artwork and layout in relation to the lens centre.

Rostrum stand and camera

Although professional animation is made using hired or in-house specialized rostrum stands and cameras, it is possible to make a

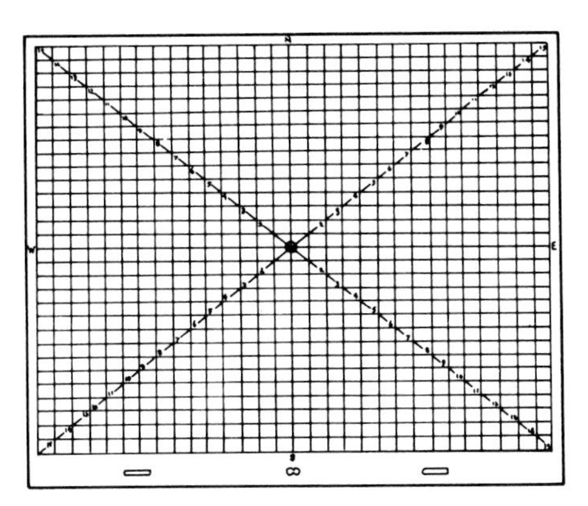

Above: A typical graticule, printed with a fine grid so that the size of the area to be photographed can be checked precisely.

stand for personal use. Both 8mm and 16mm cameras have become relatively cheap if bought second-hand. The inimitable Bolex is the favourite, although like all non-pin-registration cameras, it suffers from some inaccuracy of frame frequency. Pin-registration cameras have a pin in the gate which engages with the film sprocket, holding the film firmly in place as the exposure is made. If the camera does not have a pin, when a number of exposures are made with the camera running forward and reverse, the frame may not always return to exactly the same position.

The simplest of rostrum stands can be made by cutting a hole in a wooden box and fixing the camera in this hole. The base of the box serves as the table top. This system does not permit movement of the table, but by using a zoom lens the field size can be altered. Lights can also be fixed to the sides of the box in the correct alignment to the ersatz table top. A rostrum is similar in many ways to a photographic enlarger, and a heavy-duty enlarger can easily be adapted for rostrum purposes. It is important, however, to fix the column firmly to a wall.

Single-frame video

Single-frame video is an ideal medium for learning and producing animation. Unfortunately, the costs put it outside the range of the individual animator. However, it seems likely that the costs will fall as the technology develops.

Sound and editing

Sound production and editing are areas which can be costly. Simply animating to a pre-recorded soundtrack is often the best answer for the beginner. The development of sophisticated computer packages, however, has added a new dimension to this aspect of animation production, making it possible to produce complex soundtracks at low cost.

The cost of purchasing editing equipment can be considerable and even renting rates are often prohibitive. There is a range of equipment available for the amateur 8mm and Super 8mm market; 16mm production is less well served. It is possible to plan the animation so that it is shot exactly as required and there is no need for editing. But even so, a splicer and a synchronizer of some sort will prove invaluable.

Computer programs

There are increasingly useful programs available for personal computers, especially Atari, Amiga and Archimedes. They fall into two categories, paintbox programs and animation programs. It is important if possible to try out these programs before purchase, to ensure that they are appropriate. Bear in mind that when the animation is produced, it will have to be saved, either through hard copy or by frame-grabbing on to video. The hardware for either of these tasks can be expensive.

The Basic Production Process

The production process which developed out of the studio system is still the most widely used in animation. Individual animators adapt it to their own needs, as do those working with model and handmade animation techniques.

An animated film is first developed from the initial idea through to a strip-cartoon version, the storyboard. Once this has been finalized, the soundtrack is recorded, initially consisting of music, voices and effects on separate tracks. The soundtrack is broken down, analysed and transcribed to bar charts as a guide for the animator.

The animator or animation director then works with a layout artist to produce a detailed breakdown of the action. This is used by the background artists to draw the backgrounds and by the animators to produce the key drawings – those drawings which are at the extreme position of each movement. These key drawings are then in-betweened by the assistant. In a complex production, the movement may have further in-betweens added by an in-betweener. The drawings are then filmed to see if the movement works. If the results of this line test are good, the animation goes on to the next stage of production.

The conventional method of producing the final artwork is on cel or clear acetate. The animation drawings are traced on to the cel, which is then painted on the back by the painters. Different parts of the picture appear on different levels of cel in a single frame. So for a figure, the body may be on one sheet, the arms on another, the eyes on a third, and so on. All the levels combine to make a complete picture.

The cels, together with the backgrounds and the instructions for the shooting (called dope sheets or exposure sheets), then go to the camera. When the scenes have been shot they are sent for rush prints – ungraded prints produced quickly by the laboratory. These prints are then used by the editor to lay the soundtracks and edit the picture, making what is called the cutting copy. When this has been done, the sound is mixed (dubbed) on to a single magnetic soundtrack.

The picture is then sent for negative cutting. The original negatives are cut to correspond to the cutting copy. The sound is also transferred to film, making an optical sound negative. The sound and picture negatives are then printed together to make a married or combined print, and this is colour-graded until the correct print has been achieved. This is the final print for release, and the information for all consequent prints can be obtained from this master.

This process is broadly the same whether the film is 8mm, 16mm or 35mm. However, the development of computers and video systems has produced significant changes in some aspects of the process. A great deal of animation for commercials is now shot partly on video and then combined with conventional film footage. This opens up a range of possibilities at the video-editing stage, such as the introduction of computerized images, the manipulation of images by paintbox systems and the enhancement of frames.

But although new technology has become an essential part of the production process and computer animation is becoming more and more sophisticated, the fundamental character of animation remains. It is a construction made up of very many different parts. This building up of images through time is what makes the discipline so applicable to different technologies as they develop.

USEFUL ADDRESSES

Manufacturers and Suppliers

Animation Equipment Engineering
8 Barnhill, Pinner, Middlesex HA5 2SX, UK
Tel: (01) 868 762

Art Colour Products
12455 Brandford St, Arieta, CA 91131, USA
Paints and cel vinyl.

Birns and Sawyer Inc
1026 N. Highland Ave, Hollywood, CA 90038, USA
Computer animation equipment.

Arthur Brown & Brothers
2 West 46th St, New York, NY 10036, USA
General art suppliers.

Cartoon Colour Company
9024 Lindblade St, Culver City, CA 90232, USA
Cel vinyl and animation suppliers.

Chroma Colour
Cartoon House, 27/29 Whitfield St, London W1P 5RB, UK
Tel: (01) 636 2103 Telex: 298 668
Supply a vast range of equipment and materials for animation and provide demonstrations of equipment.

Eos Electronics AV Ltd
Weston Sq, Barry, South Glamorgan CF6 7YF, UK
Tel: (0446) 741212 Telex: 497223 EOS G
Manufacture single frame video unit.

Film Sales
145 Nathan Way, Woolwich Industrial Estate, London SE28 0BE, UK
Tel: (01) 311 2000 Telex: 941 9814 FSL G
Suppliers of cel paper and specialized paint.

Adolph Gasser
5733 Geary Blvd, San Francisco, CA 94121, USA
Basic cel animation suppliers.

Alan Gordon Enterprises Inc
1430 Cahuenga Blvd, Hollywood, CA 90028, USA
A major supplier of motion picture equipment for purchase or rental.

IIMC
Wellington House, Wellington St, Thame, Oxon OX9 3BU, UK
Suppliers of the NAC Quick Action Recorder, the computerized line testing unit.

Langford and Hill
10 Warwick St, London W1R 6LS, UK
A wide range of general art materials.

Lyon-Lamb Video Animation Systems
4531 Empire Ave, Burbank, CA 91505, USA
Single frame videos and encoders.

NAC Inc
17 Kowa Buildings, Nishi-Azabu 1-Chome, Minato-Ku, Tokyo, Japan
Manufacturers of the NAC Quick Action Recorder and suppliers of motion picture equipment.

Nielson Hordell
Central Trading Estate, Staines, Middlesex TW18 4UU, UK
Rostrum camera manufacturer and supplier of motion control equipment as well as studio equipment.

Oxberry
180 Broad St, Carlstadt, NJ 07072, USA
Manufacturers of animation stands and cameras.

Transilwarp Inc
14335 Iseli Rd, Santa Fe Springs, CA 90670, USA
A major supplier of acetate cels.

Organizations and Colleges

ABC Entertainment
2040 Ave of the Stars, Los Angeles, CA 90067, USA
Tel: (212) 887 5000 Telex: 422 003
Mrs Jennie Trias, vice-president of children's programs

American Film Institute
John F. Kennedy Centre, Washington, DC 20566, USA

Antenne 2
22, ave Montaigne, 75387 Paris Cedex 08, France
Tel: 45 55 92 90

ASIFA International (International Association of Animated Film)
Raoul Servais, 3 Dimmereieweg, 8432 Middelkerke, Belgium

BBC Enterprises
Television Centre, Wood Lane, London W12 8QT, UK
Tel: (01) 743 8000 Telex: 934 678
Mr James Arnold Baker

Bilifa
West Surrey College of Art & Design
Falkner Rd, Farnham, Surrey
Roger Noake, president
Information on schools, colleges, courses and workshops in the UK can be obtained from Bilifa.

British Film Institute
6 Stephen St, London W1P 1PL, UK
Tel: (01) 255 1444 Telex: 27624 BFIL DNG

Buzzco Associates Inc
Kraemer Marilyn, 870 Seventh Ave, New York, NY 10019, USA
Tel: (212) 586 6333

California Institute of the Arts
Bob Winquist or Jules Engel
24700 McBean Parkway, Valencia, CA 91355, USA

Emily Carr College of Art
Animation Department, Hugh Foulds
1399 Johnston St, Vancouver, BC, V6H 2R9

Channel 4
60 Charlotte St, London W1P 2AY
Tel: (01) 631 4444 Telex: 893 355
Mr Paul Madden, animation consultant

Columbia College,
Film & Video Dept, Barry Young
600 S. Michigan, Chicago, IL 60605, USA
Tel: (312) 663 1600 ext 311

Computer Animation Laboratory Gmbh
Beethovenstrasse 4, 6000 Frankfurt 1, West Germany
Tel: (069) 74 05 71 Telex: 176997639

Finnish Broadcasting Company/TV2
Tohlopinranta 31, 33270 Tempere, Finland
Tel: (931) 445 455 Telex: 22-176
Mr Pertti Nykänen, director

FR3
116, avenue du Président-Kennedy, 75790 Paris Cedex 16, France
Tel: 42 30 22 22 Telex: 630 720F
Mrs Mireille Chalvon

HTV Limited
Television Centre, Culverhouse Cross, Cardiff CF5 6X5, UK
Tel: (0222) 590 590 Telex: 497 703
Mr Derek Clark, senior producer

International IMC
Wellington House, Wellington St, Thame, Oxon OX9 3B4, UK
Tel:(0844) 217333 Telex: 837 354
Mr Alan Neal, director
Mr Robert Wheeler, animation manager

INA
Tour Gamma A, 193–197 rue de Bercy, 75582 Paris Cedex 12, France
Tel: 40 04 64 00 Telex: 214 422

Kask
Academiestraat 2, 9000 Gent, Belgium
Tel: (091) 23 52 31

Liverpool Polytechnic
Graphic Design Dept, 2A Myrtle St, Liverpool L7 7DN, UK

Middlesex Polytechnic
Cat Hill Barnet, EN 48th Hertfordshire, UK
Tel: (01) 440-5181

MTV On Air Promotion
1775 Broadway, New York, NY 10019, USA
Tel: (212) 713 7281 Telex: 424 804
MTV UI

New York University
Institute of Film and TV, John Canemaker
65 South Bldg, Washington Square, New York, NY 10003, USA

Office National du Film Canada
a/s Bureau des Festivals, ONF, BP 6100, Montreal, Quebec, H3C 3H5, Canada
Tel: (514) 283-9805 Telex: 05 82 66 80
Natfilm Mtl

Polski Film
Rue Mazowiecka 6/8, Varsovie, Poland
Tel: 268455 Telex: 813 640

RAI TV 1
Viale Mazzini 14, 00195 Roma, Italy
Tel: 06 368 64 127 Telex: 436 144 32
Mr Luciano Scaffa

Rhode Island School of Design,
Film/Video Department, Yvonne Andersen
2 College St, Providence, RI 02903, USA

Royal College of Art
Kensington Gore, SW7 2EU London, UK
Tel: (01) 584 5020

San Francisco Art Institute
Larry Jordan
800 Chestnut, San Francisco, CA 94133, USA

Sheridan College of Applied Arts and Technology
School of Visual Arts, Tom Halley
Trafalgar Rd, Oakville, Ontario L6H 2L1, Canada

Sogitec
32, bd de la République, 92100 Boulogne, Billancourt, France
Tel: (1) 46 08 13 13 Telex: 260 922

Thames Television International
149 Tottenham Court Rd, London W1P 9LL, UK
Tel: (01) 387 9494

UCLA Animation Workshop
Dept of Film & TV, Dan McLaughlin
405 Hilgard Avenue, Los Angeles, CA 90024, USA

West Surrey College
Falkner Rd, Farnham, Surrey GU9 7DS,
Tel: (0252) 72 2441

Zagreb Film
Vlaska 70, 41000 Zagreb, Yugoslavia
Tel: (041) 275559 Telex: 21 790
Mr Bruno Gamula

Festivals

Annecy International Animated Film Festival
dir Jean Luc Xiberras
BP 399, 74013 Annecy Cedex, France
A biennial festival held in early June. The most prestigious of the competitive animation festivals, with a great deal going on, it can be overwhelming.

British Animation Festival, Bristol
dir Irene Kotlarz
41B Hornsey Lane Gardens, London N6 5NY, UK
A non-competitive festival with an excellent venue and good programming. It takes place biennially in November.

Hiroshima International Animation Festival
1–1 Nakajima-cho, Naka-ku 730, Japan
A very interesting new festival which takes place biennially in August.

Los Angeles Animation Celebration
2222 S. Barrington, Los Angeles, CA 90064, USA
The only US festival which attracts international films.

Ottawa International Animation Festival
c/o Canadian Film Institute, 150 Rideau St, Ottawa, Ontario K1N 5X6, Canada
A new festival held in September.

Zagreb World Festival of Animated Film
dir Borivaj Dovnikovic
Nova Ves 18, 41000 Zagreb, Yugoslavia
A biennial competitive festival alternating with Annecy. A smaller event, it is particularly strong on documentation.

There are also festivals in Stuttgart, Amsterdam, Esphino (Portugal) and, to mark the 60th year of the Shanghai Studio, in Shanghai. Information on these and other events can be obtained from ASIFA, the international organisation for animation (address above).

GLOSSARY

Aerial image
A method by which previously processed film is projected from beneath on to an under-lit ground glass surface, and combined with titles and other graphics, which are inked and opaqued on transparent cels placed on top of the surface and illuminated by overhead lighting units. The combined imagery is then photographed from above in a stop-motion process to produce a wide variety of unusual illusory effects.

Animatic
A filmed version of the storyboard, also known as a Leica reel.

Animation
Derived from the Latin word *anima* meaning 'life' or *animare*, 'to breathe life into', this general term describes a wide range of film-making techniques shot frame by frame to create the illusion of motion.

Back lighting
Also known as bottom-lighting or under-lighting. A method of illuminating artwork from below, as opposed to above, when photographing a scene. It is used to create effects such as stars and glowing letters.

Bar chart
A printed chart used by directors and animators in planning the movement of art and camera. All the elements of a film – music, voices, sound effects, visuals – are noted frame by frame in their relationship to time.

Cel
A sheet of thin, transparent acetate on to which the animator's final artwork is drawn. When the cel is placed over a background and photographed, the clear cel does not show, thus creating the illusion of characters within a setting. Frosted cel is now available, which makes it possible to use crayons instead of paints to colour the artwork and creates a frosted or misty effect.

Claymation
An animation technique using pliable clay figures whose positions are manipulated fractionally before each exposure.

Cut
A direct or immediate transition from one scene to the next which may or may not require the removal of unwanted footage during the editing process.

Cut-outs and collage
An animation technique using cut-out and jointed figures which are manipulated slightly between each exposure. The figures can be either designed by the animator or lifted from magazine artwork and other sources. Collage is a method of combining a variety of images, both original and found, to create a montage effect.

Cycle
A series of drawings that are photographed over and over. The final drawing of the cycle moves logically into the first, to achieve the appearance of continuous repetitive motion. Cycles are usually used for movements that are repeated without variation, e.g. walks or runs.

Dissolve
A visual effect in which one scene gradually fades out as another simultaneously fades in to replace it. This technique is commonly used in animation to suggest changes in both time and location.

Dope sheet
A visual synopsis of the animation sequence prepared by the animator. It details the position of each level of artwork in relation to its background, in conjunction with dialogue and sound effects, etc.

Editing
The arranging, assembly, splicing, synchronizing and general preparation of the various film elements into a logical flow of picture and sound information to create the finished film.

Fade
A camera effect in which the image either gradually appears from black (fade in) or disappears to black (fade out).

Field size
The area covered by the camera lens and, therefore, the area within which the animator must contain his artwork. TV cut-off titles and other artwork prepared for televison must be confined to the 'safety field' – i.e. an area comfortably within TV transmission limits. See GRATICULE.

Frame
An individual photograph on a strip of film. When the film is projected each frame is normally seen for one twenty-fourth of a second, but one twenty-fifth of a second for television.

Graticule
A punched sheet of heavy acetate printed to indicate the sizes of all standard fields. When placed over the artwork, it indicates the area in which the action will take place. It is used by the director, animators and camera operator to check the size of the area the camera will photograph. Also known as field guide or field chart. See also p. 145.

In-betweens
The intermediate drawings that fall between the extreme points of a movement. In studio animation these drawings are done by an assistant animator or 'in-betweener'.

Key drawing and extreme
The key drawings and extremes, drawn by the

animator, show the principal points of each movement and how it will be continued. Spacing guides are added by the animator to show the assistant the timing and spacing of the in-between drawings.

Line test
Before the production of the cel artwork begins, the animation drawings are shot on film, video or Quick Action Recorder to test the movement. This is called a line test.

Lip sync (synchronization)
The matching of the characters' mouth movements to the recorded dialogue on the soundtrack.

Matte
An opaque shape which blocks out part of the film, stopping it being exposed. A new image can then be inserted in this unexposed area.

Merchandizing
Term used to refer to the promotion of products linked to characters in animated films – for example soft toys, T-shirts, posters and greeting cards based on cartoon characters such as The Care Bears, Henry's Cat, Snoopy or Heman and Masters of the Universe.

Mixing
The combination of the various soundtracks, dialogue, music, sound effects, etc. re-recorded on to a single soundtrack that is used to prepare the composite print. In Britain, mixing is often called 'dubbing'.

Model sheet (character sheet)
A reference sheet for the use of animators to ensure that a character has a consistent appearance throughout a film. It consists of a series of drawings showing how the character is constructed, its size relative to other characters and objects, and how it appears from various angles and with various expressions.

Multiplane camera
A special animation stand developed by Lotte Reiniger in the 1920s and at the Disney Studio in 1937. The artwork is divided into foreground, middle and background elements and placed on glass frames several inches apart, thus creating an illusion of realistic depth and changing perspectives.

Pan
A visual technique in which the camera appears to move horizontally or vertically. In animation this effect is achieved by moving artwork under the camera on panning pegs.

Panning or travelling pegs
Specialized moveable pegs on the camera table, calibrated and controlled by dials which allow the artwork to be moved to accommodate moving shots such as pans.

Peg bars
Strip of metal or plastic with fixed pins used to keep drawings, cels and background in precise registration with one another. Identical to set-up on a camera table. See also p. 144.

Pixillation
A stop-motion technique in which objects and live actors are photographed frame by frame to achieve unusual effects of motion.

Platen
A heavy sheet of glass used to hold cels and other artwork flat in position during filming. Eliminates shadows from painted areas and cut-outs falling on the background art.

Production
a) *Pre-production* Term used to denote work to be done on a film project before the artwork stage, e.g. research and planning, budgeting, equipment and personnel.
b) *Production* Term used to describe all the procedures required to complete the visual and audio material for a film, e.g. storyboarding, scripting, character design, sound recording, titles, filming, processing and print.
c) *Post-production* The work done on a film project once photography has been completed, such as editing, special effects, soundtrack spotting and mixing.

Quick Action Recorder (QAR)
A specially designed unit which photographs animation frame by frame. Its instant-replay facility makes it particularly useful for line testing. The images are digested by a computer and stored in a frame store, allowing the user a high degree of manipulation.

Registration
The exact alignment of the various levels of artwork in precise relation to each other, made possible in animation by the use of the peg-bar system.

Rostrum camera
A motion picture camera with single-frame and reverse capabilities for animation work. It can be mounted on columns and suspended directly over the artwork to be filmed. It can also be mounted on a flat bed for optical work. This system enables the camera to move vertically in relation to the artwork.

Rotoscope
A device patented by Max Fleischer in 1917 that projects live-action film, one frame at a time, on to a glass surface from below. When drawing paper is placed over the glass it allows the animator to trace off the live-action images as a guide to complicated movements.

Shorts and features
Short Animated film anything from one to 33 minutes in length.
Feature A full-length animated film, usually 60–120 minutes long.

Show reel
A compilation reel of an animator's film work used as a portfolio. Nowadays show reels are generally presented on video cassettes.

Single-frame video
Video rostrum camera attached to a computerized unit which facilitates frame-by-frame recording, making it particularly suitable for animation intended for television transmission.

Storyboard
A series of small consecutive drawings plotting key movements in a film narrative, accompanied by caption-like descriptions of the action and sound, which are arranged comic-strip fashion and used to plan a film.

Superimposition
A method of combining two or more film images to create a composite image. This can be achieved at the filming stage by back-winding the exposed film in the camera and re-exposing it, by using the aerial image unit, or as a laboratory process during post-production.

Tracing back
Sometimes part of the animation remains unchanged from one drawing to the next. In such cases, the animator may leave it to the tracer to complete the drawing by 'tracing back' that part of the animation from a previous drawing.

Wipe effect
A transition in which one scene appears to advance on to the screen over another; the leading edge may be straight line, or it may describe a shape.

Zoom
An effect in which artwork within the shooting field of the camera is made to appear progressively larger or smaller by moving the camera closer to or further away from it.

FILMOGRAPHY

The Adventures of Prince Achmed (Die Abenteuer Das Prinzen Achmed) Germany 1926
Dir Karl Kock, mus Wolfgang Zeller, magic & scenery Walther Ruttman, Berthold Bartosch, Alexander Kasden, story based on *The Arabian Nights*, title decorations Edmond Dulac, typography C. F. Parkins, prod Comenius-Film. 16mm, b/w, 63 mins.
The adventures of Prince Achmed, Aladdin and the Princesses Peri Banu and Dinarzade as a result of the evil machinations of a wicked sorcerer. Silhouette animation.

Babylon UK 1986
Dir Peter Lord, David Sproxton, scenery Lowe Howard, des Andrew Franks, ani Peter Lord, Richard Bolesxoaski, Nick Park, bkg Chris Lyons, Michael Wright, ph David Sproxton, ed Dave MacCormick, mus Martin Kiszko, v Tony Robinson, prod Occam for Channel 4. 35mm, colour, 14½ mins.
A diffident waiter observes an assembly of arms dealers. The conclusion is an inevitable holocaust.

Begone Dull Care Canada 1949
Dir Norman McLaren, Evelyn Lambert, mus Oscar Peterson, prod NFBC.
One of the best examples of McLaren's technique of drawing on film.

Binary Bit Patterns USA, 1969
Dir/prod Michael Whitney, dis Arts Council of Great Britain. 16mm, colour, 3 mins.
An early work by the son of John Whitney, without doubt the most famous pioneer of computer film. Following his father's lead, Michael Whitney produced this film which is an exploration of formal abstraction using geometric configurations.

The Black Dog UK 1987
Dir Alison de Vere, prod Lee Stork, dist Film Four Int, tel: (01) 621 4444, telex: 892355. 35mm, colour, 18 mins.
A woman accompanied by a black dog moves about in fantasy places, space and time.

Breakfast on the Grass USSR 1988
Dir/sc Prit Pjarn, des Prit Pjarn, Miljard Kiljk, ani M. Aruljep, M. Busman, T. Juring, E. Kurg, mus Olav Ehala, cam Jano Piljma, prod Tallinfilm. Colour, 26 mins.
An animated fantasy based on the famous painting of Edouard Manet. One of the new critical works from Estonia, the film won the Grand Prix in the Zagreb Festival 1988.

Damon the Mower UK 1972
Dir George Dunning. 35mm, b/w.
An enigmatic film by the director of *Yellow Submarine*, based on four poems by the seventeenth-century metaphysical poet Andrew Marvell.

Dancers USA 1987
Dir/sc/ani Susan Van Baerie, des Susan Van Baerie and Steve Depaola, cam Ariel Shaw, prod Computer Graphics Laboratory, New York Institute of Technology. B/w, 4 mins. Computer animation.
Three statues perform a dance in a large bay window, the fourth does not know the steps and improvises. Made using a programme designed by Dick Lundin and David Sturman on a Vax and using U8's NYIT Software.

Dimensions of a Dialogue Czechoslovakia 1982
Dir Jan Svankmajer, ani Vlasta Pospisilova, cam Vladimir Malik, mus Jan Klusak, ed Klara Stoklasova, prod Kratky Film, Praha. 16mm, colour original version without commentary.
Two heads, one made of vegetables and the other of kitchen implements, constantly devour and regurgitate each other.

Dreamless Sleep UK 1986
Dir/ani David Anderson, sc/p David Hopkins, cos Maggie Hayes, prod Occam for Channel 4. 35mm, 9 mins.
An experiment in texture, marrying technical innovation with a story that explores a couple's sleepless fears.

Egged On USA 1926
Dir/sc Charles Bowers, Harold Muller, Ted Sears. 35mm, silent, b/w, 20 mins.
An early use of pixillation, for a story in which an inventor's egg-laying machine suddenly begins to lay automobiles.

Felix Makes a Movie USA 1924
Dir Pat Sullivan, ani Otto Messmer. 16mm, silent, b/w, 10 mins.
Animation's first star, Felix, decides to make his own movie. But he gets into trouble when his children turn the camera on to Felix while he is flirting in the park, and his wife sees the results.

George and Rosemary Canada 1987
Dir/sc/des/ani Alison Snowden, David Fine, sound David Fine, Patrick Godfrey, cam Pierre Landry, Jaques Avoine, Robin L. P. Bain, prod Eunice Macaulay NFBC, dist NFBC. Colour, 9 mins.
George Edgecombe harbours a secret passion for Rosemary Harris, the lady who lives across the street. He imagines different ways in which he might approach her and keeps trying to muster up the courage to do so.

Getting Started Canada 1979
Dir/sc/des Richard Condie, mus Patrick Godfrey, prod NFBC. 16mm, colour, 12 mins.
To some degree everyone shares the common human condition of procrastination. In this film a pianist attempts to practise his repertoire before an important concert.

Great UK 1974
Dir/ani Bob Godfrey Movie Emporium, sc Colin Pearson, Bob Godfrey, Richard Taylor, Robin Smyth, Paul Weisser, Colin Pearson, mus Jonathan Hodge, ed Peter Hearn, Tony Fish, voice Richard Briers (Brunel), Barbara More, Harry Fowler, Angus Lennie, ph Julia Holdaway, Kent Houston, Alan More, prod/dis Bob Godfrey Films, 55 Neal Street, London WC2 (01 240 1889). 16mm, colour, 30 mins.
Oscar-winning tribute to the great Isambard Kingdom Brunel.

The Great Cognito USA 1982
Dir/prod Will Vinton, des Laymation, ani Barry Bruce, sc Susan Shadburne, John Morrison, mus/effects Bill Scream, voice John Morrison, dist Pyramid Films. 35mm, colour, 4½ mins.
A night club performer dazzles his audience with amazing impersonations of the men and events of the Pacific War.

Hunger Canada 1973
Dir Peter Foldes, prod National Film Board of Canada, dis National Film Board of Canada/Contemporary Films/Scottish Film Library. U-matic colour, 12 mins.
Award-winning film from the late Peter Foldes. Perhaps the most accomplished of those early computer films which attempted to use computer-generated key-frame animation. It is also one of the few computer films which attempts to put across a message through its metaphorical story and imagery.

I Fly to You in my Remembrance (Ya k vam lechu vospominanyem) USSR 1977
Dir/sc Andrei Khrzhanovsky, des V. Yankilevsky, Yu. Batanin, cam I. Skidan-Bosin, S. Kashcheeyeva, mus A. Schnitke, prod Soyuzmultfilm. 35mm, colour, Russian language version 30 minutes.
The first part of a poetic film based on Alexander Pushkin's drawings and manuscripts.

Jude USA 1982
Dir/sc/prod Drew Klausner.
Jude's subject matter is the holocaust. As time passes the events of the past, horrific as they are, change in our minds and an effort of will is required not to forget. The film combines documentary footage with hand-drawn rotoscoped animation.

Luxo Jr USA 1986
Dir/ani John Lasseter, prod Pixar, San Rafael, California. U-matic colour, 2 mins.
Award-winning film about an angle-poise lamp, its child and a ball! The piece displays superbly realistic rendering, lighting and movement. Its character animation is perhaps the best yet achieved in computer film.

The Man Who Planted Trees Canada 1987
Dir/sc/des Frederic Back, story Jean Giono, ani Frederic Back (assisted by Lina Gagnon) mus Normand Roger, voice Philippe Noiret, sound Michel Descombes, dist Les Enterprises Radio Canada, 1055 Est, Bd Dorchester, Quebec, H2L 4S5 Montreal, Canada. 35mm, colour, 30 mins.
The story of a man who devotes his life to bringing back life to a deserted landscape, oblivious to wars and setbacks, which seem petty in comparison to his creation.

Neighbours Canada 1952
Dir/ani/prod Norman McLaren, cam Wolf Koenig, mus Norman McLaren.
The first film to be wholly pixillated, though the technique was used in early trickfilms.

Night on Bald Mountain France 1934
Dir Alexandre Alexeieff, Clair Parker, dist BFI. 16mm, b/w, 6 mins.
An experimental fantasy based on Mussorgsky's music. Made on the pinboard apparatus invented by Alexeieff and Parker, in which the animated image is produced from the shadows of thousands of pins.

Oilspot and Lipstick USA 1987
Dir/sc/des/ani/mus/effects/cam/prod Disney Computer Animation Late Night Group, dist Buena Vista Distribution. Colour, 3½ mins, computer animation.
This early morning visit to the junk yard features a whimsical version of man's best friend: Oilspot the junk-yard dog and his ladyfriend Lipstick.

One of Those Days USA 1988
Dir/sc/des/ani Bill Plympton, mus effects Phil Lee, cam John Schnall.
A humorous point-of-view film which shows the worst day in anyone's life.

Pictures from a Gallery USA, 1976
Dir Lillian Schwartz, mus A. Millar, prod Lilyan Prod Inc, dis Lillian Schwartz, 524 Ridge Road, Watchung, NJ 07060, USA. 16mm, colour, 6 mins.
Highly influential early film from one of the pioneers of computer-generated art. A move away from the total abstraction displayed in the first computer film of Lillian Schwartz. Picture processed photographs from the artist film-maker's family are abstracted in a divisionistic manner.

Poligon USSR 1978
Dir A. Petrof, sc S. Gonsovski, des G. Barinova, prod Gosinko. 35mm, colour, 10 mins.
The story of a monster which turns against its creators.

On Probation UK 1986
Dir/sc/ani/prod Peter Lord, David Sproxton, bkg Chris Lyons, ph David Sproxton, ed Dave MacCormick. 16mm, 5 mins.
A film based on a soundtrack recorded in a probation centre for young people.

Rehearsal for Extinct Anatomies UK 1988
Dir/sc/des/anim Brothers Quay, mus Leszek Jankowski, effects Larry Sider, cam Brothers Quay, prod Keith Griffiths, Konnick Studios for Channel 4. Object and model animation.
The film is dedicated to an anonymous anatomical specimen – to the single hair, still dreaming on its brow, with its desire to disturb the wallpaper and things outside.

Set in Motion USA 1987
Dir/sc/des/ani/cam Jane Aaron, mus Donald Fagen. Colour, 4 mins.
A rhythmic, free-flowing vision of moments from daily life using cut-out and object animation.

Snow White USA 1933
Dir Max Pleischer, 16mm, b/w, 7 mins.
Betty Boop stars in a spooky version of the fairy-tale. With music by Cab Calloway.

The Snowman UK 1982
Dir Dianne Jackson, supervising dir Jimmy T. Murakami, mus Howard Blake, ed John Carey, cam Peter Turner, exec prod Ian Harvey, prod John Coates, Snowman Enterprises for TVC. 16mm, colour, 26 mins.
Christmas special telling the story of a small boy who builds a snowman for Christmas. The snowman comes alive and leads him off on a journey through the night skies.

The Sound Collector Canada 1982
Dir Lyn Smithani, cam Pierre Landrey, mus Norman Roger, ed/effects Ken Page, prod NFBC, Dist NFBC. 35mm colour, 12 mins.
Leonard is a six-year-old with an unusual hobby. His older brother ridicules him and his father says he is a daydreamer, but the boy has a wonderful way to liven up every day. He collects sounds.

Stanley and Stella: Breaking the Ice USA 1987
Dir Larry Malone, des Robert Fusfield, ani, char Craig Reynolds, ani Phillippe Bergeron, prod Michael Wahrman, Prod Co Symbolics Inc, Graphics Division, Los Angeles, CA. VHS video, colour, 1 min 52 secs.
The additional representational complexity of this recent film is provided by the simulation of the motion of flocks of birds and schools of fish. Symbolics' Craig Reynolds developed the experimental programs in behavioural simulation utilized in this piece.

Tango Poland 1981
Dir Zbigniew Rybcinsky, dist BFI. 35mm, colour, 10 mins.
Award-winning tour de force of timing by the Polish experimental film-maker.

Tale of Tales USSR 1979
Dir Juri Norstejn, sc Juri Norstejn, L Petrusevskaja, des Juri Norstejn, F Jarbusova, mus M Meerovic. 35mm colour, 27 mins.
A story which meditates on the transience of time and the memories which remain as it passes.

Top Priority Canada 1982
Dir Ishii Patel, mus Norman Roger, prod NFBC.
The story of a poor Indian family's wait for water during a drought. Instead they receive a gift of equipment for military use. The technique is Plasticine on glass.

Three Inventors (Les Trois Inventeurs) France 1979
Dir/sc/des Michel Ocelot, mus Christian Maire, sound Robert Cohen-Solal, prod AAA. 5mm, colour, 13 mins.
A family of inventors work on fulfilling their dreams in a room full of white lace. People do not appreciate their attitudes which differ from their own.

Ubu UK 1978
Dir/des Geoff Dunbar, sc Alfred Jarry, ed Terry Brown, prod Grand Slamm Animation, dist Arts Council of Great Britain. 35mm, colour, 20 mins.
Based on the play *Ubu Roi* by Alfred Jarry. The film uses a brutal graphic style and a language of sound to re-create the meaning of the original production.

The Victor UK 1985
Dir/sc Phil Austin, Derek Hayes, story from a documentary film *Guinea Pig Soldiers* (1976), ani Gaston Marzio, Bill Majee, Kevin Molloy, Anna Brockett, Gary McCarver, mus Dirk Higgins, voice Robert Llewellyn, David Tate, Shaun Curry, Prod Animation City, 16/18 Beak St, London W1R 3HA, UK, dist Channel 4, 60 Charlotte St, London, UK. 35mm, colour, 14 mins.
A film about experiments with drugs on GI volunteers. Is Jimmy Mullen the object of an obsessive punishment or a horrific military experiment?

The World of Children UK 1984
Dir Vera Neubauer, cam Bill Boulk, mus Gary Carpenter, prod Simon Hartog (Spectre Productions). 16mm, 14½ mins, live action/animation.
How does the environment affect the child? Is it possible to learn to talk without the prejudices built into the language?

Zoom and Bored USA 1959
Dir Chuck Jones, prod Warner Brothers, 16mm, colour, 7 mins.
One of Jones's personal favourites of all his Roadrunner films; the Roadrunner's unexpected 'beep-beep's nearly drive the poor coyote insane.

BIBLIOGRAPHY

Blair, Preston *Animation* Walter Foster Art Books 1949
The bible for animators. Preston Blair animated Red in *Red Hot Riding Hood* by Tex Avery.

Godfrey, Bob *Film Animation Book* BBC Books 1974
An entertaining introduction to animation techniques, with many personal insights.

Grush, Byron *The Shoestring Animator: Making Films with Super 8* Contemporary Books, Chicago 1981
A useful book on simple techniques such as cut-out and making light boxes and rostrums for the amateur.

Halas, John *Masters of Animation* BBC Books/Salem House 1987
Published in conjunction with a series of video study tapes, this makes a very useful resource, bringing together animation film extracts which can be difficult to locate.

Hayward, Stan *Scriptwriting for Animation* Focal Press 1984
A step-by-step approach to the technicalities of scripting for animation.

Heath, Bob *Animation in 12 Hard Lessons* Robert P. Heath Productions, New York 1972
Almost a study resource book, this contains exercises which are designed to help assistant animators.

Jankel, Annabel and Morton, Rocky *Creative Computer Graphics* Cambridge University Press 1984
A lively and lavishly illustrated work by the creators of Max Headroom. More technical in some areas than others, but a good background to the way this important area has developed.

Laybourne, Kit *The Animation Book* Crown Publishers, New York 1979
One of the best of the how-to-do-it books, with information on most conventional techniques. Unfortunately now out of print.

Levitan, Elil *Electronic Imaging Techniques* Van Nostrand Reinhold 1977
By the author of *Animation Techniques and Commercial Film Production*, which was a standard work, this book extends the approach into the area of new technology. This part of the work has dated, but the section which deals with animation production is still applicable.

Masden, R. *Animated Film: Concepts, Methods, Uses* Interland, NY 1969
A wide-ranging useful book for both ideas and techniques. Unfortunately now out of print, it remains a basic text.

Perisnic, Zoran *The Animation Stand* Focal Press and Hastings House 1976
A guide to the rostrum camera by one of the foremost experts in special effects.

Reiniger, Lotte *Shadow Puppets, Shadow Theatre and Shadow Film* Batsford, London and Watson-Guptil, NY 1970
Though the book deals with Reiniger's technique of silhouette film, the information can easily be applied to the production of cut-out animation.

Salt, Brian *Basic Animation Stand Techniques* Oxford, Pergamon Press 1977
A detailed technical guide to preparing camera movements and working out timings. His further work, which gives tables for such breakdown, *Movements in Animation*, is used mainly as a reference work for camerapersons and students.

Solomon, Charles (ed.) *The Art of the Animated Image: an Anthology.* Los Angeles, American Film Institute 1987
Essays on animation from film-makers, historians and others in the field.

Solomon, Charles and Stark, Ron *The Complete Kodak Animation Book* Kodak 1983
An excellent guide to animation, with illustrations and stills and many interviews with animators. Very useful.

Thomas, F. and Johnston, O. *The Illusion of Life,* Walt Disney Productions 1981
The major work on all aspects of the Disney Studio – the process, productions and individuals, crediting the artists. Written by two of the group of nine animators responsible for the majority of Disney films.

Whitaker, Harold and Halas, John *Timing for Animation* Focal Press 1981
A clear, concise guide to one of the most difficult and elusive areas of animation.

White, Tony *The Animator's Workbook* Phaidon and Watson-Guptil Publications, NY 1986
A good up-to-date guide to drawn animation techniques which concentrates on animation production, with exercises for each step of the process.

History

There is no comprehensive history of animation in English though there are some excellent works on specific areas.

Adamson, J. *Tex Avery* Popular Library 1975
A lively and readable history of the work of Tex Avery which includes interviews with Warner and MGM personnel.

Crafton, Donald *Before Mickey: The Animated Film 1898–1928* The MIT Press 1984
The book is exemplary in its approach and rigour, and has made a very real contribution to the serious study of animation history.

Curtis, D. *Experimental Cinema* Studio Vista 1971
One of the major works on experimental film, including detailed discussions of the work of film-makers such as Fischinger and Len Lye.

Field, R. *The Art of Walt Disney* Collins 1948
Though old-fashioned and long out of print, this book gives a fascinating view of the Disney Studio. It deals with the early shorts and features up to 1940, but tends to credit Disney himself as the sole creator.

Halas, J. (ed.) *Computer Animation* Focal Press 1974
A selection of articles on the state of the art in 1974. Inevitably the work has been superseded; nonetheless some useful essays.

Hayward, S. *Computers for Animation* Focal Press 1984
A simple introduction to animation methods is followed by a presentation on the applications of computer animation. Again, the speed of development in the field dates some of the material, but the background remains valid.

Holloway, R. *Z is for Zagreb* Tantivy 1972
A portrait of the Zagreb studios, the films and artists. The studio is an exemplary small unit of production.

Lenburg, J. *The Encyclopedia of Animated Cartoon Series* Da Capo 1981
A detailed filmography with credits and release dates of many American animated cartoons. Though aimed at animators and cartoon fans, it contains essential reference information on silent, theatrical and television cartoons.

Maltin, L. *Of Mice and Magic* Plume 1980
A good survey of the American cartoon studios, which made significant inroads in unravelling the history of this area.

McLaren, Norman *Exhibition and Films* catalogue, Scottish Arts Council 1977
A detailed account of McLaren's production and techniques, as well as a picture of the film-maker himself.

Peary, G. & D. *The American Animated Cartoon* Dutton 1980
An excellent anthology of essays on the history of the American cartoon which includes the important essay 'Meep Meep' by Thomson, and Susan Elizabeth Dalton's 'Bugs and Daffy go to War'.

Richard, V. T. *Norman McLaren* Ontario Film Institute 1982
A good example of a history of a single film-maker, in this case a central figure outside the studio system.

Russet, R. and Starr, C. *Experimental Animation* Van Nostrand Reinhold 1976
Now out of print, this important work deals with the history of experimental animation and current practice by concentrating on 'authors'.

Schickel, R. *The Disney Version* Simon & Schuster 1968
One of the major works on Disney and the Disney Studio. Not illustrated.

Shale, R. *Donald Duck Joins Up* UMI 1982
This deals with one of the most interesting periods of American animation production, the Second World War, and the perception of the role of animation as a propaganda weapon.

Stevenson, Ralph *The Animated Film* Tantivy 1973, 1977
Based on his earlier work *Animation in the Cinema*, the book tends to favour the European Art animators at the expense of the mainstream commercial animators; it does, however, cover a great deal of important ground.

There are a number of magazines which appear more or less frequently: *Anifafilm*, the journal of ASIFA, the new *Animation Magazine* and in the UK the chatty *Animator.* Festivals often have useful documentation.

INDEX

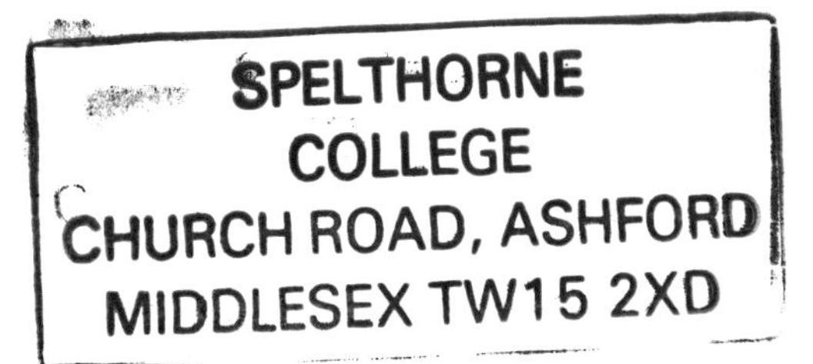

Acknowledgements

The author and publishers would like to thank the following individuals for their invaluable contribution to this book:

For the author's photograph: Fran K. Jones
For special photography: Susanna Price
For additional photography: Tim Searle

The publishers would like to thank the following for supplying the photographs reproduced on the following pages:

Introduction Marcin Gizycki; 6 Arts Council of Great Britain; 7T Museum of Modern Art; 7B Pierre Courtet-Colh; 10T British Film Institute; 10B Harold Whitaker; 11L Museum of Modern Art; 11R, 12 and 13B BFI; 15R Arts Council of Great Britain; 19T BFI; 28 Khitruk Film-Makers Association; 30T and 33T BFI; 33B Khitruk Film-Makers Association; 43L BFI; 43R Cecile Starr; 46B and 47R National Film Theatre; 63B Arthur Melbourne-Cooper Collection; 64 and 65B BFI; 68 Cinémathèque Québecoise; 70 and 71T Rasker Groep BV; 71B and 72T Khitruk Film-Makers Association; 72B BFI; 73 Bristol Animation Festival; 74B and 78T BFI; 87R Cinémathèque Française; 89B Joel Finler Collection; 94B London Film-Makers Co-Operative; 95L Bristol Animation Festival; 98 Cinémathèque Québecoise; 99L Cecile Starr; 99R Bristol Animation Festival; 105B photo Baxter Photographics; 112R photo Ivan Vít; 119T, 120L, 121T, 122R, 123L photo Bernard Hedges; 125T BFI; 125C and B American Federation of Arts Film Program; 126B London Film-Makers Co-Operative.

T = top
B = bottom
L = left
R = right
C = centre

Every effort has been made to trace the copyright holders of photographs and films; we apologise for any unintentional omissions and would be pleased to insert the appropriate acknowledgment in any subsequent edition of this publication.

The author would like to thank Fran Jones, Tony Fish, Peter Hearn, Joanne Gooding and Andy Darley for the enthusiasm and expertise which they brought to the project. Thanks too to the many studios and individuals who participated, particularly Maggi Allison, Bob Godfrey, John Coates, John Challis, David Anderson and Aardman. Also the staff and students at West Surrey College of Art for their support; Sarah for her relentless pursuit of the pictures; for their continued interest and encouragement my mother and father; and Prince Achmed, who kept us on our toes.